ENDORSEMENTS

When I met Dennis Tinerino at the health club in Beverly Hills, I almost gave up my own attempts at bodybuilding, thinking, *What's the use? I'll never look like that!*

I recognized Dennis as a former Mr. America and Mr. Universe, and had read articles and seen pictures in which he was considered a peer and competitor to Arnold Schwarzenegger and others. I imagined that Samson in the Bible must have looked quite a lot like Dennis did then.

As he recounts, I certainly couldn't share any bodybuilding tips with him, but I did share with him my knowledge about the Creator of bodies, the One who fashions us in His own image. As it turns out, Dennis was indeed fertile soil, in which the Master Sower could plant His seed of life.

Since then, Dennis has grown spiritually in a way that surpasses even his physical being. He's a man of God, a man of ministry, and I'm proud to call him "Brother."

—Pat Boone

I believe this book will reveal powerful truths and inspiration, and release a greater measure of faith to every man or woman who is serious about pursuing their divine destiny and developing godly character.

—A.C. Green
Renowned Christian speaker and
professional basketball player

Super Size Your Faith is an amazing testimony of God's transformation power. Your faith will be strengthened and hope rekindled as Dennis shares his story of new beginnings.

—G. Craig Lauterbach, Senior Pastor
Lambertville Assembly of God

Although Dennis' testimony will appeal especially to men, anyone who wants to know about the limitless power of God's love will be blessed by this book. As Dennis shares his story, see how God's grace and mercy have changed his life forever.

—Kenneth Hagin, Jr.
Pastor, REHMA Bible Church
President, Kenneth Hagin Ministries, Inc.

Through Dennis Tinerino's ministry at our church, my son Dominic, at the young age of 12, had a supernatural experience with God that has marked his life forever. Since that moment, Dominic has gone on to be a world changer. This summer alone he will speak to over 100,000 internationally as an evangelist for Jesus Christ. Dennis, we love you!

—Dominic Russo, Senior Pastor
Oakland Christian Church

Dennis Tinerino was one of the best bodybuilders of his era. His blend of size and shape was a classic combination that took him to Mr. America, Mr. World, and Mr. Universe titles. But his greatest victory has been in the way he climbed from rock bottom to become the inspiring person he is today.

—Joe Weider, Trainer of Champions
Father of Bodybuilding
Publisher, *Top Fitness Magazine*

The story of Dennis Tinerino is remarkable, beginning with his youth in the projects of Brooklyn, New York through his bodybuilding journey and his days living a life of crime. I'm grateful I was given the opportunity to lead him to Christ and to mentor him. He has changed from a man with an empty, restless heart to a Christian champion legend in his time. Many thousands of lives have changed through his powerful testimony and anointed ministry.

—Pastor Ray McCauley

As you read this book, you will see how God miraculously transformed Dennis to a man who is committed to seeing individuals saved, healed, and delivered by the power of God. He has a compassion for the lost, and his heart is to see lives totally changed for the glory of God

—Dr. Jerry Savelle

I am thankful that I had the privilege of mentoring Dennis in bodybuilding as a teenager through adulthood, and seeing him overcome many obstacles to become a worldwide bodybuilding champion.

This book will inspire you to fulfill your destiny and achieve great heights.

—Bill Pearl
One of the "bodybuilder greats"

Dennis is a man of passion and power. Our church calls him the "Sermonator" because of the intensity and impact he carries when preaching. Dennis is a modern-day, Saul-to-Paul story. His dramatic testimony is only trumped by his knowledge of the Word of God and the accuracy of the prophetic word that he proclaims. What I appreciate most is his love for God and his family—his greatest success. Jeannie and I have the honor of being the pastor of their daughter, Tara, and her husband, Eli. The true value of a man's ministry can be measured in his children. Dennis and Anita are godly, sincere, anointed people of God whom we consider friends.

This book will read like a novel. Its thrilling moments and painfully truthful experiences will intrigue you and hold you in suspense. Please remember—it's true; and in the end, God's truth prevails. Dennis lives to share this powerful testimony. Someone has said you live only once—true, that is, if you don't read biographies. You can live many lives through others, so get ready to live and learn from one of the most fascinating people you'll ever meet.

—Pastor Phil and Jeannie Munsey
Life Church

SUPER SIZE YOUR FAITH

Tapping Into God's Miracle Power

SUPER SIZE YOUR FAITH

Tapping Into God's Miracle Power

Dennis Tinerino

Destiny Image₀ Publishers, Inc.
P.O. Box 310
Shippensburg, PA 17257-0310

"Speaking to the Purposes of God for this Generation
and for the Generations to Come."

For Worldwide Distribution, Printed in the U.S.A.

ISBN 10: 0-7684-2408-9

ISBN 13: 978-0-7684-2408-9

This book and all other Destiny Image, Revival Press, MercyPlace, Fresh Bread, Destiny Image Fiction, and Treasure House books are available at Christian bookstores and distributors worldwide.

For a U.S. bookstore nearest you, call
1-800-722-6774.

For more information on foreign distributors, call
717-532-3040.

Or reach us on the Internet:
www.destinyimage.com

1 2 3 4 5 6 7 8 9 10 11 / 09 08 07

ACKNOWLEDGMENTS

WORDS seem inadequate to express my deepest gratitude to the extraordinary individuals who have invested prayer, tears, sweat, and contributed financially to the publication of this book.

I must first acknowledge my loving family, a power plant of inspiration, joy, and yes, nagging. My precious wife, Anita, you have shown enduring strength throughout our marriage. Your steadfast patience has been a guiding force, as this project demanded so much of our attention and—it seems like—an eternity of your data input skills on the computer. Thank you for watching my back and never leaving me. I love you always and forever. My oldest daughter, Tara, your personality and spirit resemble mine. I love you dearly. Marissa, your effervescent personality and spirit are graced by God. I love you big-time. And my son, DJ, you are my Elijah, my Timothy—I am proud of you and love you. You all have challenged and encouraged me to tell this story. You have lived it with me.

A special thank you to my greatest fan and mentor, my dad, Carmine, who gave me his genes, his love for family, relentless drive, enthusiasm, energy, and will to succeed; my mom, Mary, always there with her quiet love and devotion, and the strength to cook the innumerable ten-course meals I needed to build my physique; my brothers and workout partners, Salvatore and Larry; Uncle Bill Porfido, a Vaudeville strongman, who was my early workout partner and introduced me to Charles Atlas. My success is yours.

My deepest gratitude to my bodybuilding heroes for the priceless inspiration they gave me: Jack LaLanne, Steve Reeves, Reg Park, Bill Pearl, Joe Abbenda, Larry Scott, Tom Sansone, and others—Peary and Mabel Rader, Bob Hoffman, John Grimek, Joe Weider, Dan Laurie, and Oscar Heidenstam. Thanks to John Balik for publishing health magazines. Your publications gave me inspiration, loads of insight and knowledge, and worldwide exposure. I commend your efforts. To my close friends and mentors, Joe Abbenda and Bill Pearl, you were the potters, and I was the clay...without you, my championship dreams would have never been fulfilled.

Special thanks to photographers Doug White, Cliff Swan, Artie Zeller, John Balik, Jim Caruso, Russ Warner, Harry Langdon, and Leo Stern who captured the greatest highlights of my physique career. Your true artistry will never be forgotten.

I must give my heartfelt thanks to my spiritual heroes and early mentors for the priceless wisdom, revelation, and character I have drawn from them: Ray McCauley, Kenneth Hagin, Ken Hagin, Jr., Oral Roberts, Dr. Jerry Savelle, Reinhard Bonnke, Ed Longshore, Tommy Barnett, Dr. Ed Cole, and many other ministers who have blessed me beyond words.

Thanks to my neighbor and encourager, Eve Cohen; to Paul Fabian and Paul Crouch at TBN, the first to see the vision of this book; Pat Boone and Rosemary Bix, for your bold witness; Ray McCauley, my spiritual father, whose anointed words touched my heart when my life was in despair; my "Homeboy"—Jo Jo Sanchez, who printed tens of thousands of testimony tracts and a poster for our early crusades, and said, "Next, Dude...a book!" Edward Dalcour, for your faithfulness, love, and help;

my friends, Bud Keilani, for your constant prayer and encouragement, and Paul Drumm, my intercessor and prayer warrior, a constant voice of counsel and imparter of wisdom and direction; Pete Samra, a true friend—we both came into the Kingdom at the same time—you're a loyal friend and mighty man of God; Michael and Dru Hammer, for your wisdom, guidance, and encouragement. Big-time thanks!

Special thanks to those who prayed and financially contributed to this project. Kingdom blessings now and forever to Ben Ferrell of BMC Advertising; Jim Kerby, for assisting in transcribing my thoughts from tape to paper and organizing the first draft; and Jackie Lusk, for polishing the final draft. Loads of thanks to my gifted assistant, Carol Hurley, who took this project and ran with it, and made me focus. Carol, you were in the trenches with us, praying, writing, and rewriting, even from thousands of miles away, and now we're going over the finish line. Jill Austin, bless you for introducing me to Joel Nori, Jr., of Destiny Image. Joel, thank you for seeing the nuggets of biblical truth in my story, and choosing to make it available to those who need to transform their lives. Thanks to Don Milam and his staff at Destiny Image for bringing this book in for a landing.

Finally, thank You, Lord, for gracing me to glorify You in my story.

—Dennis Tinerino

TABLE OF CONTENTS

FOREWORD

THE amazing story of Dennis Tinerino is also my story. I have known Dennis for over 36 years and have been married to him for 33 of those exciting years. I remember the moment I set my eyes on him and instantly knew that someday he would be the man I would marry.

Being a romantic, I chose Valentine's Day to tie the knot at a little Catholic church in Queens. It was a rainy day, and we were soaked. When I said my marriage vows, I knew that this girl from Astoria, New York who sang in the choir at St. Francis of Assisi Church would need the strength of the Holy Spirit to stand with her man through the years. But abuse, uncertainty, fear, and financial ruin were not among the expected challenges I was thinking of on that day. As I recited, "For better, for worse, for richer, for poorer," I had no idea of the roller coaster ride I was committing myself to.

Filled with drama, adventure, intrigue, action, and glamour, the life of Dennis Tinerino is an amazing testimony of conversion and faith. It is also the story of a partnership of two people who grew up together spiritually as if God did not just join us together, but molded us into His divine plan. Yes, meeting Arnold Schwarzenegger, Lou Ferrigno, and other famous bodybuilders and celebrities was exciting, and watching Dennis win his titles and being inducted into the AAU and IFBB Hall of Fame was thrilling, but watching him spiral downward and being hauled away in handcuffs was equally devastating.

Many women would have walked away from a marriage for indiscretions that were far less than those I endured, but I learned to trust God to get us out of each and every crisis. And look at what I would have missed if I had left this man...witnessing God turn calamity into miracles time after time, building a worldwide ministry for the two of us, blessing us tenfold for every step we have taken in the right direction. Had I given up on this marriage, the precious family we hold so dear would simply be "what might have been." Fortunately, what would have been the end for most couples was truly a new beginning for us.

While Dennis's early life, bodybuilding career, show business experiences, and criminal activities are eventful and bigger than life, there's no comparison with the extraordinary accomplishments of the miracle ministry in America, on the mission fields of the world, and wherever the Lord takes him on a given day. As you read about 25 years of ministry, you will literally get a glimpse of God's divine intervention in the lives of those he touches.

Super Size Your Faith is the story of a young boy's journey from the grit and grime of Brooklyn's projects as he transforms himself into Mr. Universe. It is also the story of a world champion who fell from grace, only to be transformed yet again into the man I lovingly call "the mighty man of God."

—Anita Tinerino

Chapter One

MR. AMERICA—
A DREAM COME TRUE!

The marquee outside Veteran's Memorial Auditorium in Columbus, Ohio, read...

1967 MR. AMERICA, June 12, 8:00 p.m.

At the prejudging, for most of the day, three thousand people had watched state and regional bodybuilding title-holders flexing and posing for the judges, vying for the chance to compete against the best-built men in the United States to become the AAU national champion, acquiring the prestigious title of Mr. America.

Now, more than an hour before the final competition was to begin, the place was packed to the rafters. Excited family members and friends of the various competitors had come to cheer their favorite on to victory. Bodybuilding enthusiasts had gathered from across the nation for the crowning event of the year—the "world series" or "super bowl" of amateur bodybuilding. There was also a large crowd of local people, curious to see what the sport was all about.

Dennis wins Mr. America 1967

The press was clustered down front—writers and photographers from radio and TV stations, newspapers, and various sports publications. Also ringing the stage was the inevitable corps of "groupies"—girls and women hoping to attract the attention of one or more of the muscular, near-naked giants on stage and perhaps be invited to bask in the presence of—maybe even to "entertain"—some of the handsome celebrities.

Backstage was near pandemonium, with scores of contestants nervously preparing for the big show! Almost every square foot of the stage wings was filled with bodybuilders stretching, warming up, flexing before full-length mirrors, and practicing their posing routines for the thousandth time.

Some guys paced back and forth, talking under their breath. Others stood staring into space, oblivious to the commotion and hubbub around them. Still other contestants had begun rubbing oil all over their arms, legs, and torsos to make their well-tanned skin shine and glisten, highlighting the definition of the bulging muscles and veins just below the surface.

Younger competitors peeked through the stage curtain, amazed at the size of the capacity crowd, buzzing and twittering, waving to acquaintances in other sections, and fanning with already dog-eared programs. Most of these guys had never competed in front of so many people before, and the prospect made them feel even more nervous and uptight.

More experienced, veteran contestants finished their preparations and tried to relax, greeting other bodybuilders they'd met and competed against over the years, or talking and laughing with friends and well-wishers who'd found their way backstage.

Meanwhile, Mr. America contest officials twisted their way through the maze of people, passing along last-minute instructions, answering questions, and trying to be sure all the final entrants were present and would be ready to go when the curtain went up.

My dad, Carmine Tinerino, had traveled with me from New York for the big event. We'd arrived a day early so I could familiarize myself with the auditorium facilities and get acclimated to the new, strange surroundings as well as assess how to avoid the crowds and choose a place backstage to warm up and get ready. We both felt that I'd made a good showing in the pre-judging competition—I'd been awarded a trophy for "Most Muscular." For months the bodybuilding publications had called me one of the favorites to win the Mr. America title, despite my disappointing sixth-place finish the year before. In a little over three years, I had won more than a dozen titles, including Junior Mr. USA, Teenage Mr. America, Junior Mr. America, and Mr. USA.

Ready for the "Big Time"

I was an experienced competitor. I'd entered my first competition when I was 16, placing third. I won my first event three months later at the age of seventeen, and then competed as often as I could. I knew how the game was played and felt I was ready for the big time. For the past five months, I'd been training especially hard, three to four hours a day, five days a week. Now 21 years old, my body had grown and matured. I weighed 212 pounds, and my arms measured 20 inches around—almost unheard of at that time. I could dead lift a bar loaded with 550 pounds! I could do multiple-repetition arm curls with 225 pounds and bench press more than 400 pounds.

I felt great. There are no words to describe how it feels to call upon your body to perform some prodigious feat and have your limbs and muscles respond smoothly, easily, like a well-oiled machine. I was pure, lean muscle mass—less than five percent body fat. In bodybuilding jargon, I was "ripped to the bone"—crisscrossed by bands of muscle tissue below the skin so hard they felt like spring steel. When I worked out, I could almost feel the blood coursing through my veins, each muscle and ligament rippling into action. I actually got an adrenaline kick from working out that was as potent and pleasurable as the "high" from any drug.

I knew I was ready. My body was tuned and polished to perfection, and every muscle group looked just the way I wanted. I was ready—a lean, mean, fighting machine. My posing routine was dramatic and powerful, synchronized perfectly to an absolutely compelling piece of music.

Despite his pride and confidence in me, Dad was becoming nervous and antsy in the midst of the tension-charged atmosphere. So I told him it was time for him to go find a good seat and cheer me on to victory. I didn't want his agitation to rub off on me—I knew I had to stay cool and focused.

"Places, everybody! Get ready to go. Five minutes to curtain!"

The milling around intensified as the finalists finished last-second preparations and looked for their places in the lineup. I found my spot and stood quietly, exhilarated and ready, but calm. This was it—the opportunity to fulfill a dream that had consumed my thoughts and energies for more than nine years.

My Ticket Out of the Ghetto

In those final moments before the curtain went up for the Mr. America competition, my mind thought back to the first time Dad had taken me and my brothers to work out at the Brooklyn Central YMCA. A driven, disciplined man, who followed his own fitness program of running, boxing, and calisthenics, Dad wanted to teach us how to defend ourselves through boxing, while also fulfilling his dream of becoming a professional athlete through his sons. Instead of being enthralled by the boxers, however, it was the huge, muscular guys I saw in the weight room, lifting enormous weights and pushing themselves through strenuous bodybuilding routines, who fascinated me.

The attraction of bodybuilding, I believe, is its creative challenge and its unswerving demand for purity and discipline. Each bodybuilder starts with a lump of raw material—a mass of tissue and tendons, fat and fiber, muscle and bone. Using only diet and exercise, he builds and develops, sculpts and shapes each limb, each muscle group, each part and section of his body, changing it from what it was into what it ought to be. And to a great extent, the bodybuilder is in total control of—and solely responsible for—how his body turns out...what it looks like...what it can become. Bodybuilders are real physical architects using their God-given gifts and genetics to reach their full potential.

Potential was something that had never entered my mind in my early years. I was a skinny 12 year old, second son of a poor Italian dockworker. We lived on the "mean streets" of New York, in a dirty, dilapidated, and dangerous public housing project of tall tenements filled mostly with black and Puerto Rican people. Beatings, muggings, robberies, and killings happened often. Every day was a fight for survival. And not yet a teenager, I was already looking for a way to escape—to get out.

At 12 years of age, I weighed 112 pounds. I looked at my body in the gym mirror and compared it to the guys lifting weights. "I'm so skinny I could duck raindrops," I told myself disparagingly. "My shoulders are so narrow they choke my neck!" "If my body could talk, it would say, 'help'!"

But rather than making me want to give up, seeing my skinny, under-developed physique gave me a challenge and a goal. I determined that someday I would be a champion—a super-strong, best-built guy like Steve

Reeves or Reg Park, the superstars of bodybuilding who played Hercules in the movies. With Dad's coaching and motivation, and my ability to work hard, we would keep on pushing until I accomplished something big—until I was the Joe Namath or Muhammad Ali of bodybuilding. I wouldn't stop until I became Mr. America! That would be my ticket out of the ghetto and into the big-time world of fame and fortune.

And for nine long years, I had worked toward that goal, working out for hours every day, learning what to do and how to eat to turn my body into peak performance material. No matter what, I was constantly training, sacrificing, and disciplining myself in order to accomplish my goals and dreams. I had competed in every event that would accept me until I had finally earned the right to take a shot at...

"OKAY, PEOPLE, HERE WE GO!"

A music fanfare blared, and Len Boslin, the announcer on stage, declared, "Ladies and Gentlemen, welcome to the 1967 Mr. America competition. Join me in giving a big round of applause to the top bodybuilding champions in the United States who have come here tonight to compete for the title of...MR. AMERICA!"

The curtain went up, the stage manager gave the first guy in line a shove, and soon all the contestants were making their way onstage to thunderous applause. The judges immediately began to observe the first round, which consisted of comparative poses, to evaluate physique. Each contestant stood naturally, no flexing, showing front, side, and back. Points were awarded for symmetry, muscularity, and proportion. There were also points for posing routine and stage presence. Posing individually, each contestant was given his moment in the spotlight.

The next competition involved comparisons of bodybuilders exhibiting basic, compulsory flexed poses—front, side, and back. At this point, the judges called for pose-offs between pairs of contestants so they could see them side by side. In the meantime, the crowd had chosen their favorite contenders and were cheering them on, while the judges called out their choices time and again for comparison with others. I was asked to step forward numerous times to flex and pose with various competitors.

Each judge then tabulated the points he had awarded and combined his evaluations with the rest of the panel. The field was then cut by about half...and I had made the cut! I was over the first hurdle and was already imagining my hands on the trophy. But first, I had to focus on winning.

Reaching for My Dream

Each of the remaining contestants was allowed to present his posing routine, set to music. This was the dramatic, artistic, expressive part of the show. There were many styles of posing—some emphasizing size and power with bold, almost mechanical changes; others displaying grace and poise, with smooth, fluid position changes, as one motion flowed into the next.

The posing routine was always my favorite part. While I enjoyed the head-to-head competition, the music routine allowed me to use my body as a fine instrument to project my emotions and state of mind. To me it was almost like poetry in motion, combining strength and grace, power and sensitivity. I felt isolated from everything around me, almost lifted out of my body, yet totally in control of the muscles rippling under my oiled skin, turning and gliding continuously like a perfectly tuned machine.

When I finished my routine and the music stopped, the audience surged to its feet and gave me a thunderous standing ovation! I felt goose bumps of excitement up and down my spine as the applause went on and on. I knew I'd turned in an exceptional performance and the crowd appreciated it. But would it be good enough to win?

When all the posing routines were finished, the judges called for some final pose-offs, carefully comparing their top-ranked contestants. I was called forward again and again to pose against one or two others at a time.

Finally, the judges were finished and retired to calculate their final tabulations. Meanwhile, the finalists were allowed to take their places in the lineup to wait for the judges' decisions.

In those long, suspense-filled moments, my mood vacillated from confidence to anxiety. The contest was over. There was nothing I could do now to change the outcome. I'd done my best and would soon know if my nine years of hard work had paid off.

"The judges have just handed me their list of winners in this year's Mr. America contest," announced the emcee. "I'll call the names of the top-ten places in reverse order. In tenth place...." And the countdown began. "Ninth place...eighth...seventh..." and on up the line.

The third place winner was Will Whitaker, and my friend, Jim Haislop, was second.

Then looking out into the audience, I saw my dad on his feet, hands clasped overhead, beaming in joy! His eyes caught mine, and he yelled in exultation. I could read his lips as he shouted, "You did it, Dennis. You won!"

And the announcer confirmed his declaration: "Ladies and Gentlemen, in first place, our 1967 AAU Mr. America champion...DENNIS TINERINO!" There was a roar of approval and delight from the crowd, then explosive applause.

So many people had told me I would win. But when it finally, officially happened, I was so thrilled I could hardly stand it. My arms shot into the air in a V for victory salute as elation lifted me so high that my feet barely touched the stage. Other competitors were yelling, cheering, and whistling.

Strobe lights flashed and photographers captured this triumphant moment as I made my way to the top of the podium, flanked by the second and third-place winners; and sponsors and dignitaries pumped my hand and shouted congratulations over the tumult as they presented me the official medal and trophy.

I smiled and cried at the same time, savoring the most exciting and satisfying, most wonderful moment of my life.

My dream had come true! I was Mr. America!

Chapter Two

A Heritage of Strength in a Land of Hopelessness

I was born in Manhattan to third-generation Italian-American parents—Carmine Tinerino and Mary Teresa Porfido. Their grandparents—my great-grandparents—had come to America from the old country, from Sicily and Naples. We lived on the Lower East Side, on Mott Street in Little Italy's Knickerbocker Village.

I spoke Italian at home until I was eight years old. Then my grandfather said, "Hey, you were born in this country. You're an American citizen. Speak English from now on!"

Both the Porfido and Tinerino families were large—my dad had six brothers and two sisters, and Mom's family consisted of six boys and four girls. So, there were lots of uncles, aunts, nephews, nieces, and cousins. They were gregarious, noisy people, filled with passion and pathos, laughter and tears.

On most Sundays, after Mass at St. Joseph's Church, we'd gather at my grandparents' apartment for a delicious nine-course real Italian dinner. You could gain weight just from the aromas of homemade Italian bread, pastas, and desserts!

Afterward, the men would walk down to Mutchie's Bar and try to out-drink each other. The women and girls stayed at home, but the boys would tag along. We'd mill around underfoot, watching and listening to the bragging and to the drunken stories. We boys got to meet some very colorful characters while hanging out at Mutchie's. Included in this "Den of Thieves" were the "Wise Guys from Mulberry Street," who were bookmakers, loan sharks, and enforcers for the "family," plus an assortment of longshoremen and teamsters. Once, when somebody challenged my dad to dive off the Recreation Pier into the East River, he said, "That's no challenge!" and the next thing I knew, he was in the water!

Among their ongoing commentary about the numbers and the "merchandise" for sale in the back room, which just happened to fall off a truck, the men talked about the horses they'd bet on, what was going on in the neighborhood, or listened to sporting events on the radio. Many times, friends and family having civil conversations eventually led to disputes, which turned into senseless brawls. I saw many cops come by to pick up envelopes, while turning a blind eye to what was going on.

Sooner or later, someone would start bragging about his sexual exploits with his *goumada*—his girlfriend or mistress. Then another would try to top that story, only to be interrupted by someone else's boastful tale. Many of these married men actually seemed *proud* to claim they had women on the side. What they didn't understand was that over the years, their actions were actually shaping *our* lives.

Life in the Projects

When I was about eight, we had to move out of Little Italy to the Brownsville area of Brooklyn, into the Van Dyke public housing projects, which they called the Black Projects, on Sutter Avenue. Even though our family was of a different ethnic background than the other tenants, one thing was the same—everyone was poor. That was the common background we shared. We were all just trying to make it.

My dad was a loyal Teamster who worked as a packer for Selig Paper Company for many years. He filled orders, loaded trucks for delivery, and sometimes delivered paper stock as well. He never made much money, and often spent his evenings and weekends working various odd jobs to earn extra money.

Most Friday nights, Dad would have an all-night poker game at our house. Usually someone brought a bottle of Scotch or some other kind of booze, and the room was full of tobacco smoke and noise. Friends and relatives would crowd around the kitchen table, eating and drinking, excitedly anticipating a big pot, sometimes arguing noisily into the wee hours of the morning.

If Dad won at cards, the next day he and his friends would go to Aqueduct or Belmont racetrack and spend half the day betting on the horses. Almost everybody I knew was caught up in gambling. Many poor people in the housing projects barely existed from paycheck to paycheck. Sometimes, just to get by, they borrowed money in desperation from loan sharks at exuberant rates, which were impossible to pay back. Then, they had to endure the pressure and threats from these loan sharks, and would often scam and scheme, robbing Peter to pay Paul, just to pay the interest if they didn't want their legs broken. Their hope was to win big in a card game, make a hit on the numbers, or to score big at the track with a trifecta. Unfortunately, most of their hopes turned into living in fear and bondage. Occasionally, someone in the area would make a big score. A week later they'd show up to pay off their loans, wearing fancy clothes or driving a new car.

Life at 390 Sutter Avenue was noisy, crowded, and full of attitudes. There were lots of unhappy people crammed into the projects, which had

Dennis' 1st Communion

virtually no amenities or recreational facilities—not even a safe place for children to play. Everything happened on the streets. It was a rough place, and kids soon learned to survive by using their wits...and their fists.

In fact, growing up in Brooklyn—especially the rough-and-tumble Brownsville area—you almost had to be trained for guerrilla warfare. Just going to school meant you had to look out for kids carrying switchblade knives, brass knuckles, and zip guns. Even the stairwells were dangerous.

Because the elevators were slow, we kids preferred to run up and down the stairs. But while the stairwells were our favorite meeting places, unfortunately they were also hiding places for rapists or muggers trying to shake us down. Several times, confrontations would end up with us running for our lives, bullets flying over our heads. Dealing with violence, intimidation, and fear was part of our daily lives. We had to earn respect.

The streets were battlegrounds for various gangs of rebellious, confrontational youths defending their own "turf." Even the local swimming pool was full of racial tension. One day, a lifeguard had to save me from being drowned by a rival gang. I was on the wrong side of town and was fighting for my life. Later in the same day in the locker room an entire gang mugged me, taking my shoes, my belt—everything they could grab. I pulled out my knife when a city worker came in and broke up the fight. I learned quickly who belonged in the neighborhood and who was an outsider. Every stranger was a potential threat...or a potential victim.

One evening when I was about 13, while on the way home from the pizza parlor, I witnessed something I'll remember forever. Halfway down the block, I saw a guy on the steps in front of a brownstone. He was kissing a girl good-bye, and as he turned to leave, a van pulled up to the curb and two guys started shooting. The girl was wounded...the guy was dead.

I ducked behind a car, holding the pizza boxes in front of my face. The first thing that came to my mind was the warning my dad and uncles had repeatedly drilled into my head: *Mind your own business!* So, while confusion and excitement erupted on our street, I slipped through the gathering crowd of onlookers, into our building and upstairs to our apartment.

"Hey, Dad," I blurted out excitedly, "I just saw a guy get killed! Are we gonna call the police?"

"Shut up! What are you talking about? Where'd you see this?" Dad and Mom then immediately went down to find out who had been shot. When they came back, they warned us kids to be careful when we went out, and my father warned me, "Don't tell anybody what happened. It's none of our business. That's how they deal with one another. They're a bunch of dirty rats! That's the way they settle disputes—with violence."

"But that's not right, Dad!" I responded.

"I'll handle this. Trust me. You don't want to get involved. It's just one wise guy taking care of another. The consequence of their choice of an evil life. They're in their own dark world."

I learned right there that bad choices with evil people could get me killed.

Later on, I understood my dad's position. Witnesses also got killed in our neighborhood.

On the Other Hand...

Being poor and Italian did have some perks, however. At Christmastime, Dad always had good connections with the Catholic charity organization that provided gifts for less-fortunate Italian-American children. When we'd show up, the sponsors would say, "Oh, yeah, Tinerino, pick out whatever you want." Our family always seemed to get more toys, clothing, and gifts than the other families received.

In addition, our extended family was close and supportive, and we were often included in our relatives' activities. If an uncle was taking his kids to the circus or rodeo at Madison Square Garden, he'd finagle extra tickets so that my brothers and I could go too. Or a cousin would take us along to a basketball or hockey game, which was a rare treat.

When we weren't on the streets, my brothers and I watched TV quite a bit, and also enjoyed going to the movies. Number one: it was cheap entertainment, and number two: the pretend world of films offered a temporary escape from the drab reality of the grinding poverty, dirt, and danger that constantly surrounded our lives in the inner city. Movies also gave us heroes to look up to.

In the Name of the Father

We were Italian, therefore, Catholic. My dad wasn't very religious, but he and Mom did their best to see that the whole family got dressed up and went to Mass on Sundays. If we kids were noisy or disrespectful, we got the backside of a hand against the side of our heads. We also participated in other church-sponsored activities, like Bingo, raffles, and festivals. (My brothers and I liked the family gatherings with the card games, booze, and Italian food more than the church services!)

When I was very young—maybe three or four years old—I remember my mother dropping me off at a pre-school held in the Catholic Church. I remember seeing statues of Mary and various saints, a crucifix with Jesus bleeding, a basin of holy water, and dozens of flickering candles. There were confessional booths and "spooky" stained-glass windows—it all gave me the creeps. When Mom left, I cried, and a sister came over to my little bench and said, "Everything's going to be okay. Your mother left you here because she can trust us. We're here to help you and to serve God."

I remember another nun taking an interest in me, telling me that Jesus loved me. She taught me some simple things about God and helped me understand the Catholic religion.

Although she wasn't super-religious, Mom did pray for us kids. She was a typical Italian wife and mother. She never really talked a lot and wasn't a great communicator. Her whole existence revolved around being a housewife, cooking, cleaning, being a good wife and mother. She also read the catechism lessons to us from a little book, put olive oil on our foreheads, and prayed in the name of the Father, the Son, and the Holy Ghost. Praying the rosary was part of her family tradition. She asked God's protection over her sons and over her entire family.

Hearing God's Voice

"Many are called, but few are chosen." (Matthew 22:14). *"My sheep hear my voice. I know them, and they follow me."* (John 10:27).

My brothers and I attended Catholic school and went through the various religious classes. I was impressionable and sensitive, saying I wanted to be an altar boy or usher. I was always asking questions: "Why do we pray to Mary and to dead saints? Why do I confess my sins to you, Father? Why do my family members go to confession, and receive forgiveness for their sins, then go out and do the same things again? Why can't Jesus change them? Didn't Christ overcome sin and evil?" This religious stuff ain't workin!

At our family gatherings, it was common to hear husbands, wives and family members arguing, and children crying...mostly because the men's adultery and illegal activity were being exposed. Women would pray their rosaries and make the sign of the Cross and men would try to defend their actions. I was so confused. It seemed as though everybody I knew looked over their shoulders. They thought they had to compromise to survive.

In bed at night, I cried out to God, "There's gotta be a way out! Everyone is so unhappy. I don't want to live like them." The answer to my prayer came in a most unusual place.

When I was twelve, I made my first Holy Communion, along with several other kids my age. It was a big deal! I wore a white jacket and tie and received my own ceremonial catechism book. I went before the priest and confessed that Jesus was Lord and that He died for my sins. Then I received Holy Communion.

Afterward there was a family party at my grandparent's home to celebrate the big event, "When Dennis made his Holy Communion." My parents and I were on the BMT subway on the way to Little Italy in New York City when suddenly I sensed that the Spirit of God was around me, communicating with me! This would be a profound and defining moment in my life that would change my destiny...something I could not deny, and always remember.

I turned to my father who was sitting next to me on the train. "Dad, I heard the sound of God's voice. He spoke to me!"

"Well, Dennis, what did he tell you?"

"He told me that it doesn't matter what you do in this world. Life will pass and only knowing Jesus and what you do for Him will last. I think God is calling me to do His work—maybe as a priest, or to serve in the Peace Corps." To a twelve year old, the Peace Corps seemed to be a worthy, noble calling, a suitable way one could serve God.

My dad was quiet for a moment, then he replied, "Well, you know, there's a time for everything. And someday you might be able to do that. But I think God has given you a talent and a gift to become a great athlete. And that could be what you're really supposed to do, to serve God through sports." Twenty years later, this ability to hear the voice of God would save and change my life forever.

A Mistake or the Will of God?

Sometimes, circumstances can affect the course of your whole life. Soon after I heard God speak, I was involved in a misunderstanding at my Catholic school. A guy at school was bothering one of the girl students and making her life miserable. Apparently, one of the nuns confused me with this other guy, and honestly thought I was the culprit. We never could get it straightened out. In the end, my parents felt it would be best if my brothers and I just left and enrolled in public school. That was the end of my religious training. The path I took after leaving the Catholic influence may have been less religious, but I believe the end result brought me into some priceless spiritual reality.

Confusion, Compromise, and Contradictions

Following the incident at school, most of my ethical and moral training came solely from my father, other relatives, and books I read. Dad wanted the best for his family and constantly cajoled his sons to make good choices and try to treat everybody right. He spelled out a simple code of right and wrong and warned us to avoid troublemakers on the streets. He taught us about the peril of drugs and even urged us to steer clear of his personal vices—periodic drinking and gambling. It was the classic line of "do as I say, not as I do." My conscience would tell me what was right or wrong, but I had no one to teach me how to live a life above reproach, a life of integrity and honesty.

For instance, there was a lot of drug use in our neighborhood. There was always marijuana around, and we noticed lots of people shooting up with heroin. As kids playing in the alleys and exploring dilapidated buildings, we saw junkies and dealers everywhere. But even with this accessibility, I never wanted to get involved in drugs. I dabbled with cigarette smoking a little just to fit in and be accepted, but that was about it.

I remember when some of the guys I went to public school with started sniffing glue. It was deadly stuff, often causing brain damage. "Huffers" were easy to spot—with their spaced-out, glassy-eyed appearance, they looked like zombies. Even as a kid I could see what those toxic fumes were doing to them; fortunately, seeing the effects that drugs had on other people's lives kept me from using them.

My dad came home crying one evening. "What's the matter?" I asked.

"Did you hear about your friend Buddy at school?" he responded. "He was sniffing glue and tried to hitch a ride on the back of a bus. He fell off and got run over. He's dead!"

The news hit me hard. Nobody had realized that Buddy had started sniffing glue. He was the fat Italian kid—I was the skinny one. He was always full of laughs. We'd played stickball and marbles together and gone to movies, and our parents knew each other. I'd always thought he was smart and would be really successful in life. Now he was gone...his future snuffed out in an instant. I started crying too because this was one of the first people I knew really well who had died. Furthermore, I was afraid to go to the funeral.

Drug use was only one of the many problems a kid in the projects had to deal with. In a melting pot like New York, you're surrounded by people of all colors, speaking different languages, and they all have different customs and religions. As the "token whites" in a predominately black and Puerto Rican neighborhood, we often experienced the "culture clash" and were made keenly aware that we didn't belong...we didn't fit in with most of the people around us. However, we soon earned respect from our neighbors.

Although we heard lots of name-calling and racist language, Dad tried to teach us not to be prejudiced. "Don't judge people by their color or their nationality," he said. "People are people. They all bleed the same color. Make up your mind after you find out what kind of individuals they are."

Dad once saved a little black girl from drowning in a nearby apartment. As he was walking through the neighborhood, a fire alarm went off in an apartment building, and a woman came out screaming for help. "My little girl fell in the bathtub and drowned!" she cried. "She's not breathing. Won't somebody help me?"

Nobody moved, so Dad ran inside the building. When he got to the apartment, the mother was shaking the apparently lifeless body of her daughter. "She was shaking her like a rag doll, but nothing was happening," Dad remembers. He took the child in his arms and began giving her mouth-to-mouth resuscitation and heart massage. By the time the fire department emergency crews arrived, the little girl was breathing again.

The newspaper reported his heroic deed, and Dad received a civilian citation from the fire department. He later received a personal letter of commendation from President Richard Nixon. It was a big deal. That's the kind of man Carmine Tinerino was.

Dad regularly had to rescue my older brother, Sal, and me from one thing or another. One time, we had "borrowed" a rowboat and became stuck on an island across from Canarsie Pier in Brooklyn. It was growing dark, and we were getting really scared, when my dad appeared out of nowhere in a motorboat and saved us.

In fact, Dad helped "save" lots of kids by helping to steer them away from trouble and redirecting their energies into more constructive activities than hanging out on the streets. He had eyes that could see trouble coming a mile away—in time to get out of harm's way. During the summer, Dad started the East New York Softball League, and he also organized and directed neighborhood stickball and baseball leagues for kids who were the ages of my brothers and me. (In fact, my older brother, Sal, and I were known as the "home run kings." Many coaches thought we had pro-potential.) In any case, Dad was no angel, and you could get the back of his hand easier than a kiss any day of the week; but by his actions, you knew he had a big heart.

I think my dad hoped that his sons would live out his unfulfilled dreams and ambitions. He wanted us to have better lives than he had, and the quickest road to success he could envision was through professional athletics. He was a former Golden Glove boxer who had dreamed of becoming a professional fighter. He always believed he could have been another Rocky Graziano or Rocky Marciano, but he never received encouragement or support from his immigrant parents.

Dad loved to tell us about some of the classic big league games he'd seen and the great baseball heroes—his all-time favorite was Joe DeMaggio, the "Yankee Clipper." One of the highlights of my life was when he took me to see the Dodgers and Yankees play at Yankee Stadium in the Bronx—"the house that Babe Ruth built."

So, as I searched for God and the Truth, my role models, other than my dad, were longshoremen who endured hard physical labor on the docks, and Teamsters and truck drivers—tough guys who sweated and strained all day, lifting, shoving, loading, unloading. They worked hard...and they played hard. When they had time off, they met with their friends to laugh loud, drink long, and gamble with money they couldn't afford to lose. If they were lucky enough to scrounge a few extra bucks, maybe they'd take their *goumadas* to a restaurant or club on the weekend and, hopefully, "get lucky" later in the evening. It was a rough, sordid lifestyle, but they didn't know anything else. Fast living was an accepted part of our Italian heritage. My uncles would say, "You gotta take care of your family first, but a guy's also gotta have time for fun. There's nothing wrong with having a woman on the side." But for me, it was another contradiction. I knew I didn't want to wind up like these guys, but I turned the wrong way in spite of my determination and because of my confusion. Nobody taught me to how resist temptation.

The Brownsville Boys

To survive in Brooklyn, you had to belong to a gang. If you didn't belong to a gang, you didn't get respect. You didn't even have an identity.

So, when I was twelve Salvatore and I, along with a guy named Mario Schosek, gathered up some other "misfits" from the neighborhood and started our own gang called the Brownsville Boys. We wore black leather jackets and carried switchblades and brass knuckles so we could defend our "turf" and protect ourselves against the other gangs.

We all had nicknames—Mario was Tarzan, Sal was Reno, and I was Dino. The three of us would always pal around together, even when we weren't with the rest of the gang. My brother Larry was younger than the rest of us and had different interests. He was into popular music and had organized his own singing group that performed at weddings, bar mitzvahs, and holiday parties. So he wasn't a part of the trouble we got into...at first.

Sal was another story. Although he had the intelligence to excel at school and easily could have been a professional boxer or bodybuilder, he was more interested in chasing girls and acting cool. He was hotheaded, with a vicious temper, and if provoked, which was often, would fight until he was the last guy standing. Being the oldest brother, he considered it his job to protect Larry and me. He constantly had a "chip on his shoulder," and it almost seemed that he was always looking for trouble.

For example, there was a policeman we called "Jesse James" who patrolled our neighborhood, whom Dad had once told, "If you see my kids doing anything wrong, you have my permission to give them the beating of their lives." So, Jesse James was pretty pushy around us, and Sal didn't like him one bit.

One day, as we were laying on some chaise lounges, catching some sun up on "tar beach" (the roof of our building, above the 12th story) and listening to the radio, Sal looked down and saw Jesse James coming down the sidewalk below. He then quickly spied an old TV set someone had discarded on the roof because the trash men wouldn't haul it away.

Sal decided to lift that old TV set up on the edge of the roof and waited for the cop to get closer. When I protested what he was about to do, Sal reassured me, "Don't worry, I'm just going to scare him." When Jesse was almost directly beneath us, Sal then pushed the heavy appliance over the side. It hurtled down 12 stories and smashed into the sidewalk—two feet in front of "Officer James." When the TV crashed to the ground, this cop was scared to death. He pulled his gun, screaming wildly and looking for the culprit. Of course, by that time, we were long gone! I was never completely sure whether Sal intended to hit the guy or not.

Three Against Twenty

Once, Larry and I, wearing our leather jackets, went to meet Salvatore after school. When Sal came out from the building, we were confronted by a large gang who demanded to know what we were doing on their turf.

Sal always said, "Don't wait for a fight. If it looks like there's no way to stay out of a fight—start it!" So, we did! Sal grabbed a milk crate from the alley beside a deli and started bashing guys in the head with it. Simultaneously, he yelled at me to grab another crate and join him in the fray. When I grabbed a heavy wooden box and lifted it over my head to hit one of the gang members, I thought, *My God, if I hit this guy, it might kill him!* So, I hesitated for a second.

Sal then screamed at me, "Hit him—it's either you or him!" So I smashed the crate into the Puerto Rican's face just as he lunged at me with his knife. The blade ripped through two thicknesses of my leather jacket and sliced downward, as my attacker crumpled up on the sidewalk.

I heard Larry yelling, "Come on, you guys! Run! Run!" So we took off down the block, with at least a dozen angry Hispanics in hot pursuit. Sal tipped over the trash cans outside a store as we ran past, hoping to slow down our pursuers. But they kept coming.

Then someone shouted, "Look out!" Suddenly something hit me with crushing force, and I fell sprawling to the concrete. My head seemed to explode, and I felt a hot, gooey, smelly liquid coming out of my hair and running down my face.

Someone had thrown a bucket of tar off the roof, and it had landed on my head! Sal pulled me up and screamed, "Come on, we've got to keep going. Let's go, Dennis! We've got to run!" Somehow I managed to take a few staggering steps, and my brothers grabbed my arms and half-pulled, half-dragged me down the street.

When we reached the Junius Street Bridge, I knew we were going to make it. A hand-painted "Brownsville Boys" sign pointed to the neighborhood where all our buddies were waiting...on Brownsville Boys' turf. And sure enough, when the Puerto Rican guys saw us on the bridge, they stopped and turned around.

My brothers tried to clean me up when we got home, but it was no use. My whole head was covered with tar and blood, and the gash in my scalp wouldn't stop bleeding. When Dad got home, he was very upset.

"What did you do...pick a fight with an entire army? What are you... stupid?"

I had to go to the hospital and get stitches in my head. But first the doctors had to scrape off the gunk and shave my head. When I went back to school, everybody said I looked like Yul Brynner, the actor in "The King and I." I kind of enjoyed all the attention and hearing my classmates buzz about how Tinerino and his brothers were so tough they had taken on a whole gang. At the time, it all seemed humorous, but in reality, we could have all been killed!

Destined for Trouble

Dad was constantly trying to make sure we stayed out of trouble...but it was a losing battle. There was no way he could watch us all the time, and there was always something going on. Somebody would come around the neighborhood trying to steal a bike or a car, sell drugs, or hassle the girls, so...Reno, Dino, and Tarzan took it upon themselves to run out the troublemakers. We kept the peace, but at the same time we found plenty of opportunities to vandalize and steal. Then the storekeepers, in an uproar, would usually point their finger at us, and Dad would try to calm everybody down. Then he'd say, wearily, "You guys are trying to drive me crazy."

Another day, Mario, Sal, and I decided to go to the movies in New York, on 14th Street, Union Square. We really didn't start out to make trouble, but as we were watching the show from the balcony, about 15 Puerto Rican guys from the infamous Mau Mau gang noticed our black leather jackets with the "Brownsville Boys" insignia, crowded around us, and began trying to intimidate us.

Again, we didn't wait for someone else to throw the first punch. And in no time we were involved in a fight to end all fights. We saw right away that this brawl would soon get out of hand because the other guys were carrying blackjacks, clubs, chains, and knives. So, Sal grabbed a guy in a chokehold, then pushed him over the edge of the balcony. I grabbed the guy's feet and held him upside down over the edge.

"You guys better back off," Sal yelled. "Back off or we'll drop this guy over the balcony. And if he goes over, he's dead!" People were screaming and cursing while ushers rushed off to call the police. People down below were looking up and shouting insults at the punks interrupting the movie, and people on the balcony were shoving and pushing to get out of the conflict. The whole theater was caught up in the chaos while we remained in a standoff.

The Mau Maus started to back off and waited to see what we were going to do with their friend who was hanging over the balcony, screaming in terror. Sal then looked at me with a wild look in his eyes. "Drop him anyway," he snarled. "Let him fall!"

But my conscience wouldn't let me do it. Instead, I pulled the guy back over the railing and shoved him toward his buddies as hard as I could. Instantly the fight started up again, but Sal and I managed to climb over the seat backs and get to the exit. Mario wouldn't run, though, and eventually three or four guys cornered him down by the edge of the balcony. So, Mario climbed over the railing and jumped down to the main floor below, landing unhurt in an empty section of seats. We ran out of the theater, the Puerto Ricans in hot pursuit. Sal led us to some stairs that descended to a BMT subway station, and our tormentors followed. We could easily have been killed down there, but fortunately, there happened to be a policeman by the token booth. He stopped us and wanted to know what was going on. We stayed close to him until the Mau Maus gave up and went away. We were very happy that one of New York's "Finest" was in the right place at the right time!

Rumble at Times Square

"Dad's working late tonight, then he's going to meet the guys afterwards." Little did Mom know what that one sentence started!

Soon afterward, Sal, Mario, and I started off with our favorite caper, jumping the turnstiles in the subway. Then, on a dare, Mario gave everyone a heart attack by jumping on to the back of a train and defying death by hanging on with his bare hands all the way to the next stop. Needing more excitement, we became Robin Hood and his Merry Men by "relieving" a guy of his cash. Subsequently, we found ourselves a dice game. After playing for a while and continuing to lose big-time, we figured out that the other guys were using fixed dice. When we confronted them about running a crooked game, they refused to give our money back. So, we started slapping them around.

One guy got scared and took off, leaving his partner there alone. We roughed him up a little, then took our money back, plus a little extra. Finally, we let him go, laughing and congratulating ourselves for being such tough guys.

Suddenly, all hell broke loose. The guy we had slapped around was now coming after us waving a stiletto screaming, "I'm going to kill you guys!" And just in case we didn't understand him the first time, he added, "I'm going to cut you to ribbons!"

"Let's teach this jerk a lesson," screamed Sal, instantly enraged. We spread out, breaking radio antennas off parked cars to use for weapons.

Realizing he was outnumbered and in trouble, the guy jumped and slashed at me. The blade of the stiletto cut through my leather jacket and shirt—an inch away from my heart. It was the second time my jacket had protected me from an attacker's knife. But rather than being frightened by the attack, I became even more angry.

Soon the three of us were giving the man with the knife an awful beating. Huge red welts were swelling up across his face, and he began screaming in pain and fear. We might have killed the guy, or been killed ourselves, but in the midst of the beating, out of nowhere came a Catholic priest. He started saying a prayer and tried to break up the fight. "You guys are crazy," he exclaimed. "You're full of the devil."

Then the police showed up, and all four of us were arrested—the guy with the knife, Mario, Sal, and me. The cops talked to the priest and took down his name as a witness. Then they hauled us off to jail.

When we were allowed to make our one phone call, I called Dad. "Come get us—we're in jail," I said.

Because we were juveniles, we got bailed out, and my dad called an attorney in New York to handle the charges against us. Then he tried to persuade the priest to be a witness on our behalf, but he wouldn't do it. "The boys were beating up that poor man pretty badly," he said. "I don't know...I don't think I can help them other than to pray for them."

As I look back on these and many other stories from my youth, I realize that to have survived everything from knife fights to being pushed off the roof of a building to being shot at and shoved in front of a train, "The Man Upstairs" was definitely looking out for me, and keeping me alive for a purpose.

Chapter Three

THIS CAN BE MY TICKET OUT!

"**A**RE you sure you can do this, Dennis? We sure don't want to get way up there and fall!"

My younger brother, Larry, was on my back, holding on by wrapping his arms and legs around me. He looked at the rope in my hands, which stretched upward some 40 feet to a BMT train bridge where it was tied underneath to a cross-tie beam. "That looks awful high, Dennis. Maybe this is too dangerous!"

"Relax, Larry. I've climbed this rope lots of times. It's a piece of cake. Hang on now—we're going!"

Grasping the thick hemp rope with my hands, I heaved my body upward as far as I could, then clamped my feet around the rope to hold me steady while I moved my hands up to get a new grip. The weight of Larry's 150-pound body pulled heavily on my arms and shoulders. Maybe this was going to be harder than I thought it would be.

I *had* climbed the rope many times—alone, pulling myself up hand over hand until I was almost to the top, while the elevated train thundered by a few feet over my head and street traffic moved below me. It was a thrill—and a great way to condition my arms and upper body.

After climbing the rope for a couple of weeks, I then started tying dumbbells around my waist to make the ascent more difficult. After several slips and a couple near falls, I finally mastered the technique of climbing with the weights.

I'd gotten the idea from an article in one of the bodybuilding magazines about a local guy named Larry Cianchetta, an International Federation of Body Builders (IFBB) champion who used some flashy, unorthodox training methods. He had paddled a surfboard for long distances around Staten Island and climbed a rope hanging from a railroad trestle. He had also tied weights to his waist before climbing. I admired him because he was Italian and had broad shoulders and similar physique to mine. We eventually became good friends, and he was the godfather at my first daughter's baptism.

But not even Cianchetta had ever tried climbing up and down a rope with another person on his back. Now, about a third of the way up, pausing to gasp for breath, I could understand why.

"You're already tired out, Dennis, and this is getting really scary," said my brother. "Let's go back down!"

"Hang on, Larry. We're doing fine. I'm going to make it." And slowly, hand over hand, I kept on pulling us up the rope. My arms felt like they were being pulled out of their sockets; my lungs burned and screamed for more air. It seemed as if Larry was getting heavier by the minute.

But I refused to stop, determined to accomplish a feat no one else I knew had yet attempted. And after climbing for what seemed like an eternity, we reached the top. Anchoring my feet on the rope to hold the weight while I rested a minute, Larry and I twisted slowly around, getting a bird's-eye view of the cityscape below from a lofty new perspective.

Our outlandish feat had attracted a crowd of curious onlookers. Wearing shorts and a tank top, I kept the muscles rippling in my arms, torso, and legs, eating up all the attention, fantasizing that I was the next Tarzan in the movies, performing some heroic deed.

My brother relaxed a little when we got to the top. "This is kind of fun," he said. "At first, I didn't think you were going to make it."

Going back down was much easier, although my arms became very tired, and I could feel the muscles about to go into spasms of protest. When we were almost back to the ground, we noticed a policeman there waiting for us.

"Are you guys nuts or what?" he bellowed. "Somebody called in to say two crazy kids were about to break their necks climbing a rope. What's the matter with you?"

Relieved and flushed with new confidence, I assured the officer that our feat was perfectly safe and that we were never in any danger. I don't think either of us really believed it, though.

———◦———

I'd been working out at the Brooklyn Central YMCA since I was 12 where my dad had taken my brothers and me two or three times a week.

The YMCA was a good facility, with volleyball, an indoor track, boxing, tumbling, gymnastics, weight lifting, and fencing, as well as saunas, a steam room, and showers. I soon met some other aspiring young bodybuilders there, and we became friends. I was the youngest of them all and was always watching what they did and asking questions. Subsequently, I began to develop my own workout program. I also started buying *Health and Strength*, *Ironman*, *Muscle Power*, and *Muscular*

Development magazines as well as bodybuilding booklets to learn about the various muscle groups and development techniques.

Before long, it was obvious to almost everybody that I had been bitten by the "iron bug." They used to call me the "one-man gang" because I'd go to the gym with my dad early on Saturday morning...and stay all day. I'd work out, using all the weights and each apparatus, trying every exercise I could think of doing. I wanted to be the best at everything.

When I wasn't at the gym, I did chin-ups and dips on the monkey bars at the neighborhood playground. I also used the chinning bar I had installed in my bedroom doorway and various pulley and spring devices I had bought with money earned from shining shoes on the street. I even sent off for mail-order products I had read about in the magazines—different vitamins and protein supplements.

And within a few months, my body began to respond to all the vigorous exercise and training. I could see my body growing broader, thicker, bulkier, stronger. And so could everybody else—especially the girls at school and in the neighborhood. I always had an eye for the girls, and the attention I got when I flexed my biceps, did a "strong man" pose, or beat someone at arm wrestling was something I really liked.

When I was about the age of ten, people began to notice that I resembled the pop stars Fabian and Frankie Avalon. I had the same dark, olive complexion, and I deliberately wore my hair in an exaggerated pompadour style. "He's a good-looking kid," my aunts and uncles would say. "Maybe he'll grow up and be a movie star." I knew a little about music and would sing along with all the pop songs and took pride in dressing sharp, even though my family didn't have much money to spend on clothes.

At school I was always cracking jokes and acting "cool"—anything to be the center of attention. And as my body developed from the rigorous training at the gym, I gained new confidence that I was not reluctant to flaunt. The more the girls noticed me, the better I liked it.

When they were around I'd strike a pose, expanding my chest and flexing my biceps. In the gym, I'd load all the weights available on the school's rinky-dink barbell set and pick it up with one arm. Then I'd bask in the glory of the inevitable oohs, aahs, and giggles.

Setting New Goals

Soon everybody was aware that I had decided to become a body-builder. Meanwhile, I continued with my workout regimen. I watched the Jack LaLanne exercise show on TV and picked up some of his techniques, and somehow I managed to get hold of a 110-pound barbell set from the Dan Lurie Company in Brooklyn. I kept it under my bed, dragging it out to do extra sets of repetitions of basic exercises whenever I was home, and I would follow the wall chart of exercises that other body builders demonstrated.

To keep me from becoming too satisfied with myself, I kept a collection of photos of bodybuilding champions—guys like John Grimek, Bill Pearl, Larry Scott, and Larry Cianchetti. I also had a poster of Steve Reeves on my wall, with a cut-out photo of my head pasted over his, captioned: "FUTURE MR. UNIVERSE, UNDER CONSTRUCTION." In addition, I started keeping a chart of my measurements—the size of my arms, chest, waist, thighs, and calves—to keep track of my progress.

When I reached a sticking point in my personal workout program—where it seemed I was making no progress—I went to the older guys at the YMCA and asked what I needed to do. A competitive bodybuilder named Kenny Hall, who continued to compete well into his 60's, was a big help and positive influence on my life. When he advised me that I needed greater power in my legs and more mass in my upper body, I added the discipline of power lifting—the dead lift, bench press, and squats—to the competitive weight-lifting routines I was already doing. It was tough, hard, grueling work, and I remember standing in the gym, soaked with sweat, muscles trembling from exertion and exhaustion, saying to myself, "I must be crazy to do this."

But watching my muscles ripple in the mirror as I moved through my workout, feeling the blood coursing through my veins, and sensing the increase of strength and power in my body made it all worthwhile.

My First Competition

I entered the Mr. Hercules bodybuilding competition when I was 16. Somebody said—on a whim, and almost like a dare—"Hey, Dennis, you might be good enough to compete in this. What do you think?" So, of course, I had to do it.

The competition was a promotional event for the Steve Reeves/Reg Park/Mark Forrest Hercules films. The local sponsors were Loew's movie theater on Pitkin Avenue in Brooklyn and Vic Tanny's Empire Health Club. They provided trophies, month-long movie passes, and free gym memberships for the top three contestants.

When the day of the competition rolled around, I was so nervous I could hardly stand still. I really didn't know what to expect or exactly what I was supposed to do. The only help I'd had was studying pictures of bodybuilders in magazines and talking to the guys at the "Y." I knew I was supposed to have a front pose, a side pose, and a back pose in which I flexed the various muscle groups to show off their development and definition. But I really didn't have a set program or choreographed routine.

When my name was called, I heard the cheers and encouragement of my friends from school and the neighborhood, and of family members who'd come to see me in my very first competition. I simply walked out and flexed, made a quarter turn and flexed, made another quarter turn and flexed. That was my standard scoring routine. Then I was supposed to do a random routine to show my posing ability. I was so dazzled and intimidated by the noise and exuberance of the crowd that I'm not sure exactly what I did. Basically, I did the same poses again in a different order, plus a few others, then got back in line. That was all I knew to do.

A little while later, the emcee came on and began announcing the winners in traditional reverse order. "Ladies and Gentlemen, our third-place winner in the Mr. Hercules competition—MR. DENNIS TINER-INO!" The crowd exploded in thunderous applause. I stepped out to the front of the stage to receive my trophy and certificate, exhilarated and intoxicated by the lights and the noise. In fact, I was so excited I barely noticed who came in second and first.

The only thought that came to mind was, *I love this—the attention, the recognition, the applause. This is something I can do—and in time I'll do it better than anyone else has ever done it. Someday I'll be Mr. America, Mr. World, Mr. Universe! Watch out for me—Dennis Tinerino. I'm going to be a champion!*

In addition to the recognition and the boost to my self-assurance that came from placing among the winners in my first competition, the prize of a membership at the Empire Health Studio was a really big deal. The first time I walked into this big, fancy, spa-type gym with its carpeted exercise areas, juice bar, trainers, a full array of benches and machines, and racks of chrome-plated weights, I realized there was a whole new level of training available to me. This was a place where the elite, the champions trained. I gazed around, and they looked mighty impressive to me—a "wannabe" kid from the projects.

Compared to where I had been, this was definitely upscale, big time. I began to see my dream of a career in bodybuilding from a totally different perspective. There was a whole new world out there—big, bewildering—but available to me if I was willing to work.

And I wasn't afraid of work. Even before placing in the Mr. Hercules competition, I'd started following a very regimented, very disciplined lifestyle of training. I felt that bodybuilding could be my ticket out of the projects. Somehow I knew there had to be a better way of living; and to find it, I'd have to be ready when the opportunity came. So, training became almost an obsession—something I could give my whole life to.

New York's Street School

New York was a terrific place for an aspiring bodybuilder. While there was little coverage of the sport on television, in the city there were numerous health clubs and national organizations that conducted bodybuilding shows and competitions.

One Friday night per month there was a bodybuilding show somewhere in one of the city's five boroughs, and I went to these competitions to observe how the shows were conducted, what posing routines bodybuilders were using, and also to check out the competition. Although I had only limited knowledge about the sport in the beginning, I soon picked up on the terminology and what the judges were looking for in a winner.

Some guys were just massive hulks, with broad shoulders, arms as big as tree trunks, and bulging thighs and legs. They did indeed appear to be "muscle-bound," lumbering along, gorilla-like. Others were not so huge but had impressive muscularity. The best of them, however, had symmetry and proportion, "cut," with sharp, well-defined lines between the various muscle groups. If a competitor had a problem area or was less developed in one muscle group, it was easy to spot.

I also noticed that good competitors were aware of the best parts of their bodies and had developed poses and moves that showed off these features to their advantage. They displayed their compulsory poses, then moved smoothly to poses that accentuated their strengths and best features.

Sometimes my bodybuilding buddies, my brothers, or my dad would go to these shows with me. We'd sit up in the stands and engage in a running commentary regarding each competitor. "Look at that bum, Dennis," Dad would say. "You could beat him without trying—why didn't you enter this contest?" Or "Wow, that guy is awesome. Watch him move—he looks really good!"

Comparing myself with each contestant was part of my education. I could see what the competition was like—what I would have to do to be successful. In a sense, being a spectator at the shows was a way for me to test the waters.

A few months later, my buddies said, "Hey, Dennis, you need to enter the big competition that's coming up. You're pretty good, and you've probably got as good a chance as anyone. Go for it!"

The "big competition" was a combination contest—Mr. America, Mr. Universe, Miss America—sponsored by the International Federation of Body Builders (IFBB). I picked up an entry form, filled it out, and submitted it. I was too naïve even to be surprised when I was selected.

The show was held at the Brooklyn Academy of Music, and again my family and friends came out to see me compete. They were lost in the crowd of five thousand screaming fans who'd come to see some really good bodybuilders. The place was loaded with movie personalities, and the media were as thick as ants around honey. The atmosphere took on the dimensions of a circus, with guys like the Mighty Adam, who pulled a carload of people with his teeth!

I was underdeveloped and totally unprepared for this kind of competition I was facing. And I was totally in awe to be close to—posing with— bodybuilding heroes whose pictures were now hanging on my wall!

Larry Scott won Mr. Universe, and Reg Lewis won Mr. America in that contest. Chuck Sipes posed and gave a "feats of strength" show. The deafening applause the audience gave the winners and other bodybuilding stars like Larry Scott was awesome.

I could see I had a long way to go before I was ready to compete with these great champions, but I didn't let it intimidate me. I resolved then and there not only to continue competing, but to win.

Subsequently, I joined the Amateur Athletic Union (AAU), which promoted the original Junior Mr. America and Mr. America competitions. Getting good enough to compete in these contests and win these titles was a major part of my goal. Because of its involvement with the Olympics committee, the AAU required its bodybuilding contestants to participate in one or more other athletic sports. Placing in one of the top three spots in your chosen event was worth five points for athletic ability in the Mr. America competitions. You had to have those five points to have a chance of winning because the judging was always very tight.

I concentrated on becoming a competitive weight lifter and power lifter, both qualified amateur sports, and I did well as a weight lifter, winning many regional and national competitions as a heavyweight.

I was also interested in fencing and participated on the varsity fencing team at East New York Vocational High School, determined to help my team win. My strength, speed, and natural aggressiveness, as well as my focus and flexibility served me well. I won several championship matches for my school and could have accepted a full athletic scholarship to college. I still remember the satisfaction of carrying the fencing foil in an athletic bag onto the BMT subway on my way across town to inter-school matches. In my imagination I felt like one of the Three Musketeers on my way to participate in some grand new adventure.

The important thing was that it soon became obvious that fencing would enable me to earn the full five points required by the AAU. Having accomplished that, I could then apply all my efforts to developing my physique to a new standard—an unprecedented level of development that would bring new respect and honor to the title of Mr. America.

Dad and Mom's Sacrificial Support

I was blessed to have a family who was totally supportive of my dream. Once my dad saw that I was fully committed to bodybuilding, he was with me 110 percent, helping me in every way possible. He often went with me to the gym to offer encouragement, or sometimes to serve as my "spotter" as I worked with heavy weights. He also helped me get the vitamins and supplements I needed.

When I began competing in various shows, Dad was nearly always there, cheering me on if he possibly could. And when the competitions were in other states—and later, other countries—he helped pay my travel expenses.

My mom was also a trouper, cooking incredible, prodigious amounts of food to satisfy my voracious appetite. When I was in heavy training, I

Dennis' parents, Carmine & Mary

sometimes consumed 8,000 calories a day...or even more! So when I was home, Mom lived in the kitchen. Breakfast included a full dozen eggs, potatoes, meat, toast, and all the trimmings. Lunch could be pizza, soup, sandwiches, salad, or leftovers. And dinner might be one or two steaks, spaghetti, meatballs, lasagna, or some other pasta dish, vegetables, bread, and dessert. Then somehow, Mom managed to come up with as many snacks as I needed—fruit, pastry, you name it. My folks teasingly called me "the garbage dump" or "the bottomless pit." Dad even encouraged me to find a girlfriend whose father owned a restaurant!

Because my body had a very high metabolism, I had a hard time gaining weight or "bulking up." Even when eating enormous amounts of food, I stayed very muscular and wiry. I even tried what was called "force-feeding," setting an alarm to wake up at three o'clock in the morning to make a high-calorie protein shake for myself. I would wake the whole household, fumbling with the alarm, turning on the lights, running the blender, and drinking the shake. Then it was back to bed.

Providing just the food and financial assistance to help me reach my goals was a tremendous sacrifice for my folks. But they never complained, and they were always there for me. Without their support, it would have been virtually impossible for me to become a bodybuilding champion.

Back to Basics

At first, I thoroughly enjoyed working out at the Empire Health Studio. The equipment was great, and the staff helped me put together a solid workout program. In addition, several of the guys at the gym were accomplished body-builders; however, they didn't seem to have much time for me. They were pretty much "into themselves," too busy doing their own thing to offer much help. But I still was able to watch what they did and occasionally pick their brains by asking questions.

More often than not, I'd end up back at the Brooklyn Central YMCA, sharing the information I had gathered with my old training partners. By teaching them the new concepts I'd learned, I was able to make sure that those techniques were even more deeply ingrained into my own mind. Even when we weren't working out, my training partners and I would still hang out together. We were young and strong...and pretty impressed with ourselves, even pulling stop signs, encased in concrete, completely out of the ground just for fun!

We were constantly finding ways to show off and demonstrate our strength. One night in Greenwich Village, four of us picked up a Volkswagen "Beetle" that was parked beside the curb and carried it up to the steps of the owner's brownstone. Then we rang the doorbell and ran, laughing like crazy. When the guy came out, there was his car parked on the steps to his house! I wish we could have seen his face!

Testing the Waters (Ready for the Competition)

When I was 17 and as strong and conditioned as I had ever been in my life, I decided to enter the Junior Mr. Metropolitan competition. I'd been working diligently for two years, implementing every aspect of what I had learned since my first competition, and by experimentation, I had discovered which exercises and training methods worked best for my body. Using tips I had picked up from watching others compete, reading my magazines, and observing champions at different health clubs, I'd put together a better posing routine, choreographing my best poses and moves to music. In addition, I had focused on my tan and learned how to oil my body to highlight my muscles.

As the prejudging began at the Junior Mr. Metropolitan contest, I felt a tinge of anxiety and uncertainty in the pit of my stomach, but as soon as I heard my friends and family speaking words of encouragement, my confidence returned.

And the minute I stepped onstage I felt even better. I had practiced each move a hundred times. I knew every note of the music and what I was supposed to be doing when I heard each part of the melody. I'd visualized myself going through each pose, each flex, each turn. And from the enthusiastic response of the crowd, I sensed that they liked me.

When my music stopped and I stepped back in line, I was elated to hear a thundering ovation from the crowd. I knew I had done well—I would not be satisfied with anything less than winning.

And when the awards presentation was made, I was not disappointed. After the top-place finishers were named, the music fanfare surged to a crescendo, and the emcee shouted into the microphone—"JUNIOR MR. METROPOLITAN IS DENNIS TINERINO!"

My first win! My first championship! I looked around and saw my dad out front, laughing for joy! I then recognized other friends in the crowd, guys who had pushed me on at the YMCA and at Vic Tanny's gym—they were also sharing in the thrill of my victory. The spotlight hit me, and the roar of the crowd hit my ears. It was time to celebrate!

And there *was* celebrating that night, Italian style, with food, drinks, laughing, and a throng of family, friends, and well-wishers...including more than one pretty girl. For a few magic hours, the months of exhausting training, the sweating and straining, the discipline and determination all seemed worthwhile.

But there was not time to celebrate for long. After reliving and savoring the thrill of my first victory for a few days with my friends in the neighborhood and at the gyms where I worked out, it was time to start preparing for a new challenge. I became eager to compete again, and as a winner, I was now eligible to participate in an upcoming bodybuilding event that included contestants from all over the city—the Mr. New York City competition.

By this time, there were more people at the gym interested in watching me work out, and some of the guys who hadn't had time for me before, now came around to offer suggestions and wish me well. In fact, it seemed everybody wanted to help me, and I was given lots of advice on how to polish my routine and make it sharper and more impressive. Suddenly, I had the respect and recognition of my peers, and training became a lot more fun with all the extra attention.

I felt that the Mr. New York City contest was a more important event, certainly the biggest competition I'd ever been part of. When it was held at the 125th Street YMCA in Harlem, there was a capacity crowd watching. And once again, against a solid field of quality competitors, I won the contest! I had now captured a third place and two outright wins! I was ecstatic.

Later that year, I was named the AAU's "Outstanding Bodybuilder" for 1964 and won the "Mr. Eastern America" regional title. I was definitely on track, and my plan was working.

Winning a bodybuilding contest is heady stuff. You know you look good—everybody's admiring your physique and muscles, and you feel good from all the conditioning and dieting. And after months of near isolation in a stuffy gym, you're suddenly onstage, in the spotlight, taking bows before a demonstrative crowd of well-wishers.

If you're fortunate enough to place among the finalists—or to win—the attention and adulation goes straight to your ego! Photographers snap picture after picture, asking you to pose. Friends pound you on the back,

Dennis wins his first contest — Mr. Brooklyn

and total strangers shake your hand. And there are always the girls hanging around, smiling and flirting.

Although I was certainly not immune to temptation, my personal goals were well-developed enough in my mind to help keep me focused. I had a burning desire to succeed—an attitude of winning at any cost. Every day I thought about becoming a champion bodybuilder and using that success to get out of the poverty-stricken, crime-infested projects of East New York. I dreamed of seeing my picture in *Health and Strength* and

Iron Man magazines, of getting paid big money to make commercials and ads, endorsing products, and even making it in the movies!

Overcoming Distractions

To be a champion, I knew I had to be disciplined in my training. My father had taught me from an early age that respect and discipline go together. However, there were so many distractions. The neighborhood, my old friends, and even my family were constantly tempting me to compromise my goals and ideals. I owe a huge debt of gratitude to an AAU judge by the name of Dick Shatel who took it upon himself to act as my "big brother," often taking me to meets and driving me home from the gym. He became like part of the family to me, and to a great extent was responsible for helping me resist the urge to compromise and possibly ruin my career.

Considering my questionable activities as a member of "The Brownsville Boys" and as a teenager looking for trouble on occasion, I knew it was only a matter of time until someone got hurt—or we got caught. The risks were simply too great. The longer I stayed around East New York, the greater the probability that I'd never get out. So I renewed my resolve to use my physical talent as a ticket out of the ghetto. I determined to work even harder—to let nothing distract me or become more important than achieving my goals. That driving ambition helped to some extent to prevent me from getting sidetracked.

Chapter Four

MENTORS, MEDALS, AND MAYHEM

"**H**OW would you like to meet Mr. America?"

I looked up from my plate of spaghetti and meatballs at my friend Roger, the manager of the deli where I ate lunch almost every day. "Yeah, sure," I said in disbelief. "Why don't you also set me up an appointment with the President of the United States?"

"Hey, man, I'm serious. I work out with this guy all the time—he's my best friend. Joe's main job is teaching school, but he trains a lot and stays in shape. And he really did win the Mr. America title a few years ago.

"What's his name?" I asked.

"Joe Abbenda—I think he'd like to meet you."

I was really excited at this news. *Of course* I wanted to meet Joe Abbenda. At the time, he was one of only two Italian-Americans involved in bodybuilding at the championship level. Abbenda was Mr. America and twice Mr. Universe, and the other guy, Tom Sansone, had also been a Mr. America winner.

"Why do you think Abbenda would want to meet me?"

"Well, you're looking pretty good, Dennis. You've won some important contests, and I can see you're working hard and eating right. Let's face it—your whole life revolves around becoming a champion. I think you've got the potential to follow in Joe's footsteps. You could make it if you had the guidance and training of someone who has already reached the top— someone like Joe Abbenda!"

At the time, Joe was in Europe for the summer, conducting fitness seminars, appearing in posing exhibitions, and judging several bodybuilding contests. I could hardly wait until he returned home.

What an amazing turn of events! I had been working after school as a packing clerk for a company in Astoria-Queens, handling 50-pound boxes of bolts, nuts, and screws. I loved the job because it was physical; even when I wasn't at the gym, I still could get a workout! I'd put in my hours working, then I'd go eat at a little Italian-American delicatessen close to my job. Afterward, I'd take the train all the way back to Brooklyn to work out at the YMCA there. After two or three hours, I'd go home to sleep. Early the next morning I'd start all over again.

It was at the delicatessen that I got acquainted with Roger. Now, he had just offered me the chance of a lifetime! I told my parents, my friends, my brothers, anyone who would listen, and most of them thought I was making it up, especially the guys at the gym!

After waiting for what seemed like an eternity, the day finally came. I was standing in front of one of my heroes—someone I had idolized for years! To my joy and amazement, Joe and I hit it off immediately. He was a tremendous man, intelligent, well-educated, and in superb physical condition. With his Italian heritage and experience as an accomplished bodybuilder, we discovered right away that we had much in common. He was one of those people you meet and feel that you've known all of your life. He took an immediate interest in me and my dreams and goals.

Joe invited me to come work out with him in his folk's one-car garage that he had converted into a makeshift gym. To my surprise, it was within walking distance of where I worked. The gym certainly wasn't fancy. In fact, it was a "Flintstone special"—primitive as a cave. You had to crawl through a small, low, improvised door. There was no ceiling—only exposed rafters. The walls were rough, the floor unfinished concrete, and the equipment consisted mostly of crude but workable benches and racks. I remember the "pulley" for the "lat" pull-down was a butcher's hook fastened to a beam with a cable running through it. The only heat came from a small, open-flame gas stove—and the body heat we generated as we worked out. It was great because there were no distractions, although it was like being in a dungeon. But still, Joe had all the free weights, dumbbells, and basic equipment we needed, and he knew a great deal about the sport of bodybuilding.

The first time I worked out with him, I demonstrated about every exercise and lift anyone had ever shown me, including all I knew about weight lifting, power lifting, and bodybuilding. When I was finished, Joe led me out of the gym and into the basement of the house, next to the winepress where his father made his famous Italian Chianti. There, in the faint light coming from a hallway bathroom, Joe asked me to do my posing routine for him. Wanting to make a good impression, I asked, "Don't we need more light?"

"Don't worry about it—just pose."

So I did, demonstrating the posing routine I'd used in winning my last couple of competitions.

When I stopped, Joe just shook his head. "Your routine needs lots of work, Dennis, and so does your training workout. You're doing a lot of stuff that's either repetitive or unnecessary, wasting too much time and energy. You need to concentrate on the building blocks—the basic things that really count. If you'll do this, you could be Mr. America and Mr. Universe—a true world champion, like me. I'll help you if you want me to."

If I wanted him to? Of course, I did! This was the first time a real champion and an AAU judge had ever given me any personal attention. So we started working out together, with Joe acting as my coach. Joe was the mentor, I was the protégée, and he let me know the rules right away. "You do exactly what I tell you and how I tell you to do it. No lip service. The first time you complain or don't follow my rules, you're outta here. Got it, kid?" At that point, I became a member of Joe's warm, gregarious family, sharing fine Italian meals and laughs as well as our workouts.

Four days a week, we would head for the dungeon, turn on the light and the radio, and train nonstop, set after set, rep after rep, increasing the weight as we went along. Usually we worked at least two hours, and often three. Monday was a killer day, working on my chest, shoulders, and triceps. Tuesday we worked on my legs, back, and biceps, averaging twenty sets per body part, which really finished me off. We did waist and calves every workout. By Wednesday, I was more than ready to rest and let my exhausted body recuperate. We completed the entire workout again on Thursday and Friday. Over the years, I've found this to be a highly successful routine for developing strength and size, and I've recommended it to many bodybuilders.

Joe Abbenda was noted for being very strong. He could squat with more than 500 pounds any day of the week. So I really had to work hard to catch up with him. At first I could barely keep up, but after only six months on Joe's training and nutrition program, my body was making dramatic improvement. I had gained size and strength and was more muscular. Not only could I *feel* the difference, but it was also apparent by looking at me.

Competition Beckons

At that point, Joe felt I was ready to start competing again. So he helped me develop a totally new posing routine and coached me on how to present myself to the judges. He stressed that rather than a series of utilitarian muscle flexes, my posing routine should be a dramatic performance with meaning and showmanship. Setting this routine to music, turning, reaching, moving—at times I almost felt like a dancer. But after the initial sense of awkwardness, posing became exciting and fun!

I became aware that my personality and inner feelings were positive gifts I needed to use to my advantage to infuse my performance with confidence and *life*. My posing routine could become a platform to display a winner's image—an expression of originality and vision that could set a new standard of excellence and pride.

But before I started up the ladder of competitions leading to the Mr. America contest, I needed experience. It was another part of Joe's strategy: training, nutrition, experience, posing, and pre-contest diet. This strategy made me ready to step out on stage with the confidence and assurance of a champion.

Having won the Mr. New York City contest, I was eligible for the Mr. Eastern America competition, which attracted the top contenders from all of New England and the Eastern seaboard. With months of conditioning and coaching by Joe Abbenda, I went into the contest totally prepared and with enthusiastic confidence. And I won that regional competition handily. The Tinerino name was beginning to be recognized and respected

Dennis (center) wins Mr. New York City

throughout the New York area. My family—especially my dad—was very proud of my achievements.

Abbenda's strategy was working, and I had a definite advantage. Not only was Joe my friend, my training partner, and my coach, he was also a highly respected world champion bodybuilder and AAU judge. With Joe as my mentor, I received immediate credibility. The talk in the gyms and even in the magazines was that Joe had found someone with great potential, and was molding him to follow in his footsteps.

With each win, I gained more confidence, more polish, more assurance. In fact, I was enjoying my new status as a "star" athlete to the hilt. It was a thrill to be "somebody"—not just another Italian ghetto kid from the projects, running around with a gang and staying a half step ahead of the law.

The Majors

Following the Mr. New York City title, I won the AAU Outstanding Body Building Award. Now, Abbenda felt I was ready for national competition and entered me in the 1964 Teenage Mr. America contest in Chattanooga, Tennessee. I was 18 years old, and this was to be my first trip on an airplane. Because of the expense, no one else from my family could afford to go with me. Furthermore, Joe was working full-time as a schoolteacher and couldn't get away. So I went alone.

Chattanooga was like another planet to me. I'd never seen so many trees and mountains. There were pickup trucks everywhere, and Southern guys drawling, "Whurh ya'll frum? Why're yuh dressed that way?" I'd never seen or heard anything like these rednecks. They reminded me of the "locals" in the movie *Deliverance*—like they still went hunting for lunch. Actually, they were hunting for a fight! Before I could get my bearings, they came at me with insults about my clothes, my looks, and my "Eye-talian" heritage, trying to goad me into fighting them. Luckily, Ralph Countryman, an AAU judge, arrived at the airport in the nick of time, and whisked me to my hotel before they pushed me too far.

The contest was tough. The favorite was Bud Shozak, a guy known for his huge, muscular legs, calves, and thighs. His upper body wasn't as developed, but he ultimately won Teenage Mr. America that year. I came in third. I was shocked and bitterly disappointed by the loss.

A Victory in the Midst of Defeat

The highlight of the trip for me was meeting Paul Anderson. Actually, I was trying to get acquainted with his daughter, a pretty blonde girl, when he came over and started talking to me.

"Dennis Tinerino, my name is Paul Anderson," he said. "You've got a pretty good physique, son." Paul Anderson was an Olympic gold medal champion weight lifter, a legendary competitor who was often called the strongest man in the world. In fact, many of his records still stand. Paul overcame many adversities, including severe physical illness, to achieve his goals, and was always steroid-free.

"I believe if you stick with what you're doing, you're going to go all the way," he said smiling. Then, suddenly serious, he said, "But remember one thing. It's great to win contests and titles, but don't forget to give the glory to the One who deserves it—the Lord Jesus Christ. Always remember to praise Him for the gifts He gave you, Dennis." He continued, "I'd rather burn out for Jesus than rust out living for the devil."

And the legendary Paul Anderson began to witness to me about the Lord. He told me about the Christian boys' home he had set up not too far away and how working for the Lord was the most important thing in his life. I couldn't remember anyone ever talking about God and Jesus to me the way he did. I was reminded of the time on the train when I was 12 years old and heard an inner voice speak those wonderful things to me about serving God. When I shared my experience on the train with him, Paul told me that this was just another confirmation of the calling that God had put on my life. He urged me to surrender my life and my career to the Lord. By speaking to me about these things, Paul planted another *seed* in my heart, but one which would not sprout for many years.

I was fascinated by what I was hearing. I realized that Paul Anderson had something I didn't have. I could sense his inner peace and great faith. Although I didn't understand all he was saying, I respected him for his sincere testimony. His final words to me still resonate in my heart. "Dennis, to be a real man, you have to meet Jesus—the man from Galilee." The men whom I knew had only an outward strength, but I knew way down deep that Paul Andersen had inner strength. I had grown up under the influence of people who had no real sense of values, but Paul was showing me another way to live.

Although my life at times was to be filled with sin and degradation— plunging me to the depths of despair—I never forgot the light and the witness I received from Paul Anderson, a true "strong man" of faith for God.

Back to the Drawing Board

Back home in New York, my family was disappointed that I hadn't won. On the other hand, Joe Abbenda was tremendously encouraging. "Don't worry about it, Dennis," he said. "I think you should have won, but it's history. Just get back to work. Next year the contest is in Philadelphia, and you're going to win! Don't get discouraged. In the meantime, let's go for the Junior Mr. America."

And to everybody's surprise, even though most of the other guys in the contest were older than me, I did remarkably well, placing second. The muscle magazine write-ups increased, and so did my confidence.

Then I focused my attention on training and preparing for the next Teenage Mr. America competition. I made a poster of a picture of myself in a strongman pose, including a giant-sized caption—DENNIS TINER-INO, TEENAGE MR. AMERICA. I hung a copy on the wall in my room at home and another in Joe Abbenda's dungeon. Every time I went to the gym to work out, I was reminded of my goal. Every time I went home at night to sleep, I remembered what I was striving for.

A Champion at Last

In May 1964, I graduated and received my general diploma from East New York Vocational High School. My vocational major was electronics, although I had no interest at all in spending the rest of my life sitting at a bench repairing TV sets and hi-fi equipment. Dad wanted me to get a job with security...maybe even have a retirement pension after 20 years. I wanted to travel the world, meet successful and interesting people, and make my mark.

At that time, the fitness business wasn't all that great. A few made money in the relatively new business of product endorsements, doing photo shoots for magazine ads and making spots for radio and TV, but there was no big commercial market for bodybuilders, even titled champions. Some got bit parts in Hollywood movies, maybe even a starring role in a "B"-grade film. But the key word was "few."

Dad could never understand what was motivating me—why I wanted to take such a long shot in the dark. In his sincere efforts to be a good parent, he encouraged me to settle down and make conventional decisions, but he also remained supportive of my efforts in the bodybuilding field.

The next year, in Philadelphia, I was as prepared as could be for the Teenage Mr. America contest. I had made great improvement since the year before; my body was in superb condition; and I was mentally ready.

Because Philadelphia was relatively close to New York, my dad and mom both were able to attend. They knew how much this competition meant to me, and they wanted to be there, cheering me on.

The pre-event rumor mill had it that the top two guys in the competition both had the potential to go on to win Mr. America. And the experts thought the top two guys were Boyer Coe, a talented young man from Lafayette, Louisiana...and Dennis Tinerino.

When the posing was over and the judges completed their scoring tabulations, the contestants lined up on stage for the announcement of the final placements. The announcer said, "And in second place...Boyer Coe!" The crowd applauded as he took his bow. I then looked out to find my mom and dad. "Marone," Momma screamed, "my son is the champion. My son is the champion!" They already realized what the announcer was about to say—"Ladies and Gentlemen, the 1965 Teenage Mr. America is...DENNIS TINERINO!"

A wave of exhilaration and deep satisfaction swept over me. Here was a milestone—a really significant achievement! Teenage Mr. America was a national competition. My name was in the record books, and my picture would be in all the bodybuilding magazines. I would now be favored to win Junior Mr. America, then Mr. America!

This victory was different from all the other competitions I had won. Because it was a national event, winning the Teenage Mr. America title gave me instant status and recognition wherever I went. People were now even asking for my autograph!

One victory led to another, paving the way to three more major titles: Mr. North America, Junior Mr. USA, and Mr. East Coast...totally unheard of in bodybuilding until now. I was officially on my way to the top! What a year!

A Bunch of Wild and Ca-ray-zee Guys

Bodybuilding was no longer just a hope-filled dream or a way up and out of my surroundings—it had become an all-consuming passion, a way of life. Bodybuilding was not something I did—it was who I was! However, all training and no play was not a part of my vocabulary. I was happiest and completely at ease when I was hanging out with my body-building buddies.

In the summertime, a bunch of my friends from the YMCA and the neighborhood would take a trip to Coney Island to escape the heat. We'd all ride the same BMT subway together. Each of the guys would wait at their various stations until they saw others of us on the train. Those of us already on the train would stick our heads out the windows and shout, "UMGAHWA!" That was their cue to jump on board.

Guys from East New York, Benton Hurst, Burrough Park—all the stops along the way—would pile on the same car. There was more than a dozen altogether. We'd all be wearing tank tops, shorts, and sandals, doing push-ups between the seats, and pulling ourselves up on the bars at the top of the car. We didn't care what other people thought. We were looking for excitement and craving attention. And to make sure we had everyone's attention, we'd even sing songs we'd heard in the *Hercules* movies.

We're 230 pounds of muscle and steel,
We have 20-inch arms—we know we're for real.
We're coming on strong, staying long, talking loud,
And winning the crowd.
We're the first, the last, the best, and the most—

Dennis & Tommy Aybar at Coney Island

The girls all love us from coast to coast!
And we will win the championship crown.
We're the mighty men of Hercules.
We fight for the rights of men,
And we will win the victory.

What we lacked in talent and musical ability, we made up for in volume and enthusiasm! Most other BMT passengers would wisely decide to let us have the whole car to ourselves. So we had a great time riding out to Coney Island—huge, muscular, young giants, Vikings, warriors, gladiators...all acting like the overgrown teenagers we were.

Coney Island had a great beach for swimming and lounging, and there were always girls in skimpy swimsuits lying in the sun. More importantly, several former Mr. Universe titleholders hung out there. We couldn't wait to pick their brains and pose for pictures with them.

Trying to flirt with the girls and impress the onlookers at the same time, some of us would start to arm wrestle and compete in bodybuilding pose-offs. This would evolve into an outright showdown of show-offs. From handstands and chin-ups on the Boardwalk, the competition graduated to push-ups with girls on our backs and pressing a person overhead. A few of us even brought springs and other apparatus to pump up. Then we would jump into the water and swim like dolphins to cool off.

Famished from all the exercise, we'd eat mass quantities of Nathan's famous hotdogs, sandwiches, and pizza from the food stands, buy snow cones and ice cream, and drink protein shakes.

Coney Island also had an amusement park with penny arcade games, food booths, and rides like the giant Ferris wheel, fancy merry-go-rounds, Tilt-A-Whirl, bumper cars, and the famous Cyclone roller coaster. But those things were for little kids as far as we were concerned. What we wanted to do next was dance. So we'd find a spot where the jukebox never stopped playing...dancing 'til dark to songs by Elvis Presley, Frankie Avalon, The Four Seasons, Tom Jones, Diana Ross—all the Motown stars, and all the Top 40 hits.

Families spread out picnic lunches in the shade under the piers. Kids ran in the water, built sand castles, laughed and screamed and squabbled. It was the place to be.

But just like in the city, various gangs staked out their turf on the beach at Coney Island. Pier 15 was the place for all the Italians from Little Italy. The blacks had their own area and so did the Puerto Ricans. If someone walked onto the wrong section of beach, he could easily be attacked.

For the most part, my friends and I avoided the young "toughs" who were swaggering around and looking for trouble. After all, we'd already been there and done that. All we were interested in was celebrating being young and strong and full of life. We felt invincible, unbeatable—like kings of the mountain.

Chapter Five

RIDING THE
ROLLER COASTER OF SUCCESS

California, Here I Come!

S OON after I won the Teenage Mr. America contest, Joe Abbenda got in touch with a close friend of his named Bill Pearl who owned and operated a bodybuilding gym in southern California. Bill was the epitome of bodybuilding, having won every major title including Mr. America and Mr. Universe. I idolized him. He was massive, symmetrical, graceful, and perfectly coordinated, yet known as a gentleman and revered as an authority on fitness. Bill Pearl was in a class by himself.

Joe first introduced me to Bill on the phone. Then we essentially became pen pals, corresponding back and forth at least once a month. Usually my letters were full of questions about workout routines and strategies for future contests as well as the current scoop on the sport. He always wrote back to me with good advice that was both encouraging and challenging. One day on the phone Bill asked me, "Hey, Dennis, how would you like to come to California for a while? You can stay with me and train at my health club. Maybe you can even take a crack at the 1965 Mr. America contest coming up out here."

"I'd love to come," I stuttered in excitement. "Thanks for asking me…I can't wait to get there." Being invited to California was like a dream come true. Since I was 12 years old, I had fantasized about going to the West Coast. California was Hollywood—where the movie stars were and home to some of the top-rated, big-name bodybuilders. California was sunshine, ocean, and sandy beaches filled with bikini-clad girls. California was paradise!

I'd been saving up a little money from my job as a shipping clerk at the nut-and-bolt factory, and my boss had informed me, "Dennis, if you'll do a good job until it's time for you to leave, I'll buy your plane ticket to California." I was out of school, so there was nothing to keep me in New York, and I planned to stay on the West Coast at least all summer. Finally, I was taking off on a grand adventure, and I was one step closer to fulfilling my life's dream.

A Taste of Paradise

California was everything I dreamed it would be…and more. There's no way it could have been more different from New York, where I'd grown up among dark, dangerous alleys and dirty, noisy streets. In contrast, Southern California was palm trees and swimming pools, expensive foreign sports cars on crowded freeways winding through sprawling flatlands, framed by the ocean on one side and mountains on the other. I loved it at first sight.

One of the first places I asked Bill to take me was Muscle Beach, located in Venice. It was a Sunday afternoon, and the place was swarming with people. There were lots of bodybuilders there, climbing ropes, working out with barbells and dumbbells, doing dips and chins, performing strong-man feats and acrobatics. I stared in amazement as I recognized Joe Gold, Zabo Koszewski, George Eifferman, Chet Yorton, and many others. You could just feel the energy in the air. I'd never seen anything like it. People were jogging on the beach, having tug-of-war contests, and swimming. It was a fitness circus!

Bill Pearl was a great host. After one day, I felt as if I had known him all my life. He was friendly, intelligent, and a hard worker. In addition to running a successful health club right in the middle of Watts, he drove a Harley-Davidson, spent time collecting and restoring antique cars, and adding to his coin and stamp collections. He still worked out every morning, keeping himself in competition shape.

Bill really thought I was too young to do well in the Mr. America competition, but after a few days, he said, "Dennis, if your heart is really set on it, you might as well give it a try. But you've got to understand that nobody has won it on their first attempt."

If the workouts Joe Abbenda had put me through were tough, Bill Pearl's were absolutely brutal. In addition, he had an up-to-date gym with every imaginable kind of equipment for me to use. After Joe's "East Coast Dungeon," it was mind-boggling to be able to work out there. Even though it was torture at times, I still had the best time of my life working out every morning with Bill. I realized I had been given a rare opportunity—every young bodybuilder in the world would have given his right arm to train with this legendary hero.

To save money, I slept in the gym. After Bill closed down the club at ten o'clock, I'd get a pillow and blanket and lay down on a gymnastic stretching mat. I'd sleep there all night until I heard Bill's toilet flush about 5:30 A.M. That was my alarm clock!

Bill would come down and talk with me until a couple of his friends arrived. We'd all go eat a light breakfast together, then come back to the gym at about 7:00 A.M. and train for about three hours. I was strong enough and in good enough condition to really benefit from Pearl's coaching. One of the first fitness trainers NASA asked to work with the astronauts, Bill had probably forgotten more than most people ever know about physical fitness. He certainly knew exactly what I needed to do to refine and polish my body. I gained much knowledge about the human anatomy from him and why certain kinds of exercises were used to work on particular muscle groups.

About 10:00 A.M., Bill would start working in the health club and then spend the rest of the day selling memberships and assisting clients with their basic fitness and bodybuilding exercise programs. He was a complete professional, and I soon learned that he was a person of integrity, with character and good morals. He was a true role model, and I aspired to be like him.

Party Time!

Once, Bill took a day off, and I rode along with him and his friends on motorcycles to Tijuana. It must have been quite a sight—a dozen big guys wearing jeans and muscle shirts. We looked like a scene out of "The Wild Bunch," only we had massive chests and bulging biceps. In fact, we created a mob scene, flexing and posing for pictures as we crossed the border.

We had a fantastic time, eating Mexican food, haggling and bargaining with the shopkeepers as we bought souvenirs, bantering with the street musicians and vendors, trying on huge sombreros and sitting on donkeys. We even went to a bullfight. Even though we seemed to take over every place we went, nobody seemed to mind. It was an easy way to blow off a little steam without getting into any trouble. I remember the little Mexican kids staring at us with big brown eyes, slipping into the street to tug at our jeans as they got braver. They had never seen such big *hombres* before.

Then it was back to Los Angeles to get back to work in the gym, preparing for the 1965 Mr. America competition. But inevitably, I soon met a distraction...a good-looking blonde who was a bodybuilding groupie.

Cheryl had a crush on Bill Pearl, but Bill refused to have anything to do with her. When he halfheartedly introduced her to me, he did pull me aside for a few words of caution. I liked Cheryl in spite of her troubles and unhappiness. She was flashy, daring, and very experienced. She also had something I didn't have...a car! So Bill asked her to show me the sights. Soon, Cheryl, her best friend, and I were driving around in Cheryl's red Cadillac convertible, along with her big Collie dog. I can still remember the sights and sounds of my first whirlwind tour of Southern California— the cliffs and beach at Malibu, placing my hands over the handprints of Errol Flynn in Hollywood, buying fresh food at the Farmer's Market, and viewing the lights of the Valley from Mulholland Drive at midnight.

One day, Cheryl drove me down to San Diego for a photo shoot with the famous photographer and gym owner Leo Stern. After the shoot, Cheryl introduced me to a bunch of her biker friends—hard-drinking, long-haired, wild-looking guys. And there were lots of other bodybuilding groupies and beach girls around—some of the toughest-talking, hardest-faced gals I'd ever met. They were totally uninhibited. A whole group of us went nude swimming at Black's Beach. It was pretty racy stuff, even for a New Yorker like me who prided myself on being a man of the world. After a while, they all started drinking Tequila. I wasn't used to drinking much alcohol, and after just a couple of drinks, I got totally smashed and almost passed out on the beach.

That kind of indulgence doesn't mix well with bodybuilding. It wasn't long before I realized that things were getting out of hand and that I would have to be more disciplined. And sure enough, when Bill Pearl found out I had lost my key to the gym, he said, "Dennis, you've got to cool it! Don't mess up." I knew that Bill was right, so I cut back on the partying and trained diligently. And going into my first Mr. America competition, Bill and other guys at the gym said they thought I might be good enough to place high—maybe even win.

So what did I do? I walked into the competition with Cheryl and her girlfriend. Needless to say, I didn't make the right impression. What can I say? I was human—I let my ego get the best of me.

A fellow named Jerry Daniels won the Mr. America title that day, and Sergio Oliva came in second. I placed sixth, but I won trophies for Best Back, Best Biceps, and Most Muscular Man. Many observers felt that Sergio Oliva or I should have won the event. And almost everybody felt that my flamboyant behavior, particularly making a grand entrance at the contest with a blonde on each arm, had prejudiced the judges against me.

After the competition, I had more time to visit some of the other renowned gyms up and down the coast, and I had a chance to observe the training routines and techniques other bodybuilders were using. During this time, I made a lot of friendships that lasted for years—some for a lifetime.

One new acquaintance was a champion bodybuilder named Vince Gironda. He was known as the "guru of bodybuilding." He operated a well-known and respected gym and had a reputation for being an unorthodox yet excellent trainer, working with many actors, celebrities, and bodybuilders. "You've got a bright future, Dennis," he told me. "If you'll let me help you, I can make you a champion." I learned a lot from Vince, especially about diet, posing, and muscle definition, but I felt my allegiance should be to Bill Pearl if I stayed in California.

During the remainder of my time on the West Coast, I became a tourist, with Cheryl showing me around the many attractions of southern California.

At that time, Hollywood was starting to use some bodybuilders in the movies because they looked good without shirts, revealing their trim waistlines, broad shoulders, and big muscled arms. So I went to some movie studios and even met some agents, a couple whom encouraged me to stay around because they thought I was a good-looking guy and might get a break. It was like a dream come true.

In fact, MGM Filmways was just starting to cast a movie titled *Don't Make Waves*, starring Tony Curtis, Sharon Tate, and featuring Dave Draper and Chet Yorton, former bodybuilders. *Beach Party* and *Muscle Beach Party*, starring Don Rickles and Frankie Avalon, had already been box office successes a couple of years earlier. They featured performances by former bodybuilders like Larry Scott and Peter Lupus. The rumor was that *Don't Make Waves* and other upcoming films would have roles for several other bodybuilders. I've always felt that I would have gotten a part in one of those films if I'd just stayed around a little longer.

Another one of my goals was to get involved in television and perhaps create my own fitness show like Jack LaLane had done, or land an ongoing part in a TV series like Peter Lupus later did with "Mission Impossible."

I was ready to move to California permanently, but my dad was absolutely against it. He knew me pretty well and honestly felt it was in my best interest to return home. I always thought Dad was a bit overprotective, but I finally gave in. I told Bill and my other friends I'd try to come back the next summer. Then with much reluctance and regret, I packed my bags, said good-bye, and caught a flight for New York.

Even as my plane lifted off the runway at Los Angeles International and circled out over the ocean to head east, I knew one day I'd be back.

Home Again

Reality came crashing in when I returned to New York. Party time was over. I still lived on the tenth floor of a tenement building in a housing project on the east side. Talk about culture shock! Plus, I had to get back to work to earn a living.

With my previous electronics training and with the help of my friend Roger, I was able to secure a job with Olympic Radio and TV on a production line, assembling TV sets and big console stereo equipment. I really hated it. The work was easy and it paid pretty good, but standing in one place for hours, doing the same thing over and over, was monotonous and boring.

My training headquarters was again Joe Abbenda's dungeon. Occasionally I'd work out at the Brooklyn Central YMCA or R & J Health Club in Brooklyn, which was owned by Julie Levine, one of the strongest men I ever met. This was a hard-core, no-nonsense sweatshop, a heavy Iron Gym for competitive weight lifters and bodybuilders who were title winners and world champions. If you didn't bring your *Ben Gay* and knee wraps, you weren't serious. Everyone was always screaming and yelling at each other to do another rep or set—"Go heavy" was the motto, and there was an electric atmosphere that created intense training energy. On Saturday afternoons, many "stars" of bodybuilding would visit the gym, and people would double-park their cars in front of the gym to get a glimpse of the bigger-than-life characters.

Lou Ferrigno, a young, enthusiastic bodybuilder with superstar potential, trained there. He was a few years younger than me, and I tried to help him out as best I could. As a result, we became great friends, motivating one another, encouraging one another to achieve our goals. As we practiced our posing and flexing, Louie would scream across the gym, "Yo, Dennis! *Hit a muscular pose!*" and I would respond with, "Louie! Give me an *arm shot!*" We shared our hopes and dreams with each other. After our workouts, we loved to eat clams and shrimp by the dozen at Sheepstead Bay, Brooklyn, and watch the girls go by.

Because New York was the bodybuilding headquarters for the East Coast, the city had many great gyms. My brothers and I had friends who worked out at Al Fives's Olympia Gym on Freshpond Road in Queens, and we'd go over there a couple of times a month. Major contenders like Ricky Wayne and Fred Ortiz worked out there. Sometimes I dropped by the gyms on Times Square—Tom Minichello's Mid-City Gym and Sig Klein's place—just to see who was there and what was going on. I met some interesting people at those gyms, including professional wrestler Bruno Sammartino and Harold Poole, a former Mr. Universe. There were always lots of sports jocks, actors, and bodybuilders hanging around.

After numerous tries, I eventually persuaded a talent agent to represent me, and everything was finally in place! I loved showing up for auditions, even though it quickly became obvious that I would have to work as hard at show business as I did with bodybuilding. I wanted to work in magazine ads and commercials so I would be noticed and possibly break into the movies. Dealing with rejection was tough, though. Every time I booked something, I was thrilled, but for each booking, there were at least five jobs I didn't get. And I guess it was inevitable that I would be typecast as a bodybuilder. After all, you can change your voice and your look, but not your physique.

To give me more time in the day for bodybuilding—and, hopefully, auditions—I started working the night shift at Olympic Radio and TV, from 7 P.M. to 3 A.M. After working all night, I'd get home between 4 and 5 A.M., grab a few hours sleep, and head for the gym to work out for three hours. I'd get something to eat, go back home to make a few phone calls and grab a nap, then get on the subway to go back to work. It was a drag, but I was willing to do it. After all, I knew it was only temporary. As soon as I had some big wins...as soon as I got a break in the ad or movie business, I'd be out of there and on my way back to California.

But the key was to win. So training and preparing for the next level of bodybuilding competitions became my obsession. Every waking moment I thought of winning. When I was working out at the gym, I visualized myself onstage, presenting my program, posing under the lights. When I was at work, I daydreamed about delivering the best competitive routine of my life, then taking a bow at center stage as I acknowledged the cheers of the crowd when my victory as Mr. USA was announced!

The Dream Becomes Reality

The Mr. USA contest was a major event, conducted in conjunction with the Senior National Power Lifting Championship on September 3, 1966, and held at Dallas Memorial Auditorium, one of the largest auditoriums I'd ever seen. The place seated thousands of people, and it was nearly full.

My name was becoming pretty well-known in bodybuilding circles, and some of the trade magazines actually favored me to take Mr. USA on my first try. But the judges were not totally enthusiastic about me, so I had to win them over. They envisioned their champion as a well-mannered nice guy—the All-American boy next door, not some tough kid from

Brooklyn who was still rough around the edges. But Mr. USA wasn't a personality contest; it was all about the sport and who was the best. I gave a peak performance, and the judges were impressed. In fact, I won the contest hands down, a big victory for me. Just a few shining, glorious moments in the spotlight was what I needed to balance out months of exhaustive training!

Then I started getting some serious publicity—full-flexed muscle-shot photos, admiring articles by respected sportswriters, and interviews by the editors of the leading bodybuilding magazines. I felt like a movie star!

Back home, my family was excited and thrilled at my victory. My faithful friend and trainer, Joe Abbenda, was also quietly exuberant. "Okay, Dennis. You've won Junior Mr. USA and Mr. USA. Now you're ready. It's time to go win Mr. America!"

First-Time Romance

About this time, I met a really sharp girl at Coney Island. She was sitting on the beach across from me, and the minute I saw her she knocked me out. "My God," I said, "what a beauty!" She was wearing a bikini that few girls would have dared to wear—especially on a beach that didn't attract the most sophisticated and polite type of people you could find. She stuck out like a sore thumb.

Lots of guys noticed her, but she was totally aloof, refusing to respond to their whistles, comments, and come-on lines. She even ignored my attempts to start a conversation with her for a while, but I could tell she was fascinated by my physique and my zany sense of humor. And very, very slowly, she warmed up and began to talk with me.

Her name was Joanne Romano, and she lived with her sister and mother in Benton Hurst, a more prosperous Italian area. Although I'd been attracted by Joanne's figure and incredible beauty, as we talked, I found myself even more fascinated by her personality and genuineness as a person. So I asked her for a date—just a trip to the movies. We had a great time. Then I asked her out again...and again. We continued to date, and she became the first real love of my life.

I started taking her to bodybuilding shows and teaching her a little about the sport. She was amazed the first time she watched me go through a workout at the gym. She had no idea how strenuous and demanding the training for bodybuilding could be, and she was impressed with my discipline to stay on my diet and training program.

I shared my dreams with Joanne about becoming a major bodybuilding champion, then moving to California to work in Hollywood movies. If I could just get a break, I told her, I was sure to become rich and famous someday.

She understood those dreams because they were similar to hers. Her best chance to make it as a model and a starlet, she felt, would be in California. We talked about getting married and moving out there together. But neither of us had much education or resources to draw on to make our dreams reality. So we mostly just talked about them.

Big Time

I had competed in the Mr. America competition before, but this time was different. I prepared a whole new posing routine and practiced until I knew every motion I had to make with my eyes closed. I'd hit a pose, hold it for a count of five, then move into the next pose. I bought some new, even more form-fitting posing briefs and spent lots of time under the sun lamps. I felt that I was really ready, and my hopes were high.

The 1966 Mr. America contest was held at William Penn High School in York, Pennsylvania, on June 19, and my family went with me to the competition. As usual, Dad was right there for me. And like most fathers, he was never very objective. He always thought I should win and was very vocal about it!

But 1966 was not my year. Bob Gajda and Sergio Olivia won first and second. I placed sixth, although I truly believed I had done much better than that. I was told that I would have been third if I'd had the proper paperwork to confirm my championship athletic status in another sport as the AAU required. Besides, no one my age had ever won the Mr. America title.

During this period of time, Joanne went with me to various gyms and health clubs. She even started working out with weights and getting personally involved in fitness training at Mort's Gym in Queens. We also spent time going to the theatre, taking acting lessons together, and walking on the beach while we planned our future. We decided we should start out by opening a health club in New York together before moving to California to become sports fitness personalities and movie stars. That way our reputation would precede us.

Meanwhile, Joanne's mother always invited me to go to church with them. I was comfortable with that because it was a Catholic church, just like the one I had grown up in. Often, when I would visit Joanne's house, her family would be watching Katherine Kuhlman, a TV evangelist. As I would join in watching, I was amazed at the faith of this petite woman. People would testify that incurable diseases were healed as she spoke about a miracle God and how the Holy Spirit could transform the lives of people. I almost felt like God's presence would come through the TV. I knew the Lord was drawing me closer to Him, but my bodybuilding goals at the time were first place.

As I turned 21 on December 23, 1966. I intensified my training to get ready for the next Mr. America competition. I also was committed to enter the Junior Mr. America contest, which was to be held in York, Pennsylvania before a crowd of thousands. Everything went great during my pre-event training, and I went off to Pennsylvania in awesome condition, well rehearsed and supremely confident. In fact, I would have been completely shocked if I hadn't won, although there was a strong field of contenders. And at the event, I was crowned 1967 Junior Mr. America!

At night I would continue to dream of standing on stage, competing for the Mr. America title and of course winning. I felt that I knew what the judges were looking for and what I had to do to win.

Columbus, Ohio, June 12, 1967

"Somebody pinch me...I need to know this is real!" Amidst all the noise, my mind was still trying to absorb it all. I was the new 1967 Mr. America!

It was the most exciting time of my whole life, and winning the Mr. America title was—to this day—my most satisfying bodybuilding victory. The feelings I had were almost indescribable!

I still remember seeing my proud and happy dad surrounded by well-wishers after the show was over. He was thrilled and exuberant. "I'm Carmine Tinerino," he told everybody who might not recognize him. "I'm the father of Mr. America!"

Celebrating My Big Win

By the time I finally finished my shower and slipped into my street clothes, the crowd had gone. But Dad was still excited and in a celebrating mood. "Hey, Dennis, let's go to that club down the street for a little drink," he said. "This is a special night!"

So we went to a nightclub in Columbus for a little while. Dad wanted everyone around to know I was the new Mr. America, and several people came over to meet me and admire my medal and trophies.

Then after a half hour or so, as we started to make our way out of the club, Dad noticed a group of girls—about a dozen of them—who obviously were also out celebrating, because several of them were carrying trophies as well. "What are your trophies for?" Dad asked. They told him they were in town for a bowling tournament. "What is your trophy?" they asked him in return.

"Oh, this belongs to my son, Dennis Tinerino. He's a champion bodybuilder—he just won the Mr. America title!"

"Where is he?" they shrieked. "We want to meet Mr. America!" And some of the girls continued to ask, "Where are all the other bodybuilders? We want to meet all of them!" So much for heading right back to the hotel.... The next morning I barely managed to grab a quick shower while Dad packed my things. He had already made sure that the hotel limo driver was waiting to rush us to the airport as soon as I was ready, and we made our plane by about ten minutes.

Achieving a victory on this level brought with it a new level of respect and opportunities I'd never had before. I was given the opportunity to write my first full-length, by-lined magazine article. *Muscular Development* published "A Dream Come True—Winning Mr. America" by Dennis Tinerino, complete with photos of me posing in Columbus, Ohio, and receiving my trophy.

Although my picture had been in the magazines before—even on the cover—having my own article was a milestone in my mind. It meant I was somebody, that people recognized my accomplishments and were interested in my opinions. As Mr. America, I was invited to write an article at least once a month for one of the AAU publications, *Health and Strength*, *Iron Man*, or *Muscular Development*. The pay wasn't much—maybe $150 or so—but the publicity and prestige were good. And I was finally doing what I liked to do and getting paid for it.

Being Mr. America and getting some press did help me get many bookings for appearances. I was invited to pose at exhibitions for health clubs and to participate in health and fitness seminars. I also did numerous photo shoots, appearing on the covers of virtually all the bodybuilding publications.

I still had an agent working for me and was hoping for a big break, like doing a commercial or a film, something that would earn me some big money. For a while it looked like I might get a role in a play off Broadway, but that never panned out. However, I did appear as a guest on the "Merv Griffin Show" and the "Tonight Show" with Johnny Carson. They were both fairly brief appearances, mainly capitalizing on the Mr. America title and showing off a guy with big muscles and a terrific physique. Both Johnny Carson and Merv got a few laughs, contrasting their petite size against my muscularity and trying to beat me at arm wrestling.

I enjoyed being on television because I could ham it up and get lots of attention...but the guest fee for talk shows was only a couple hundred dollars. The big-money opportunities I'd expected and dreamed about were slow in coming. Consequently, I really began feeling the financial pressure as the days and weeks went by.

Tempted by the "Family"

By now, my brothers and I were constantly looking for ways to get our hands on a few dollars to spend on clothes and girls. Even in Little Italy and the Van Dyke projects we could look around and see other people who seemed to have a lot more than our family. We saw guys with cars, fancy clothes, watches, and diamond rings, and we'd ask, "How come we're always broke? Why do we never have any money to get nice things? We don't even own a car!"

Dad would say, "Don't just look at what you can see. Having money and fancy things doesn't mean everything. Life doesn't revolve around that. I'm an honest man. I live right. These guys are gangsters—they're *Mafioso*. Sooner or later, they'll pay for what they're doing. Don't look up to those guys; they're evil people. They'll hurt or kill anyone for a buck."

At the time we didn't fully understand what he meant. From our point of view, the people who went along with the Mob seemed to be making out pretty good. Growing up as Italian-Americans, we were always around relatives and friends who were involved to some extent with the underworld—bookmaking, numbers running, or some other form of gambling, or participating in some minor organized crime activity. These guys always seemed to have rings, watches, nice clothes, fancy cars, and lots of cash.

One example was my "Uncle G," who was a big influence in my life. He had been a "strongman" in Vaudeville shows, the circus, and carnival sideshows and was friends with actors in the entertainment business and in the theatre. He also was respected and reverenced by prominent and influential people, most of whom lived on the Upper East Side of New York. Uncle G was a tall, massively built man who exuded dignity, self-confidence, and brute strength. He taught me how to rip a deck of cards, tear telephone books, Indian wrestle, as well as perform self-defense moves and other "strongman" feats.

Immediately after I won Mr. America, my uncle introduced me to the legendary Charles Atlas (Angelo Siciliano), a forerunner of the modern-day bodybuilder, at the New York Athletic Club. He became famous because of his comic book ads that said, "I can show you in ten easy lessons how you can get a build like me," and he developed an isometric system called "Dynamic Tension" that became very popular with the Post World War II generation.

Being of Italian ancestry we had much in common enjoying some hearty laughs, good conversation, and "low-fat" Italian food. When Charles and I went through barbell workouts together, it was hard to concentrate—everyone wanted our autographs and pictures. People would shout, "No one is going to kick sand in those two guys' faces." I saw in him the possibility of what could happen when you parlay muscles into money through business endeavors.

With respect to Uncle G, I was also impressed with his ability to operate in two worlds. Some days he would live in the underworld, where they had their own rules. There I saw him meeting with *consigliore* or "counselors," helping plot strategies for upper echelon gangsters. At other times he would mingle with the working people, and then with the "movers and shakers" in big business and politics. His influence touched a broad spectrum of society.

And he tried to help my career with his contacts in both worlds. One time he introduced me to a big Mob boss, Four Finger Patrone, to talk about doing movie commercials and opening my own health clubs. I also spoke at a rally at Central Park for the "Italian American Anti-defamation League." I was so naïve that I didn't realize Joe Colombo, a Mafia boss, was involved in it. Nothing good came out of any of my uncle's business contacts, mostly because Dad found out about them and called an immediate halt to any dealings between me, my uncle, and the "family."

There was a period in my uncle's life when he did some real soul-searching and began writing a book entitled, "The Broken Code" about betrayal and lack of loyalty in the Mob. He encouraged me to avoid his lifestyle, and pursue my God-given gifts and heart's desire. He would tell me, "Be patient! Be content with your accomplishments. Keep your goals in sight. The money will come." He'd say, "Don't mess around with these wise guys. You don't want to wind up on a dead-end street. What I am doing—this ain't no kind of life for you, kid." He regretted many of the choices he had made, and my heart was touched that he was extremely concerned about me and my future. Interestingly, he constantly read the Bible to me. He touched on such topics as right living, salvation, and peacemaking. His favorite Scripture was Matthew 12:25, "*Every...household divided against itself will not stand.*" To my amazement, he wept as he read it to me, and I felt that he regretted many of the choices he had made. I didn't realize until later that he had sown both seeds of good and evil in my life.

After winning Mr. America, my next step was an international competition—Mr. Universe.

So I made the trip to...London.

Chapter Six

CLASH OF THE TITANS

LONDON was foggy, damp, and cold. Before I could make my way from the airport to the Royal Hotel, I was chilled to the bone. I was also feeling very alone. The trip had been exciting, but long, and I was wishing that someone could have traveled with me.

The day of the event, I was tired. Sleep had been almost impossible the night before. The thrill of being in Europe for the first time, especially for my fist international event, was overwhelming. Plus, with all the well-wishers and last-minute preparations, my mind was racing. Finally, I gave up trying to sleep and began to practice my posing routine. I was in front of the mirror for hours, until there was a knock at my door, asking me to please turn off the music. I was astonished to find it was 3 o'clock in the morning!

As I stepped outside a few hours later, the bone-chilling dampness and cold hit my muscles. No wonder Joe Abbenda had warned me to allow extra time to warm up before I appeared onstage. Following his advice, I arrived a couple of hours before starting time at the hotel's convention area where the prejudging round was to be conducted.

In spite of my fatigue, I was able to focus. Visualizing the crowd and the contest, my adrenaline took over and energized me. Slowly and deliberately I began working out with light weights to warm my body and loosen up. Then I oiled my body, and started pumping up each muscle group—calves, thighs, chest, shoulders, and arms.

Finally finding a full-length mirror in an empty bar, I started practicing my posing routine. Everything was going smoothly...I was pumped and ready, and as I checked my last pose, I suddenly saw someone else's reflection in my mirror—another bodybuilder copying my pose.

Startled, I turned around to see who was behind me. And before I could get a good look, I heard, "I vant you to get out of de vay. Dis mirror is not big enough for de two of us."

I recognized his voice immediately. It was my toughest competitor, "The Austrian Oak." Knowing his reputation for intimidating people, I immediately decided to call his bluff. "That's right," I said gruffly. "Your head's too big. Get yourself another mirror." Arnold laughingly stepped away, leaving me to continue with my routine. Grinning, I knew I had one the first round. He wasn't able to psych me out.

This guy was definitely a Goliath. He was an inch taller than me, and outweighed me by at least 20 pounds. His chest and shoulders—his entire upper body—was massive and powerful. I was no David, but I fully intended to slay him in the competition. I knew that the Mr. Universe judges were noted for demanding perfect symmetry and a balanced, proportioned physique, and for being more impressed with muscularity than bulk. My rival was huge, but not proportioned. I didn't have a rock and a slingshot, but I had the weapon I needed...I had what the judges were looking for.

Arnold and I both had received lots of press during the year, and magazines in the U.S. and Europe had chosen the two of us as the top contenders. In fact, a large number of them had already determined that I would win the competition. I could hear a buzz of excitement as other competitors were sizing me up and accented voices talked about who would win.

I'd won every amateur title I could win in the U.S., and I was the current reigning Mr. America. I was trained, conditioned, rehearsed, prepared. My posing routine was perfect—both Joe Abbenda and Bill Pearl had tweaked and polished it until they were satisfied. The only thing left to do was go out and give my best performance without making any mistakes.

The Mr. Universe contest officially began, and all the contestants were called onstage for comparative poses. After the judges gave each contestant the once-over, they began calling for pose-offs between various bodybuilders. Arnold and I were called out again and again, confirming the pre-event speculation that we were the favorites to win. During the compulsory flexed poses, Schwarzenegger and I were yet again asked to step out time after time.

Next came the individual posing routines, set to music. I couldn't have asked for my performance to go any better.

Once the prejudging was over, I had a great time meeting other contestants and visiting with people in the audience. It was very heartwarming to find a following of people out there who were rooting for me.

It so happened that the Miss International Beauty Pageant was also being conducted at the same time as the Mr. Universe competition. Some really spectacular girls were participating, including a dark-haired girl with a tremendous figure. I recognized her from her picture I had seen back home in *Health and Strength* magazine. She had already won the Miss Manchester and Miss Britain beauty contests. Her name was Lynda Thomas.

Dennis and Arnold winning Pro. and Armature Mr. Universe

As I watched part of the pageant and as Lynda took the stage, we immediately made eye contact. I was instantly attracted to her, and it appeared the feeling was mutual. So, at the first opportunity, I made it a point to look her up and introduce myself. Subsequently, we made plans to get together after the evening competition.

As we encouraged each other about our respective contests, I told her she would win the Miss International title hands down, and she told me I was sure to be the next Mr. Universe. We planned to have pictures taken together, and she invited me to come visit her home and meet her parents in Manchester. When I went back to my room to get ready for the final competition, I was feeling on top of the world.

The final competition and awards ceremony was held at the Palladium Theater, in the heart of London. This theater held about five thousand people and it was completely sold out, every seat filled. Ninety anxious bodybuilders from all parts of the world stood behind the massive burgundy curtain while fans were screaming out the names of their favorite contestants. It was total bedlam, but I could distinctly hear voices shouting, "Dennis, Dennis, Dennis!" It gave me a tremendous surge of confidence before I went onstage.

The energy from the audience was infectious, and I felt like a racehorse at the starting gate. As I looked at my fellow competitors, the best in the world, I knew that we were ushering in a new era in bodybuilding, and that I was part of a legacy. This is where I would make my mark. Winning this event would change my life!

Before I had a moment to think, I was onstage. The crowd continued to call my name as I went through my routine, and as I finished posing I received one of the biggest standing ovations I'd ever witnessed in any contest. Arnold got a tremendous response from the crowd as well, and so did Paul Grant, Mr. Wales, who later became Mr. Europe and Mr. Universe.

Then came the final moment of truth. The results were called out. Paul Grant received third place. Dennis Tinerino was second, and Arnold Schwarzenegger was Mr. Universe of 1967 in the amateur division. My good friend Bill Pearl won the professional Mr. Universe title.

I was extremely disappointed but tried not to let it show. Besides, it was such a great honor just to be there, following in the footsteps of legendary bodybuilders who had been my idols for years. I was proud to be Mr. America, representing my country in the most elite competition against the best bodybuilding competitors in the world. I knew I'd done my best. And I knew I would be back. In fact, I couldn't wait. I was certain that next year, I would be the one in the winner's circle.

Celebrating in London

After the contest, thousands of people swarmed around the contestants, especially the top three, wanting our autographs and pictures. They invited us to their homes, and I was bombarded with questions. How will you train for next year? Do you think you should have beaten Arnold? How did you get so muscular? Do you take steroids?

The media throughout Europe was interested in interviewing me, and I was invited to Spain, Italy, and other countries. In addition, I was given an open invitation to train at the best fitness centers and hard-core gyms in Europe, and many fitness entrepreneurs wanted me to give seminars and posing exhibitions. So much was being thrown at me so fast, I almost forgot that I hadn't actually won the Mr. Universe contest! I decided to enjoy the moment, for I was surely getting all the attention and appreciation that I could have ever hoped for—a well-earned reward for all my sacrifices in the gym.

As soon as I got a chance, I went to my room and called my folks back in New York. Mom and my brothers were disappointed, while Dad was irate, cussing and raving about crooked judges and dirty politics. He'd seen enough backstage incidents in my amateur contests over the years to know that the best man didn't always win.

Knowing that Dad's reaction was his way of showing his disappointment, I tried to calm him down, reminding him that bodybuilding is a subjective, opinionated sport, and that "beauty is in the eye of the beholder." I told Dad that I was scheduled to appear at some posing exhibitions with Arnold and Bill Pearl in Plymouth and Manchester, England, and then in Ireland. I explained that while I was there, I wanted to see all of Europe while I had the chance.

He wasn't in the least bit happy about it. "Why don't you just pack up and come on home? You've got to get back to work. You don't want to lose your job...." He was still going on when I hung up.

That evening, Lynda and some of her beauty-contest friends joined me for dinner at the celebration banquet for the bodybuilder contestants. Lynda had also placed second in her pageant, so we had even more in common as we commiserated with each other about how we each should have won.

Afterward, many of the bodybuilders agreed to meet in London to do a little celebrating, and we decided to go to Trafalgar Square in the middle of London, where we ran into a rowdy bunch of bodybuilders doing some really crazy things. They had ripped a mailbox out of the street, and one guy was urinating into it. Another one picked up a mini Fiat and was carrying it down the street. A couple of bodybuilders, too drunk to stand, were trying to climb a streetlight, while another guy ripped off his shirt, took a big swallow of ale, and struck a muscle pose in the middle of the street. It was total pandemonium. But even though London was not used to this kind of crazy celebration, onlookers were cheering and taking pictures.

Some of the guys in our group seemed to think that these antics were hilarious. Personally, I was embarrassed by what was happening. I knew this kind of fiasco would not be good for the image of bodybuilding, and I just wanted to get away from there before the Bobbies arrived.

Although I had not always set a good example in my youth, being Mr. America was a serious responsibility. I felt that Mr. America as well as Mr. Universe should project a moral, ethical image and provide good role models for kids to look up to and emulate. As Mr. America, I had been given a platform to inspire and influence a multitude of people throughout the world. In addition, part of my job as Mr. America was to take the sport of bodybuilding to a place of respectability. I lived for and was committed to fulfilling this increasing responsibility.

Much later that night, several of us ended up at a private party at the home of a famous London gym owner. He was a friend of Arnold Schwarzenegger and was always in the know about what was going on in the world of bodybuilding. I learned that night that steroids were very popular among European bodybuilders. Many of them talked openly about what steroid they were using, and were amazed when I told them that I was drug-free.

As Lynda, Arnold, and I talked about the posing exhibitions and seminars we would soon be participating in together throughout Europe, we noticed a few people who were starting to act kind of strange, some even passing out. It turned out that some of the bodybuilders' friends from California had made hash brownies. They were passing them around, and people were getting stoned!

To say the least, I was very upset and disappointed about many things I saw and experienced that night. At 21, I came to the sad realization that just because a person has a strong body, it doesn't mean they have a strong mind and spirit...not even heroes.

The Traveling Circus

With the contest behind me, I was looking forward to the next day, and I wasn't disappointed! It was filled with fun and excitement. I joined up with Bill Pearl, Leo Stern, our good friend from San Diego, and Dr. Craig Whitehead, another bodybuilder, to begin our tour of Europe. Since we were already in England, we started there. Of course, our tour started with a huge laugh as we saw Bill Pearl driving up...sitting on the right side of the car! What a class act—a once-in-a-lifetime combination

Dennis, Bill Pearl & Craig Whitehead

of talent, strength, and unruliness! We called our group "Leo Stern's Traveling Circus."

We saw much of England's beautiful countryside and visited many famous and historic sites, including Stonehenge, where Bill and I posed for Leo's camera, pushing against the massive stone slabs and pillars.

Bill and I then participated in a posing exhibition in the old city of Plymouth, and I was surprised at the number of people who came out to see us, and how knowledgeable they seemed to be about bodybuilding and physical fitness. Bill was an accomplished performer, mixing in humorous stunts and amazing feats with the flawless presentation of his perfectly sculptured body. For example, he would take a metal license plate and tear it apart with his bare hands! He would often appear on stage wearing a fake handlebar mustache and lambskin trunks, emulating Eugene Sandow, a famous turn-of-the-century bodybuilder and strongman. The audience loved Bill's performance so much that I was inspired to create my own act. I would bend 60-penny spikes, tear a deck of playing cards in half, bend a steel rod around my neck, break a stack of bricks with my bare hands, and do push-ups with three or four fat people on my back!

When the traveling circus went to Manchester for our posing exhibition there, I was able to visit Lynda Thomas' home and meet her parents. Her dad worked for a famous Manchester newspaper and was, in my opinion, the picture of a "veddy" proper English gentleman.

While we were at the Manchester exhibition, I ran into some unexpected trouble. My strongman tricks included ripping a couple of phone books in half and blowing up a hot water bottle like a child's balloon until it burst. As a finale, I'd look into a lunch bag I'd carried onstage and say, "What else do I have?" Then I'd pull out a rubber chicken or rat, and say, "Oh, this is my lunch," and throw it out into the crowd. Even though it was just a gag, it was always good for a laugh.

But things went wrong in Manchester. For one thing, the English hot water bottles were much thicker and stiffer than the ones I'd used in the states. Finally, with much huffing and puffing, I managed to inflate it to the size of a large beach ball. Totally out of air and unable to make it explode, the hot water bottle got away from me and flew to the back of the auditorium. Before the laughter and applause quieted, a fellow in the audience called out a challenge to me.

"That's no big deal, mate. All you American guys are just a bunch of hot air!"

Not being experienced enough to know better, I took the bait and responded to his challenge. "Oh yeah? Well, if you can do any better, come on up here!"

So this scrawny little guy, all knees and elbows, who must have weighed maybe 140 pounds soaking wet, scrambled up on the stage. I had no way of knowing he was an expert at blowing up hot water bottles. He even had a plastic pipe device that connected to two hot water bottles and had a mouthpiece to blow into. He stood next to me, this seemingly skinny weakling beside a muscular giant. Then, with the greatest of ease, he blew up both hot water bottles until they exploded!

The crowd, of course, was thoroughly pleased to see me humiliated by their local hero. But that wasn't all. Next, the little guy pulled out a one-pint, glass milk bottle and challenged me—or anyone in the hall—to blow the bottom out of the bottle just by blowing into it. I knew I couldn't do it, nor could anyone else who came up and tried. When everyone else had failed, my little tormenter put the bottle to his mouth, gave a mighty puff, and the bottle broke! I've never figured out how he did it, and I've never found anyone else who could duplicate that feat.

Boy, was I embarrassed! But the whole Traveling Circus got a big laugh out of the incident. Thankfully, in a couple of days, it was time to move on. Bill Pearl and I were then scheduled to appear at posing exhibitions at the Mr. Ireland bodybuilding competition in Belfast. While there, we stayed in the opulent home of Buster McShane and his wife. Buster was very wealthy, and owned the most successful health club in all of Ireland. His home was on top of a hill that overlooked the Belfast shipyards and provided a panoramic view of the entire city.

We had a great dinner when we arrived, and I met another beautiful girl, Miss Ireland. I fell in love all over again! Being Mr. America and a Mr. Universe contender did have some *definite* advantages.

Wherever I went, there were girls. It wasn't a matter of me chasing them—they pursued me! Initially, my physique and big muscles fascinated them. Then once I'd have a chance to make a few jokes and get a girl laughing, be a little outrageous, or say a few flattering things, I could usually charm her into becoming my lover—at least for a night...or an afternoon. And that's all I wanted. I certainly wasn't interested in making any long-term commitments.

Bill Pearl and Leo Stern teased me about being the greatest playboy of the western world, having a girl in every port. It was all a joke to me—I was just trying to have a good time.

After our visit in Ireland, it was time to head back to London. We all were excited about our return trip because we were scheduled to meet the richest man in the world...J. Paul Getty. Getty was a bodybuilding enthusiast and sponsor, even handing out trophies at the Mr. Universe competition. On this occasion, he was having a luncheon for several of the top bodybuilders. A limousine driver picked us up and delivered us to the Getty mansion on the outskirts of London. Mr. Getty got a big laugh when I asked, "Is it true you have a pay phone here?" Later, as he was giving us a tour of his estate, Getty lost his footing in the garden. Bill Pearl and I managed to grab him and keep him from falling. As we were returning to the house, I laughingly said, "Hey, Bill! We helped the man when he could've gotten hurt. That's gotta be worth at least a million, right?"

All Roads Don't Lead to Rome

As Leo's Traveling Circus was getting ready to head for Rome, Bill urged me to come along with them. I wanted very much to visit Italy, the homeland of my grandparents, but my dad kept reminding me that I had used up all my vacation time and could lose my old job if I stayed away any longer. As unbelievable as it sounds, I gave up the opportunity of a lifetime because of my dad's insecurities. So, I thanked the guys for showing me such a good time and sadly said good-bye to my friends. They took off for Rome, and I caught a plane back to New York.

My job was still waiting for me. Although I was grateful for the special treatment my boss had given me, I soon moved to Kollsman Instrument Corporation to work on the calibration of the altimeters for Boeing 747 airliners. It was a better paying job and was more interesting than assembling TV sets. Plus, I could work the 7-4 night shift, which still left my days free to work out and attend auditions for TV and movie parts.

Joanne was still waiting for me as well. It was great to be with her again, but eventually our relationship began to unravel as we drifted apart. I was so busy working and training most days and nights that I didn't have much extra time to spend with her. Even though I had encountered some beautiful women as I traveled around the world, Joanne was still very special to me. After all, she was my first love. It was all very confusing. We had made so many plans for the future, but I couldn't get it together enough to make a commitment.

Samson and Hercules Hit the Streets

Determined to make my dreams come true, I decided to use the confidence, excitement, and energy that I generated for the Mr. Universe contest towards my quest for "media success." With my best portfolio in hand, I tried out for a lot of commercials, and took some additional advanced acting classes. I appeared on more talk-show programs, and gave interviews to newspapers, radio, and magazines. I even auditioned, unsuccessfully, for one of the gangster roles in *The Godfather*. Casting agents said I was too big and muscular for most parts.

At last, my efforts paid off when I got my first role in a film called *Hercules in New York*. The producer had promised the starring role to the winner of the Mr. Universe contest. That, of course, was Arnold Schwarzenegger, who changed his name to Arnold Strong for the role. And because I had come in second, I got a supporting part, playing the role of Atlas.

Hercules in New York was a low-budget, quickie movie that was completed in about two months. I didn't have many lines, and some of my scenes were cut. My big moment of glory, however, was a fight scene where we beat up the gangsters who had been menacing our brother Hercules.

I have to admit that making this film was one of the highlights of my life. When we weren't working on the film, Arnold and I spent time training with other bodybuilders at various gyms. We exchanged ideas on contest preparation, and we encouraged each other to reach for the stars.

Arnold turned out to be a lot of fun. As we went through the streets of New York together, he would flirt outrageously with the girls lining the sidewalk to watch the filming. "Hey darling," he would shout, "Hercules make love to you, okay?" Most women thought he was comical, but a few said, "Yes." And, I admit, it was easy to get caught up in it all. After all, we attracted attention everywhere we went, so why not enjoy it? Cabbies would even yell at us as they drove by—"Yo, Dennis, yo Arnold—give us a pose!" And we'd flex our arms for them.

Inevitably, all the publicity from the Mr. Universe contest and the filming of *Hercules in New York* started to attract the attention of some major players in the bodybuilding industry. At one point, Joe Weider, head of the largest bodybuilding federation in the world, wanted to meet with Arnold and me to discuss our future with his organization. His offer was simple: We had to eat, sleep, work out, and compete in IFBB events. Plus, we would get paid to appear in his magazines and endorse his products. And because he was moving his organization to California, it sounded perfect to me! While Arnold advised me to sign the contract with Weider, other advisors and associates who didn't have confidence in Joe's business ventures told me it was a bad idea. So, Arnold signed, and I didn't...but we still spent lots of time together.

One evening during this time, my brother Larry and I went to meet Arnold and Joe Weider at Joe's fancy East Side penthouse. As Arnold was putting on his shoes, he slipped, falling on a priceless antique chair once owned by Napoleon and breaking it in two. "Oh my God! You broke the chair!" Joe cried. "What am I gonna do, Arnold?" Arnold just winked at us and laughingly replied, "Who cares about a chair, Joe! I coulda got hurt! You're rich. Get some glue; we'll fix it!" The three of us roared in laughter, but Joe apparently didn't see the humor in the situation.

The next day, Arnold, Larry, and I decided to work out at Olympia Gym in Queens, and then went to my parents' house for dinner. My mother was very excited to be cooking a full Italian dinner for the "Austrian Oak." Arnold ate 12 meatballs! I had never seen anyone enjoy a meal so much. "*Minga*, he eats like he hasn't been fed in a week!" Dad said. Later, Arnold praised my mother, "Mrs. Tinerino, this is the best Italian food I have ever had. These are the first meatballs I've had that didn't fight back!" Totally stuffed, Arnold passed out on the couch in the living room. After his nap, Larry and I took him out for a night on the town. As we were leaving the projects, it seemed as though the whole neighborhood was waiting for autographs. We gave Arnold a VIP tour of New

York that night, visiting clubs, posing for pictures with policemen, and signing tons of autographs for our fans.

Filming *Hercules* was more than just a good time. Compared to my previous jobs, I made pretty good money for the amount of time I had to work. In addition, I now had my Screen Actor's Guild (SAG) card. It was fun to see how a movie is made, meet some people in the business, and be part of the hype and publicity that goes along with it. There were rumors that there were going to be several other Hercules movies made in Italy, maybe even an American TV series. And of course, I had high hopes that with my drive and determination I would star in them.

Meanwhile, I participated in a couple of posing exhibitions and body-building seminars almost every month to supplement my income. There were no competitions I wanted to enter—I'd won every amateur event there was to win...except Mr. Universe. So I trained harder than ever, with my eyes on winning the Mr. Universe title the following September in London.

In between the exhibitions and seminars, I worked weekends as a bouncer in various clubs. One time, I got a call to work the Argentina Ball during the Rio de Janeiro carnival at the Waldorf-Astoria. Mark Tendler was the maitre'd and head bouncer for the popular nightclub, P.J. Clark's, a hamburger-bar, and gin-mill hangout for the "Broadway beautiful people" crowd. Because we were friends, I worked there quite a bit. The work was usually very easy, and I enjoyed watching and getting acquainted with some of the rich and famous people who frequented the place. It was nothing to see Joe Namath, Rocky Graziano, Al Pacino, Marlon Brando, Liz Taylor, Frank Sinatra, and various other celebrities, writers, and producers at P.J. Clark's.

It's hard to imagine that I was still working a 7 to 4 night job, living with my parents in the projects, and dealing with the same old distractions and pressure from my friends and relatives. I had endless energy though, and I needed to save up enough money to go back to London, so I simply did what I needed to do. Besides, I was having an incredible year, and could have lived on adrenaline! Getting my SAG card, being in a movie, taking acting lessons—all these things were additional steps toward my ultimate goals. I truly felt on top of the world.

In addition, I felt that the sport of bodybuilding was improving over all, and that I was going to play an important part in it as it gained prominence and respectability. I told my dad, "Bodybuilding is not going to be an underground sport much longer—it's just about to explode. When it does, all of our hard work is going to pay off."

Preparing for Victory

The months raced by, and I arranged for some time off to return to California in the summer to train with Bill Pearl. He was willing to help coach and groom me for September's NABBA Mr. Universe competition in London. Being back in California was great, and I loved it just as much as before.

But this time, I was a lot more mature and experienced. I was on a mission, and I remained dedicated and committed to the job of getting my body in peak condition. Within a few weeks, both Bill Pearl and I were convinced that this would be the year for me. I was ready to win.

I felt very confident when I arrived back in London. This time I knew the local customs, how to get around, and what to expect at the competition. I did have a bit of a thrill at the airport though. I met three famous actors who were checking through customs—the three Richards—Harris, Burton, and Chamberlain. All three were very nice, and even seemed to know about the Mr. Universe competition and who I was. As an aspiring actor, I was excited to meet three such respected stars.

I was also more at ease because I knew Arnold would be competing in the professional division this year. Because my friend Bill Pearl had not entered in '68, Arnold was a cinch to win. And in New York street terminology, I "owned" the amateur Mr. Universe competition. All the magazines had installed me as the favorite, and although there were many fine athletes competing, I faced no serious threat from any other competitor.

Even so, every emotion from elation to disbelief coursed through me when the 1968 Mr. Universe winners were announced. Arnold won the professional division, and I won the amateur. And we posed together for the news photographers—two of the top bodybuilders in the world! I'd now achieved all there was to achieve and won all there was to win as an amateur bodybuilder. I was on top of the mountain. After all the celebrations, when I called home to report the good news, Dad was so happy he didn't even gripe much when I told him I was again planning to stay in England for a couple of weeks.

During this time, I resumed my relationship with Lynda Thomas, the Manchester model and beauty queen. Her parents had invited me to come to Manchester after the contest and stay in their home, and I was excited that we would be driving through the English moors, which I had read so much about in the Sherlock Holmes novels. Along the way, we stopped at scenic overlooks to admire the countryside and to eat in a beautiful restaurant. Later, as we were driving through the moors, the fog rolled in. I'd never seen anything like it before—it really was so thick you could cut it with a knife! We had to stop again for a while, then crept along at a snail's pace because we couldn't see the road in front of us. This turned out to be a blessing and a life-saving experience. We missed being involved in a deadly 40-car pileup thanks to the grace of God. We were hours late arriving at her parent's home in Manchester, but no one cared...we were alive.

Dennis congratulating Arnold on his 1967 Mr. Universe win

The next ten days were a grand adventure. My life was a whirlwind of seminars, posing expeditions, and interviews. I was even given the key to the city of Manchester and asked to be a judge in a beauty pageant and hand out the trophies. We took trips to Scotland and Wales, and Lynda also took me to Stratford-on-Avon to see a Shakespearean play. I could remember reading part of *Romeo and Juliet* in school back in New York, but it certainly sounded much different performed in the bard's own hometown by top British actors.

One of the highlights of my visit was being scheduled to appear on the David Frost TV show in England. During the interview, David asked, "How does it feel to have muscles and no brains?" I immediately replied, "How does it feel to have neither?" From that point on, I earned his respect, and the respect of the people of England.

Two weeks flew by in a hurry, and soon I was back in London, preparing to catch my flight home to New York. Lynda and I had made lots of plans and promises for the future; and after buying a few last-minute souvenirs and sharing last-minute kisses, we said good-bye, and I was on my way.

Strangely enough, the plans and promises we made were never carried out. Our hot romance cooled off, perhaps by the distance, or perhaps by the influence of two sets of overprotective parents.

To my surprise, being Mr. Universe was a little anticlimactic. Winning had been my dream, my goal, my main purpose in life for so many years. In reality, I had turned the quest for the title into my identity. But now that I had gained the title, I didn't know what to do with it. After all the congratulations from family, friends, and well-wishers, there was a big let-down.

Somehow there was an empty void in my life—something was missing. I had accomplished my goals and won every amateur bodybuilding competition there was. I was Mr. America *and* Mr. Universe. My life was filled with TV appearances and photo shoots, and even making movies. All my dreams had come true. So why wasn't I satisfied and happy?

Chapter Seven

GIVE ME A BREAK!

IF I was ever going to be a part of the film and television industry, I figured now was the time to do it. As Mr. America and Mr. Universe, I had earned the kind of name recognition that should attract Hollywood producers and directors. I told my agent to let them know I was available—and I waited for the offers.

And I waited.... But the producers and directors never called. The fact that I was a bodybuilder was obviously a disadvantage. Once again, it seemed that being strong and muscular just wasn't the "in" thing for film and television.

My "Commercial" Career

But I did have some good assignments, including magazine cover shoots, print ads, and TV commercials. One of the most famous covers I appeared on was *Esquire* magazine. Illustrating the lead article, "What Does the World's Richest Man Want?" the cover combined a photo of my

Dennis powerlifting at Lost Batallion, Queens, New York

body and Aristotle Onassis' head. Many of my friends jokingly said, "I'll bet you'd trade your body for his money!"

One of the first TV commercials I booked was for Brute, the aftershave lotion by Faberge. Another commercial required me to play Atlas, holding the world on my back. They sprayed my body with gold paint and instructed me to hold a huge globe. It was filmed in the middle of Manhattan. They also shot a still photo of the Atlas pose for a print ad. Another memorable print ad for me was an assignment working with my hero, Steve Reeves. The ad was to promote a Western movie, and we had a great time doing the shoot.

One day an old bodybuilding friend, Larry Powers, heard about a TV spot in production for Coronet paper towels. The commercial was to promote the idea that Coronet paper towels could pick up twice their weight in water. To illustrate that idea, the script called for a weight lifter to pick up two huge jugs of water suspended from a barbell. The contraption they had put together probably weighed 300 pounds or more.

Larry knew he couldn't lift that much weight, and he found out they'd already tried out several other weight lifters, wrestlers, and professional strongmen. Nobody could handle it. The problem was that the water jugs were suspended from the bar and swung back and forth, making the weight hard to stabilize. So Larry told the producers he knew someone who could do the job for them with no trouble. He gave them my name, and they gave me a call.

I knew I could lift the weight—I routinely dead-lifted 550 pounds, squat-lifted 450 pounds for 20 reps, and military pressed 275 pounds every day during my workouts. In addition, when I was warmed up, I could "clean and jerk" 375 pounds over my head at least a couple of times.

After I asked a few questions about what grip they wanted on the bar and how they planned to show the lift, I stretched and warmed up a little, then walked over and picked up the bar. The jugs of water swinging at each end made the lift really tricky. But once I felt the balance, I pushed hard...and the bar went up. Then the people on the studio set clapped and cheered, and I had the part!

During the actual commercial, I wore a very flashy silver costume, lifted the bar and the water jugs over my head, set the weight back down, then said a couple of lines. After about 20 takes, the bar fell out of my hand. The jugs smashed and water went everywhere, creating electrical sparks and shorting out the cameras. It was a miracle that none of us were electrocuted! Fortunately, there were already several good takes "in the can." Everything worked out great, and the spot ran on network TV for about a year.

At another time, during a shoot for Van Heusen shirts, I had to rip a shirt off my body to show my physique. Then in a spot for another product, I was instructed to bang on my chest and pose like King Kong.

I was glad to have the work, but I could see I was quickly becoming typecast in the bodybuilder, strongman category. Although I felt I could handle any kind of movie or commercial role—in situations that needed just a regular guy—I seldom got the opportunity. The agencies thought of me if they needed a he-man, super-brute character. But I had a vision...all I needed was a producer or writer who could develop a script or storyline that would feature a muscular hero...me!

Working nights was also getting to be a real drag because I didn't have much time for a social life. Having my days free to work out and go for auditions and acting lessons was good. But when my friends were making plans to go out to eat or to the movies or a club at 7 in the evening, I had to go to work. Basically, I had no life apart from sleeping, working all night, then going to the gym to work out. Then I'd check for auditions, try to study a little, and maybe rest an hour. Then it was time to go back to work. I was growing very disenchanted with the whole scene.

Realizing that my acting career was going to take time to develop, I decided to renew my own efforts in competitive bodybuilding and dedicated myself to winning the professional division of the Mr. Universe competition. The quest ended in another heartbreak, as I lost the 1969 pro title by the narrowest of margins to Schwarzenegger!

The Agony of Defeat

This loss put me into a tailspin. All that work, pain, and sweat! Even with my earlier wins and the status that came with them, I just felt empty and tired.

I was tired of the grind—tired of working all night doing work I detested, tired of putting up a happy-go-lucky front for my friends, when inside I felt miserable and emotionally bankrupt.

I was tired of scrimping, saving, working nights—constantly finagling and juggling my finances to keep up appearances—tired of resisting the distractions and temptations to get involved in illegal schemes and outright criminal activities.

I was tired of trying. I was ready to quit before I really got started.

"To hell with it all," I said. And for the next couple of years I set out to go with the flow, to let life happen, to do what I had to do to survive. It was time to live for the pure pleasure of it all—to look after myself and get what I could get for me.

To enhance my image, I bought a red Cadillac convertible and drove around town with the top down, summer *and* winter. I started wearing sharp clothes. I changed my working hours to a nine-to-five schedule. I dropped my acting classes and checked in with my agent only every week or so. I did keep working out, but at a less-intense maintenance level...and only because I enjoyed it.

When I went out looking for a good time, I found lots of other people like me out looking for it too. There were plenty of "wannabe" actors and actresses hanging around the trendy clubs and discos frequented by the rich and famous, hoping to rub elbows with theatre and movie stars and to be noticed or "discovered" by various agents, directors, and producers. Everybody had a script, a story, or a dream of becoming a star. Ego, pride, and narcissm were as common as salad on a dinner table!

Larry Powers and I made the circuit of the hot spots, making appearances at P.J. Clark's, Broadway Joe's, Rodney Dangerfield's place, and the Waldorf Astoria. We also went to Maxwell's Plum Restaurant at 61st and York Avenue, some of the comedy clubs, and, of course, the discos. The whole East Side was jumping. The sexual revolution was in full swing then, and you were likely to see about anything.

Larry and I liked to hobnob with the Joe Namath crowd, with champion fighters like Jake LaMotta and Rocky Graziano, and with professional wrestlers like Bruno San Martino and superstar wrestler Billy Graham. And for some reason, we hit it off with the newspaper columnists. We were more or less media celebrities, with our names in the papers at least once a month. Everywhere we went, people would ask to take pictures with us, begging us to flex and pose. People were also becoming very interested in diet and exercise, and would ask us how they could get fit. Even celebrities wanted our advice. Many asked me to train them for their next show or get them in shape for their next movie, and I was happy to do it.

As the newest New York "media darlings," we soon became part of the "in crowd," with our names added to the "A" list of private parties that were attended by the "who's who" of top celebrities, models, and the hottest entertainment artists. There were at least three or four interesting parties going on every night of the week, and even more on the weekends.

But to stay on the "A" list, you had to be seen in the right places with the right people, even if you couldn't really afford it.

One Friday night, I met my Uncle Charlie at Jillie's Restaurant in Manhattan, famous for its clientele of wealthy, influential people...and, of course, certain members of the Mob. Actually, Jillie's main claim to fame was the fact that the owner, Jillie Rizzo, was one of Frank Sinatra's best friends, and everyone knew that Sinatra was a frequent visitor to the restaurant.

As luck would have it, while Uncle Charlie and I were having dinner, in walked "The Chairman of the Board" himself, followed by the usual entourage of party animals. He shouted, "The drinks are on me!" and took his favorite table. At that point, the doors of Jillie's were closed...no one else was allowed to come in and bother Sinatra. It was an evening to remember...a loud, boisterous time was had by all. And the look on my Uncle Charlie's face spoke volumes. You would have thought he had just won the lottery!

As we left Jillie's, the scene was amazing. There was a huge crowd waiting outside...people were screaming and flashbulbs were popping as the paparazzi vied for the best picture of "Old Blue Eyes." And I must admit that my ego was taken down a notch that night. Sinatra showed me what the word "famous" really meant.

Enough Is Never Enough

My life had become one big party. But being in the swing of the social scene created a tremendous problem for me. I didn't have an allowance from a rich family or income from a trust or investment account like the people I partied with, and it seemed like I was always broke...or down to my last few bucks. Let it suffice to say that I suffered from a perpetual lack of money—but not because I wasn't making money. In fact, I was making more than I had ever thought possible. But no matter how much I made, I would spend even more! I'll never forget being at Coney Island one day, trying to make a good impression on a girl I'd met on the beach. I noticed that my picture was on the cover of a bodybuilding magazine at one of the newsstands on the boardwalk. But the irony was that I had so little money that if I had bought a copy to show her, I wouldn't have had enough money left to ride the subway home.

So there I was, burning the candle at both ends and living life in the fast lane to the fullest. The problem was, I couldn't keep up with my lifestyle. But I wasn't about to give it up because of something so minor as a lack of funds. So I had to come up with a solution, and one answer was my association with the club scene.

Because of our connections, my friends and I occasionally landed part-time jobs as bouncers, doormen, or maitre d's. And we had it made! Endless supplies of great food, throngs of pretty girls paying attention to us, loads of excitement—and we were getting paid for this! Most of the clubs were owned by Mob bosses and were hangouts for "made men" and their cronies. And our job was to keep "undesirable" patrons from coming into the clubs, break up fights inside, and throw out troublemakers. It wasn't everything I had dreamed of, but the money was steady and almost impossible to refuse. In addition, all the attention I was getting really stroked my ego.

My job also led to a few perks for other members of my family. My brother Larry was a singer, and he and his friends would often stop by where I was working to do a song or two, which led to picking up a girl or two!

Sounds simple, right? Sometimes simple becomes complicated in a few quick steps.

For instance, one night a couple of "wise guys" were having a disagreement. The other bouncer and I were watching carefully to make sure that nothing got out of control. A guy at the bar, who was obviously drunk, then got up to intervene, and we noticed that he was wearing a gun in a shoulder holster. Our boss told us to take this guy outside before things got out of hand. We wrestled the gun away from him, took him to the front door, subdued him with a couple of punches, then threw him in a cab, giving the cabbie enough cash to take the guy home. Later, at closing time, two squad cars pulled up, lights flashing. The cops got out, yelling at the manager that two bouncers had roughed up an off-duty policeman. Words and money quickly changed hands, and all was forgotten.

During this time, I became friends with a couple of the young guys in the Mob. We used to socialize often while I was working until one night, I realized that I hadn't seen them in over a week. When I started asking around about them, I was told that they had an argument over money, and they resolved the problem by shooting each other. Both were dead!

Another evening, a group of young Mafia guys were celebrating the induction of a new member. Then a college kid asked a girl to dance...what a mistake! She happened to be a girlfriend of one of those guys. That poor kid got the beating of his life. Needless to say, we never saw him in that part of town again!

Taking It to the Street

It's an amazing thought, but I was actually safer working for the Mob than walking down the street at times. For example, one night, I was out on the streets in Brooklyn with my bodybuilding buddy, Larry Powers. We weren't too concerned about our safety because we were two huge, strong guys.

While we were walking, two cars cruised by, then stopped, and six guys piled out and started following us. It was a very menacing situation.

Suddenly, one guy ran up behind me and stuck a gun in my back. Instantly, instinctively, I whirled around, grabbed and twisted the guy's wrist, and pointed the gun back into his face. "Hey punk," I growled, "don't ever do that. If you're going to point a gun at somebody, you gotta do it right!"

We stood locked together for a long minute or two. Then the other five guys began to back up and ease toward their cars, leaving their buddy behind. I looked into his face and noticed that there was sweat standing in little drops on his forehead, and his eyes were filled with uncertainty and fear. I snorted in derision, twisted the gun out of the guy's hand, and then handed it back to him. "Get out of here, punk, before I decide to hurt you!" And he took off. It seems unbelievable, but there was the former Mr. America and Mr. Universe scaring off armed street punks.

Friends in Low Places

Being a bouncer brought in more money than a regular job, but I was still trying to "keep up with the Jones's." And because I wasn't able to earn enough through my "legit" activities, the pressure was on to find some other way to finance my expensive tastes.

Other bouncers and bodybuilders taunted me about my situation. On a nightly basis, someone would say, "Here you are, Mr. Universe! And what have you got to show for it? You're wasting your time with body-building." It really got to me after a while. Where were all the big payoffs that were supposed to come after all the sacrifice and hard work? Consequently, I was vulnerable to any scheme that came along that might put a few extra dollars in my pocket. Plus, there was still a dark side of me that loved the excitement. I had been able to turn down the easy money other bodybuilders made from posing for homosexuals or even turning tricks, but I was easily swayed by another devil I was familiar with. After all, I grew up playing in the streets, surrounded by *crime*. It was only natural, I told myself. This is where I came from. This is what I know. And that's where my new friends came into the picture. They knew lots of other ways to get money.

It was simple enough at first. A few credit card scams or unloading some hot merchandise was a piece of cake. I found myself doing stuff I never thought I would do. And once you do something, even though you know it's wrong, it becomes easier each time. Then one thing leads to another, and you find yourself at a point of no return...plunging deeper into the darkness.

My friends would decide to rip off a store or warehouse, or do some other illegal deal; and as often as not, I'd end up being part of the deal just to get my hands on some quick cash. In addition, the adrenaline rush of pulling off the heist was so much like winning a contest that it filled part of the void in my life.

I loved the nightlife and easy money was hard to turn down, but I knew in my heart that I had taken a wrong turn. Even when I talked myself into joining one more questionable "job" or scam, there was an undercurrent of insanity about it all, and the confusion was overwhelming me.

Every time we'd do something crazy, I'd tell myself, *This is the last time I'll ever be this stupid. It's absolutely insane to take a chance on throwing away my whole life and all of my dreams for a few lousy bucks. I've got to get out of here before all this drags me down.*

Chapter Eight

WHAT'S A NICE GUY LIKE YOU DOING IN A BAD PLACE LIKE THIS?

THREE New York tough guys were looking down from the third-floor window of an abandoned building on the east side of Brooklyn. As they stared at a supermarket down the street, they watched intently as the last customer walked out, followed by three or four weary employees.

"That place is getting ready to close," said Nicky, with a grin. Nicky had also grown up on the mean streets of the Van Dyke public housing projects, existing among a dark and dirty maze of narrow streets and tall, shabby tenements.

"Yeah," replied Crazy Kenny, another victim of the projects. "I'll bet the night manager will be out in a minute carrying the money from the registers to the night deposit box." Kenny was being groomed by some of the neighborhood "wise guys" to be their eyes and ears and feet, running numbers and doing errands. His great ambition in life was to be a "made man," a *la cosa nostra* member who takes a blood oath—in by blood, out by blood—to be loyal to the "family."

"Let's go get what he's carrying," said the third guy. In a couple of minutes, the three had made their way downstairs and over to the store's darkened parking lot.

Nicky pulled a can of mace from his coat pocket and disappeared into the deep shadows near a couple of parked cars, while Kenny and the other guy ducked behind an old sign near the building's back door.

In a little while, the manager came out carrying a canvas bank bag and hurried toward one of the cars, and the two guys followed him as he went.

Reaching his car, the manager started to unlock the front door when suddenly, Nicky jumped out and sprayed him full in the face with the mace. Kenny and his companion grabbed the bank bag—then all three robbers sprinted away. They ran down the alley to the next street where their car was parked, laughing in excitement as they drove away.

"Man, that was so easy," said Kenny.

"Yeah," Nicky laughed as he drove away. "That poor schnook never knew what hit him."

"Let's see what we got," said the third guy, ripping the end out of the canvas bag as easily as if it were a paper sack. "Hey, there must be twelve thousand dollars in cash here—we're rich!"

The third guy had a well-built physique and huge, powerful shoulders and arms. Around his neck on a gold chain were two ornate medals—one inscribed "Mr. America," the other "Mr. Universe."

The third guy was me.

The money we had taken from the supermarket manager didn't last long. First, the three of us went out to a disco in Farmingville, Long Island called FACES, swaggering around like big shots, our pockets full of stolen cash. (Little did I know that this place would someday become a church where I would preach for over ten years...this disco where I had once been a big shot would become my pulpit). We never once thought about the seriousness of what we'd done—it was all a big joke. And besides, nobody really got hurt.

On our way back home later that night, we stopped at a Catholic church and dropped all the nickels, dimes, quarters, and dollars from the bag into the mail opening on the door of the church. Then we made the sign of the cross. We felt sort of like Robin Hood, taking from the rich and giving to the poor.

The next day we went shopping, buying fancy silk shirts and ties, new shoes—we even talked about buying a new car. My dad saw what was happening and wanted to know where we'd gotten the money. "Oh, we won it playing the numbers," we said. "We hit it big!"

Because we had pulled off this robbery so easily, Kenny, Nicky, and I started talking about another place we could rip off. Crazy Kenny knew a guy who ran an Italian delicatessen and was also into bookmaking and shylocking—taking illegal gambling bets and making loans at exorbitant interest rates. He wasn't "connected"—he wasn't a "made man." That meant he was fair game, and we could rip him off.

So, we planned how to pull off the job. We'd puncture a couple of tires on his car, then wait for him to come out the door. While he was locking up, we'd run up, put a gun to his head, rip his pockets, and take all his money. It was a good plan.

Everything worked just like we thought. We put a gun to the guy's head, cut his pockets with a knife, grabbed the thousands of dollars he was carrying, and started running down the block. What we didn't know was that Kenny's dad and some other guys were right around the corner, waiting for the newspapers to come in. Before we were out of sight, the deli guy was screaming that we had stolen his money. So Kenny's father and neighbors all started running after us. We barely managed to get to the car and drive away before they could recognize us.

We split up the money and went home. Unbeknownst to Kenny, his mother saw him hide his share of the money in his room and figured out that something was wrong. She knew he was running around with Nicky and me, so she multiplied Kenny's stash by three. Of course, it was almost exactly what the deli guy said he'd lost in the robbery.

Crazy Kenny's folks were good people. His dad was a city sanitation worker, an honest, hardworking man, and his mom was a very devout Catholic woman who was really concerned about her boy. She was almost certain we had committed the robbery and felt that she had to do something about it. So, she invited Nicky and me over for a three-course Italian dinner.

While we were eating, she told us that she knew we had robbed the delicatessen owner. She said she had prayed to Mary and had seen a vision. She spoke of seeing Kenny's face, and ours, and then the Holy Mother spoke to her, saying that we had ripped the guy off. She wept as she told the story, and said she would continue to pray for us.

We weren't sure how Kenny's mother knew what we'd done, but we didn't have much faith in her "vision." We tried to convince her that she was wrong—and we ended up giving her some money to, in a sense, pay her to shut up. She never believed us...but she did take the money.

The compassion of Kenny's mother touched my hardened heart. So, I went to confession. In the confessional, I told the priest details of my relationship with my current girlfriend, then blurted out the story of the robbery at the deli. To my utter surprise, the priest came out of the confessional, grabbed be in a vice-like grip, and ordered me to give back all the money! The man in the deli was one of his relatives! Running home at breakneck speed, I found my uncle and told him what had happened with the priest. Uncle G was even less forgiving. "You don't even know how to be a good crook," he exclaimed, giving me a smack on the head. "What are you—stupid?" I just wanted to disappear into the floor.

After laying low for a few days, Nicky, Kenny, and I resumed our three-man mini crime wave. We robbed another supermarket—which went smoothly, and again no one got hurt. Then again, we walked up and robbed a guy who was putting money in a night deposit box.

Besides getting the money we wanted, there was a weird kind of excitement associated with committing these crimes and getting away with it.

Some of my friends in the neighborhood knew what we were doing and said, "Dennis, you've got to be crazy. How could you get involved in stuff like this? You were Mr. America and Mr. Universe. If you get busted, you'll ruin your reputation and your whole career."

So I quit for a while. I'd think about starting to train for some body-building contest—then lose interest. I was on again, off again. Then, when I needed a thrill and some extra cash, Nicky and I would run some scam, steal something, or rob somebody.

I tried to rationalize what I was doing. *I've worked so hard for so long and never received anything to show for it. And we take only from businessmen who have so much they'll never miss it. And we're always careful never to hurt anybody.*

The Gang That Couldn't Shoot Straight

A few months later, I was working out at the Olympus Health Club in Queens—a really primitive, iron gym in the basement of an old building where there were just a few selector machines—plus some benches and lots of weights, wall-to-wall concrete, and rats running through the place.

That's where I met Mickey Roman. Mickey was big and tremendously strong, a power lifter with 22-inch arms. He was the one who challenged me to start training seriously again so I could go back and compete in the professional division of the Mr. Universe competition—a title I hadn't won.

One Saturday morning, as he was spotting me while I trained with 400-pound decline bench presses, I strained my left pectoral muscle. I hurt it so severely that I knew it would be a miracle if it healed in time for me to compete that year. Consequently, I had to back off and take it really easy with my chest work.

So, what does an injured bodybuilder do with his time? Find a way to have a good time—that's what.

Mickey's wife was a waitress who often worked nights, so we ran around together and had figured out how to sneak back into the gym at night through a window. Lots of times, after we'd been out on the town, we'd go back to the gym and work out at three o'clock in the morning.

We also had some guns—a couple of .38 caliber pistols, a .45 automatic, some sawed-off shotguns, and other assorted handguns. Late at night when no one else was around, we'd set up milk crates for target practice down in the gym. The bullets would ricochet off walls and miss our heads by inches. It was a big joke to us. We had no idea of the danger of our actions; we were just interested in the thrill of pulling the trigger and the sheer excitement of handling such powerful weapons.

When Mickey, our buddy Nicky, and I would hang out and shoot pistols, Mickey would talk and scheme about pulling a big job and scoring enough to buy new Cadillacs and move out of the neighborhood. He was always talking about doing a major holdup.

Finally, we decided to try one of Mickey's plans—a stickup. So, the three of us stood by the side of a building with guns, waiting for two guys to come out with a bag of money. But we were on the wrong side of the building—they came out on the other side. They were already in their car, headed for the night deposit box at the bank before we caught on. When we realized what was happening, we ran to Mickey's car to chase after them. When he threw his shotgun into the trunk, it went off and blew a hole in the side of the car. It was an absolute miracle that it didn't hit the gas tank, explode, and kill the three of us!

We raced through the streets of Queens at 60 miles an hour with a huge hole in the side of our car, trying to catch these guys and cut them off so we could pull off the robbery. By the time we found them, they had already put the moneybag in the night deposit box, and we noticed a police car sitting on the bank parking lot. We were lucky to get away unnoticed. It was a total comedy of errors.

We decided to call ourselves "the gang that couldn't shoot straight" from a movie we had seen. We made a big joke out of it and had a big laugh on our way down to Little Italy to eat Chinese food at an all-night place. Then we went back to the gym to work out. We were completely crazy...living life on the edge!

A month or so later, Mickey got a bright idea about how we could rob the restaurant where his wife worked. The police frequented this place all the time—there were always squad cars parked outside and uniformed patrolmen eating inside. Mickey thought it would be even more of a thrill to rob the restaurant while the police were there!

I said, "Mick, they know you at this place, so you'll have to stay out in the car and be our getaway driver. Nicky and I will go down the delivery chute out back and get to the basement where the manager's office is."

"No way," he replied. "If we're going to stick up this place, I've got to go in with you. I want to see that manager's face when we rip him off."

"But they'll recognize you."

"No, I'll go in disguise!" He knew I had some stage makeup from acting school, and some fake hair and mustaches we'd bought at a party shop at Times Square. So, we both put on disguises. Mickey wore a pillow around his waist and some high-heeled boots like they wore in the John Travolta *Saturday Night Fever* movies. He also wore a ski mask and heavy makeup to look like beard stubble. I simply pulled a ladies' nylon stocking over my head.

Nicky stayed in the car on the parking lot near the chute where the produce and other foods were delivered to the kitchen. He was to give us a signal. If the car lights were off, it was safe to come up. If the lights were on, someone was watching and we should stay put.

Mickey had been in the manager's office with his wife before, so he knew where we should go. Nobody saw us when we went down the chute, and we'd barely gotten inside and pulled our guns out when the office door opened and the manager walked in. I did the talking so he wouldn't recognize Mickey's voice. "This is a stickup." We pushed him down on the floor and taped him up—eyes, hands, and feet. Fortunately, the big safe in his office was already open and there was lots of money inside. In addition, we found plenty more in the guy's wallet. We then dumped all the money into a butcher's apron and headed back to the chute to climb out.

When we looked up, Nicky's car lights were on. I yelled out, "Nicky, we've got to come up."

"No, don't!" he yelled. "There's cops all over the place. Are you sure that guy didn't hit the alarm?"

We knew he hadn't—we didn't even let him get near his desk. So, we decided the only thing to do was wait for the traffic to clear out upstairs. Just then, a cook walked by on his way to the freezer. So, we grabbed him, taped his mouth and hands, and threw him inside the walk-in freezer. Then we locked the door. Things were starting to get complicated.

Back at the chute, Nicky informed us that some guy on the parking lot had recognized him—he'd met him at the gym. So, we told him to go inside for a cup of coffee and tell this gym buddy that he was waiting to meet a girl there. In the meantime, we continued to hide out down in the basement.

A half hour later, Nicky came back to the car and yelled down the chute that there were cops still milling around. We decided to take a chance and go up anyhow.

I started pushing Mickey up the chute—he was carrying the money. He was about five feet eight and weighed 240 pounds. Halfway up the chute, he got stuck and dropped the money. So, we had to go back down and repack it. Talk about nerve-wracking—I was shaking like a leaf by the time I got him out and climbed up after him. Sure enough, cops were standing all over the parking lot. We casually strolled to our car, got in, and slowly drove away. Then we went to Mickey's house and split up the loot.

Nobody found the manager until six o'clock the next morning, and the poor cook in the freezer was finally released just after that.

The cops were furious that a major robbery had been pulled off in the basement of a restaurant where they were sitting upstairs eating and drinking coffee. They tried to keep it quiet, hoping to find out if it had been an inside job.

Of course, we had a big laugh because in spite of all our problems, we got away clean.

Crazy Mickey's Lunatic Plans

Nicky and I were kind of worried about working with Mickey, though. For him, the risk and the danger was the big attraction—it gave him a "rush." And he really was crazy—his ultimate dream was to rob the Federal Reserve in New York City. Nicky and I were involved strictly for the money and didn't need or want that type of thrill. So we decided to stay away from Mickey for a while.

When Mickey heard that the police thought the robbery might have been an inside job, he came up with the brilliant idea that we should rob the joint again, reasoning that people think lightning never strikes in the same place twice! Needless to say, Nicky and I refused.

Then Mickey started casing out the business manager's house—he was also one of the owners and was pretty well off. He wanted to follow the guy home and rob him again. I said "no" to that scheme as well.

Several weeks later, Mickey came up with a new proposal, and this one sounded pretty good. He was working for a business in New York City and said, "Dennis, I know this place inside and out. Every Friday at three o'clock in the afternoon, the payroll is delivered by an armored car. It's anywhere from $30,000 to $50,000 cash in pay envelopes. We could pull this job off real easy!"

"Hey, man, you don't want to pull an inside job—it's too dangerous!" we said.

"No, I've got to be there. I'll take a couple of vacation days, and I'll wear a disguise when we go in. You can do all the talking so they won't recognize my voice."

The three of us talked about this job over and over. It would be by far the biggest robbery we'd ever attempted. We planned our every move and thoroughly cased the neighborhood. Again, our plan was for Nicky to stay out with the getaway car, while Mickey and I went inside.

On the day of the heist, we put tape on the locks of every door in the building we would need to get through so we couldn't get trapped inside. Nicky double-parked outside, and if he was forced to move and was gone when we came out, we'd take a cab.

We walked inside and went to the sixth floor, covering our faces with nylon stockings. Then we pushed the buzzer. When the two employees inside the money room opened the door, Nicky and I shoved inside, guns drawn, and snarled at the man and woman to get down on the floor. The man didn't cause any trouble, but the woman, a Filipino, started screaming at the top of her lungs, "Help me, Jesus. Oh, Lord, the evil one is trying to get me. I bind you, devil! Our Father, who art in heaven...."

"Shut up, lady," I growled. "We're not going to hurt you."

"Oh, please, don't kill me. I've got three little kids. Oh, please don't hurt me. Sweet Jesus, please help me!"

I felt a strange feeling when I heard the name Jesus. In fact, I became edgy and nervous, with sweat beginning to pour off me. When we finally finished taping and restraining her, we put her in a closet. Then we took the other guy to open the safe.

When the heavy steel door swung open, we discovered that the safe was almost empty and contained only a few thousand dollars in a bundle. "Where's the rest of the money?" I yelled.

The guy started laughing...and Mickey whacked him on the side of the head with the barrel of his gun. "What are you laughing about?" I demanded.

"I don't know what to tell you guys. Normally the payroll would be here, but the armored car company went on strike today. The money won't be coming. They're going to pay everybody with checks."

At first, I didn't believe the guy. Mickey thought that maybe the delivery was just running late and that we should wait for a while. So we taped the guy up and stashed him in the closet with the Filipino woman.

After a while, the buzzer rang. "That's got to be the money," we said. "The guy was lying to us."

But when we opened the door, we saw two other office employees, one of which was a guy who was about six feet six inches tall. Mickey was only five feet eight, and I'm about six feet tall. I knew if the guy put up a fight, one of us probably would get hurt. We stuck guns in their ribs, ordered them to do as they were told, and taped them as well. Most of them were scared stiff, but the big guy was pretty noisy.

Our plan was to be in and out of the building in a matter of minutes, and we'd already been inside almost an hour. It was way past time to get out. So, we took what money there was in the safe and started walking out of the building. Then one of the guys we'd tied up got loose, opened a window, and started screaming, "It's a robbery! Call the police!" Nicky was already upset because we had been inside so long. He'd finally parked the car in a no-parking zone...and had gotten a ticket. Now, he was worried that they'd use that to connect us with the robbery.

The newspaper headlines the next morning talked about how two armed robbers were foiled by the strike of the armored truck service.

It was another foul-up—yet another crazy adventure by the gang that couldn't shoot straight. And we all pretty much agreed we'd better quit while we were ahead.

Going From Bad to Worse

Hearing the Filipino lady pray made me realize that the devil had me in his grasp. That name *Jesus* had convicted me that I was doing evil. I wanted to change my life, but how could I get free? I was in too deep! There was no one I could turn to for help...no one who cared.

I just couldn't break away from this madness—something had a hold on me. I couldn't seem to stay away from the wrong kind of people, and it was only a matter of time until I got hooked up with Joey the Rat!

Joey was a skinny little loudmouth of a guy with a weasel face who was always bragging that his uncle was George Raft, a famous actor in gangster films. Joey owned a sub shop and a dry cleaning store in the Bronx, and was also a wholesale car distributor who dealt a lot with mobsters. New York gangsters who wanted to drive a Bentley, a Rolls Royce, or some expensive foreign sports car all knew about Joey the Rat. He sold both "legit" and "hot" cars. A client could point out a car he liked on the street; then two days later, Joey would deliver it to the guy's house—with a new VIN number and up-to-date registration papers.

Joey himself always drove a fancy car, had all kinds of money, and hung out at the top clubs. Eventually, my friend Nicky and I met him in a restaurant and then ran into him from time to time. He was a hustler to the max, and his "rap" was as strong as aluminum foil! And we noticed that he always had his pockets full of cash, so Nicky suggested, "Let's hang around with Joey the Rat for a while. We might make some easy money with this guy."

A few nights later, Nicky came over and said, "Hey, Dennis, I know this guy who wants to teach another guy a lesson. He's willing to pay to get him roughed up a little. Are you interested?" When temptation knocked, I opened the door.

Joey and I went with Nicky to meet an Armenian guy who owned a clothing store right next to Maxwell's Plum restaurant. He said, "This guy across the street—my competitor over there—I hate that guy! I'll pay you a thousand dollars right now to go beat the hell out of him."

"How bad do you want him hurt—what do you want?"

"Oh, nothing serious, just so he gets bloodied up and bruised pretty bad."

So, Nicky and I walked across the street and went into the competitor's clothing store. The two of us started fussing with the owner over nothing and picked a fight with him. When he flared up and popped off, we got on each side of him and used him for a punching bag. Nicky would slug him and spin him around, and then I'd hit him. We smashed him up pretty badly and left him lying on the floor. Then we went back across the street and collected our thousand dollars.

Before we could leave, however, the Armenian guy started talking about another job he wanted us to do. He was willing to pay $10,000 to have a building burned down. "I've got an uncle who has a store. I've got money in his business, but he's doing so bad he can't pay me back. The only way I can get my money is if he can collect the fire insurance on the place. So I want you to burn him out—but it's got to be a professional torch job so the insurance company won't squawk."

The guy was willing to pay half the money up-front and the rest when the job was done. He wanted us to call him precisely at midnight—after we had done the job—and say, "I can't believe I burned the whole thing!" There was a famous commercial on TV at that time that showed a sad-faced, fat guy holding his belly and saying, "I can't believe I ate the whole thing." The Armenian thought it would be funny if we did a takeoff on this line when we called him.

After we left, I said, "Joey, I don't know how to do a professional torch job—I've never burned a place before in my life."

"Aw, you can do it," Joey said. "It can't be that hard. Why don't you just ask around and find out what you need. It'll be an easy way for us to split $10,000."

So, I went to see my Uncle G for some information. "What would it take if somebody wanted to torch a building?" I asked. "What would it take to do a professional job that couldn't be traced?"

Of course, he caught on pretty quickly. "What's going on here? What kind of craziness are you messing around with?" Then he explained how dangerous it would be to get involved with such a job. "What if the guy puts a couple of stiffs in the basement before you burn it up? Maybe this is just a cover for murder or something. If the cops come and catch you doing the job, they could stick you for murder."

"Nah, Uncle G, I know this guy. I've worked for him before. He's okay. He just needs this place to burn down for the insurance money."

Uncle G said, "Nobody knows a strange guy that good, especially when your life is at stake!" But finally, he took me to meet a Jewish man who'd done some torch jobs for the "family." He told me what I needed, how to go about doing the job, and suggested a certain kind of chemical that burned really clean. The trick was to fill up balloons with this stuff and staple them to the stucco ceiling. When heat reached the balloons, they would burst and the highly flammable chemical would spray everywhere.

The trigger to spark the whole thing would be a lit cigar connected to a fuse running to a paper cup full of the chemical, positioned just beneath a low-hanging balloon. We had all the details planned out so that everything would happen without looking like arson.

Later, after the Armenian guy gave us a key to the carpet store and told us how to shut off the alarm, Joey and I went in late at night and attached the chemical-filled balloons all over the ceilings. Then we looked around the store to see if there was anything we wanted to steal before it burned. Everything was going smoothly so far.

When Joey lit the cigar, however, he couldn't resist doing a corny James Cagney impression, gesturing with the burning cigar. "Look, Ma, I'm on top of the world"—a line from the movie *White Heat*. A tiny piece of red-hot ash happened to drop off the glowing cigar and landed on the nearly empty chemical can we were going to carry out with us.

Suddenly, there was a gigantic WHHOOOSSH...and flames were everywhere. Joey was standing there, still holding the cigar, screaming in shock. I ran and jerked him out of the flames, and we scrambled for the door. Because we were wearing coveralls over suits, Joey wasn't hurt, and the fire never really caught on our clothes.

By the time we turned the alarm back on and removed the key from the lock, balloons were bursting and flames were roaring across the ceiling. As we ran down the alley to Joey's waiting Bentley, smoke started coming out of the building. We stashed our coveralls in the trunk of the car and drove around the block to watch the building go up in flames. It was about five minutes before midnight.

The smoke was getting worse, and any minute the flames would burst through. Then, to our horror, we saw an old man out walking his dog about a half block away, and he was coming straight toward the building.

"Oh, no, that guy's going to see the smoke and run to the fire alarm on the next block," said Joey.

"Joey, we're going to have to stop this guy before he messes everything up," I yelled.

"You want me to run him down?" asked Joey in disbelief. "We're liable to kill somebody!"

Just then the old man noticed the smoke and started to run toward us. Joey jumped out and yelled, "We called the fire department! The trucks are on the way!"

"Man, this building is going up!" the old man said.

"Yeah, I know. But the firemen are already on the way."

Suddenly there was a tremendous explosion, and the whole front of the building blew out, and the roof of the store next door caved in. Inside you could see a raging inferno. Then we heard sirens in the distance—evidently someone else turned in the alarm. We drove away before the fire trucks arrived.

I then made the call to the Armenian guy from a pay phone. As soon as he answered, I said, "Hey man, I can't believe I burned the whole thing!" He was still laughing when I hung up, screaming and yelling like he'd won the lottery.

We met the guy at his store later that night to collect the remainder of our $10,000. While he went into the back room to get the money, Joey grabbed a dozen Armani suits off a rack and put them in the trunk of the car. He figured we deserved a bonus!

A Date With the "Ice Man"

The next day, Joey checked his answering service, and listened to a call from a Mob guy named Carmine Black who worked for Onelliella

Delacrose, the boss of all the "families" in New York at that time. The message was that the "Ice Man" wanted to see Joey and the Muscle Man...and that he wasn't happy. The "Ice Man" was a nickname for Delacrose because he had a frozen face—he never smiled. Joey was the only guy who could make him laugh.

"What's he mad about?" I asked.

"Somebody told him we messed up that red El Dorado I sold him for his *gumado*—his girlfriend," Joey said.

A few days earlier, Joey and I had been riding around Manhattan in this car Joey had just picked up to deliver to Delacrose. As a lark, he decided to try and drive it the wrong way up a one-way street, with cars coming toward us. He'd had to swerve to keep from getting hit and had run up on the sidewalk. Some Mob guy had seen what happened, recognized Joey, and reported it to Onelliella.

Joey was really shook up...and I was flat-out scared. I knew that Mob bosses were completely capable of having people killed for very little provocation. And if his girlfriend's car had been damaged, that would have caused him to lose face.

"We've got to hide," said Joey. So we went over to his dry cleaning store and parked his car inside. Then the two of us spent the night inside the air-conditioned safe where people stored their fur coats in the summer. Joey called a guy to sneak over to Onelliella's girlfriend's house and check over the El Dorado. He called back in a couple of hours to say there wasn't a scratch or a nick on it.

In the meantime, I got hold of my Uncle G, the family advisor. "Dennis, you're gonna get yourself killed!" he yelled. "This Joey guy is a nut. Why are you hanging around him? You don't mess with these people. They're bad news! Onelliella will kill you at the drop of a hat—for no reason except he doesn't like the way you look. I don't know how to help you.

How did you get involved in such a stupid thing? All you can do is have a sit-down meeting and deny everything. Don't make him find you, and don't ever admit that you had anything to do with his car."

Joey got hold of Delacrose's people and set up a meeting. We then went to Little Italy, to the Ravenite Social Club on Mott Street, down the block from the Grotto. This goon ushered us into a back room, where sitting at a table with four or five of his guys around him was the boss of all New York Mafia bosses, Onelliella Delacrose.

"What's this about my car?" he said quietly. "What happened to my El Dorado?"

"I don't know what you're talking about," said Joey. "Your car is over at your girlfriend's house. It's brand-new, in perfect condition, just the way it came from the factory. You know that!"

Joey totally denied the story about the one-way street incident, and I backed him up. Then Joey clowned around a little and said, "What—do you think I'm crazy? You think a man of my character and reputation would lie to you?"

The "Ice Man" stared at Joey with no expression for a long moment, then started grinning and finally broke out into a loud guffaw. "Okay, you bum, get out of here. But I'm warning you that if anything at all goes wrong with that car, I'm gonna have your ass!"

Nicky and I made a lot of money hanging around with Joey the Rat. He was a real smooth operator. He'd keep his sub shop and dry cleaning store going, sell cars in the Bronx, and still have two or three other crooked deals going at the same time. Nicky and I were getting sucked into more and more outright criminal activities, but we kept rationalizing what we were doing, saying it was okay as long as nobody got hurt. Even though we pulled off several armed robberies, we never pulled the trigger on anybody.

Joey also knew a guy who worked in a post office in New York. He'd steal credit cards as they came through the mail and sell them to Joey for $100 each. Then Joey, Nicky, and I would use these cards to buy $400 suits and $100 ties. After a couple of hours, we'd throw one card away and use another one. We ate in the finest restaurants in New York with Joey and charged everything to hot credit cards. We thought we were a class act...living large in the Big City.

At another time, Joey somehow convinced the Harlem Mob to rob factories for him and then found ways to sell what they stole. One time, they brought him about a thousand designer label suits. They retailed for about $500 a piece at the time, and he paid $20 each for them. My friends and I bought them from Joey for $40, then sold the suits for twice that much out of the trunk of my car all over the East Side. Joey had a bunch of other guys out selling them too, who were also dealing drugs on the side.

We were partners, but I eventually came to realize that Joey was loyal to no one. He didn't care who he hurt, because he never had to deal with the consequences. Joey would turn on anybody if it came down to either you or him, and I was definitely getting paranoid.

So, Nicky and I decided to chill out and cut back on our criminal activity before it was too late. Too many people knew what we were involved in, and it was starting to get too intense. We knew we had to stop.

For once, our timing was perfect. Things were raging out of control in Joey's life, and he soon was severely wounded. It seems that that "Harlem Boys" felt they were being shorted and decided to do something about it. Joey was taken by force, pushed into the trunk of a car, and driven into the woods. His captors released him from the car, then told him to run. Joey was then used for target practice, and as he ran, the "Harlem Boys" fired off shotguns at him. At the same time the pellets were passing through his body, Joey said he saw a vision of Jesus. He stayed conscious long enough to hear the shooters say, "He's dead."

Wrong! Joey came to, and managed to crawl to the highway, seeking help. He couldn't believe it when a car stopped, and out stepped the Harlem Boys! They shot him again, leaving him for dead...again.

Miraculously, he was found and rushed to the hospital. Contrary to what the "Harlem Boys" said, Joey survived. Later, he said to me, "Dennis, Jesus gave me a second chance! It's a miracle I'm alive!"

Through divine intervention, I was not with Joey that day. Perhaps it was the result of the Filipino lady's prayers. All I know is that suddenly things started to change, and it was time for me to fade into the background.

Chapter Nine

ANITA, THE LOVE OF MY LIFE

Going undercover when you're an extremely recognizable person is not easy. I stayed in until I couldn't stand it, then I would head out with the guys...discreetly of course!

One Friday night when I was out on the prowl with my friends, cruising around various clubs and discos, and just checking out the sights, we stopped by a table to speak to some people, and I immediately noticed a strikingly beautiful, dark-haired girl who was sitting with them. She had a gorgeous soft tan complexion and dark brown eyes that snapped with intelligence. She was dressed in white eyelet lace, which on her was absolutely stunning, and there was a best-selling novel, *The Detective*, on the table in front of her.

The whole group chatted together for a minute or so. Then Anita— that was her name—looked at me and asked, "Do you know Ralph Carpinelli?"

"Oh, sure, I've worked out with him at the Mid-City Health Club on Times Square. He's an actor and model, isn't he? He told me about a girl he thought I should meet. You must be the one!"

Dennis and Anita posing for the Dec. 1971 cover of Strength & Health Magazine.

"Yeah, he told me about you too. You're the bodybuilder!" She then told me that one of her friends had dated Ralph. We continued with a little more small talk, then my friends and I moved on. I thought she was a really nice gal, and when I looked back over my shoulder to check her out one more time, she was watching me walk away.

I didn't see her again for several weeks.

Then one day I went to Aqueduct Racetrack with my dad and placed $5 on the Trifecta—where you pick the winners of the top three races. I arbitrarily chose 3-2-3...and I won $500. So that night, I decided to take my brothers and a couple of other guys out for dinner and a night on the town.

We decided to go to Maxwell's Plum, a really nice place operated by the same people who owned the famous Tavern on the Green in Central Park. There I noticed a beautiful girl wearing an unusual brown leather beret...and it was Anita!

She saw and recognized me at about the same moment. "Oh, I remember you," she said. "You're Dennis Tinerino, the guy who knows my friend Ralph Carpinelli."

We started talking for a while and discovered that we had several other mutual acquaintances. And we had other things in common—she also was into physical fitness and worked out regularly. I liked her. She was really attractive and very poised and sure of herself.

After a while, I asked Anita if she'd like to go with us over to P.J. Clark's, a popular place with the "in" crowd. "Oh, sure," she said, "that sounds like fun."

She had a girlfriend—Grace—with her, so one of my buddies came over and the four of us went off together. I had a pocketful of money and a beautiful girl on my arm...and I was the happiest guy in the world!

From that night on, we continued dating. From the beginning, my attraction to this girl was not just sexual, although she was an absolute knockout—a real beauty queen; she was so intelligent and knowledgeable about everything. In addition, I could tell her things and see that she really understood and cared. And while she was interested in me, she didn't seem to be overly impressed by my titles and reputation.

Anita had grown up in Astoria, an Italian-Irish and Greek neighborhood. Her father was Filipino, retired from the Navy and the postal service. Her mother was a Hungarian Jew who valued the traditions, culture, and religion of Judaism. She converted to Catholicism at marriage, but would still celebrate the Jewish holidays with relatives. So, Anita knew what it was like to be persecuted by the people in her neighborhood and at school. She'd had to deal with a lot of racism and prejudice.

A Beauty With Brains

As a result, Anita was a very strong person and knew how to take care of herself. I was also fascinated by her knowledge of music. She could literally "name that tune." Anita had a photographic memory and knew the lyrics of all the pop songs, plus the names of the writers and performers. She'd worked at Times Square Records for three years before moving to a job as an executive secretary for the Executone Company in Queens. She also did some modeling and was a judge in some beauty contests while competing in others, winning first place in a couple. Anita eventually joined the Olympia Health Club in Ridgewood, Queens, where I often worked out. We spent quite a bit of time together at the gym, and I helped her with her workout program.

As time went by, I told her about myself—about my dreams and ambitions, the frustrations I felt in my career, even some of the other involvements with girls I'd had in the past. I made it clear that I wasn't ready to get involved in a permanent relationship like marriage.

Anita made it equally clear that marriage was her ultimate goal—that she wasn't interested in any kind of relationship unless it was directed toward a solid, stable commitment.

"I can see that you're really a very lonely and confused guy," she told me. "You have a lot of good qualities, but people are pulling at you from nine directions. You don't know whether to be a playboy or a working-man. You haven't been able to achieve great success in movies or even in fitness, in spite of your bodybuilding accomplishments, and your relatives and friends keep pulling you back to an evil lifestyle. They're not doing you any favors. If they really cared about you, they wouldn't get you involved in illegal things. You're going to have to get over your false loyalty to this ungodly Sicilian heritage. I've seen too many people like you ruin their lives or wind up dead."

"Eventually, Dennis," she said, "you're going to have to decide to go on your own and break away from bad company. You're going to have to decide what you really want to do. The short road to success is always the longest. Follow your heart and do what you know is right. You need to face reality—then you have a decision to make before it's too late."

I knew she was right. It was time for some serious soul-searching to get my vision back. It was time to slow down, look around, and step on the brakes. My life had really been rotten—even worse than she knew. My dad had also been really worried and concerned about me, and he was always trying to give me fatherly advice about what I should and shouldn't do. He had been very concerned about what Joey and I were up to. Our brother Sal sometimes got involved in some scams and rough stuff, but nothing like the out-and-out crime wave Joey and I were causing. My dad never thought bodybuilding would be a secure career for me but had always encouraged me to work at a job that would provide a regular paycheck, some benefits, and a retirement plan for my old age.

In addition, despite his Italian heritage and very "liberal" outlook about single guys and sexual morality, Dad could see that I had no moral standards at all. When I finally came home after being "missing in action" for an entire weekend, he said, "Dennis, what are you doing with your life? Why don't you straighten up and find a nice girl to marry? You need to make a life for yourself."

Even though she wasn't Italian, Anita met with my dad's approval. He liked the fact that she went to church regularly and even sang in the choir. She even got extra points with Dad because she had been raised Catholic! He could see that she was levelheaded and a hard worker. What she wanted for her life was exactly what he thought I needed for mine. It was also easy for anyone to see that romance was in the air.

I may not have admitted it at the time, but Dad was right. Anita was right there with me as I trained...helping me stay on my diet by making me protein shakes, and giving me constant encouragement. Unbeknownst to me, she was also praying that God would touch my life.

When the 1970 NABBA Professional Mr. Universe contest was held in England, I was ready to go for the professional title again. I won the "tall class" competition, beating one of my idols, Reg Park, for the honor. However, I again placed second in the overall competition, this time to Boyer Coe. The fact that I was more muscular and symmetrical than ever only added to my disappointment.

And during the entire time I was in England, I wrestled with the decisions Anita said I had to make.

Those kinds of choices are never easy. So, while I was in London, I checked to see if my former girlfriend, Lynda Thomas, was around. I wondered how she was feeling and if I would still feel anything for her. I made

Dennis wins 1975 Mr. Universe

only a halfhearted attempt to find her, however. Although we did speak on the phone, I really wasn't anxious for us to get together. Deep in my heart, I think I already knew what—and who—was right for me.

Then later in 1970, I entered a Mr. World and Strongest Man competition, this one a professional contest held in Columbus, Ohio. One of the first contests carried on national television, covered by ESPN, it turned into a "no holds barred dogfight"—a back-alley, bodybuilding brawl. Arnold took first place, Sergio Olivia was second, Dan Draper was third, and I was fourth. In the Strongest Man division, a Russian weight lifter named Alexeev "cleaned and jerked" 500 pounds overhead for a new world record.

I was totally frustrated when I heard the results. Both Olivia and Draper were fine bodybuilders. In fact, many felt—me among them—that Sergio deserved to win the contest that year. And I knew I definitely didn't deserve to be fourth. There were TV cameras that were filming backstage when I heard the news and angrily threw down a towel. The program announcer said, "Dennis Tinerino, former Mr. America and Mr. Universe, is unhappy. You can see that he doesn't agree with the decision of the judges." What an understatement!

Although my big moment on TV wasn't the most flattering, the live telecast created a huge new audience for the sport of bodybuilding. Thanks to my television exposure, I actually ended up getting more fans and publicity from a contest I *didn't* win!

In 1971, I again entered the Mr. World contest. Although I felt I was in top condition for the show, I came in second to Ricky Wayne from Antigua. I was very unhappy about it and said so in no uncertain terms. But, of course, it didn't do any good to protest. All I accomplished was to add to my reputation for making the sparks fly when I lost.

That same night, Anita came in second in the Miss Body Beautiful Pageant. As a result, she and I were on the cover of *Health and Strength* magazine together.

Enough Is Enough!

I was becoming very dissatisfied and disenchanted with my life. My dreams of having an acting career that would evolve into a starring role in the movies were not coming to pass, and the constant cycle of auditions and rejections was beginning to wear me down—my normally exuberant optimism was wearing thin. And with certain notable exceptions, my career as a commercial actor had not been really successful either. At the time, I was very discouraged that my future prospects seemed bleak.

Then there was bodybuilding, the thing I had loved most in life. My picture had been on the cover of virtually every bodybuilding magazine—*Iron Man, Muscle Development, Health and Strength*, and others—and my articles on fitness and training were being published. I was still receiving offers to do several photo-shoot jobs and appeared at a few posing exhibitions and fitness seminars, but generally the pay was not what I had hoped for. In retrospect, I almost gave up before I really got started, just because I was impatient!

For the amount of time and struggle invested in training for the competitions, the return was just not worth the effort. Too often, it seemed, the judging was no longer fair and impartial. The selection of winners had very little to do with the physical condition and artistic presentation of the competitors, but was based on the arbitrary opinions of sponsors and judges. It seemed I had put out so much and gained so little...and now I was at the point of diminishing return. I was so discouraged that I didn't return to London to participate in the 1971 Mr. Universe competition. It was time to admit I was on the verge of being burned out.

Moving Away From Emptiness

Back in New York, I started breaking away from my old life and distanced myself from the relatives and friends who walked on the edge of the underworld. My instincts told me that I was a train wreck waiting to happen, and it was time to get off that train. I set a new goal of putting my bodybuilding experience to practical use by operating my own health club someday. And I knew I was tired of the emptiness of living life with no moral boundaries...and no commitments.

Anita and I started seeing each other full time...all the time. We talked for hours and dreamed and planned of a life together. She wanted to get married and have kids. I just wanted to be with Anita, because being with her was so great. Anita was always happy and contented, and she had a great sense of humor. Unlike me, she was well organized and had good business sense. We got along extremely well and hardly ever disagreed. Amazingly, Anita was able to overlook the fact that I often had a quick temper. Best of all...she loved to cook!

As a couple, Anita and I complimented each other—not just physically, although we did look terrific together! We loved the same things, and were always out on the town together. Going to concerts, the movies, or the theatre, followed by a fabulous meal at a fine restaurant was one of our favorite ways to spend an evening.

She also went with me to bodybuilding seminars and exhibitions whenever she could. When she met Arnold Schwarzenegger, he posed with her for a picture, and then told me, "She looks like healthy German gal. Make good babies!" Although Anita would have preferred a different kind of compliment, we all had a good laugh. Arnold was the king of the one-liners.

My family and friends loved Anita. When Anita would go with my family to competitions, she fit right in. My dad was constantly screaming and yelling, and Anita quickly learned to join him as he lambasted the judges and other competitors. Plus, Anita would watch my back...she could spot the phonies a mile away!

The early years with Anita were "boss." It was a good time, yet an opportunity to learn about myself and a chance to finally grow up and be responsible.

But somehow I couldn't seem to make a clean break from my old life, and about that time, I received a call from an old neighborhood friend of mine who had moved to California. He was a wheeler-dealer kind of guy—a macho boxer and bodybuilder. His name was Dog Man—they called him the Dog Man because he kept two, huge Bouvier des Flandres German police dogs that must have weighed 150 pounds each.

Miggs would call me from time to time, bragging about how well he was doing in California and how much money he was making. He said he'd gotten involved in an escort service in Los Angeles and was getting rich. The purpose of his phone call this time was to say he was coming back to New York to visit his folks and that he wanted to meet with the "Tinerino Terror."

So I agreed to meet him for lunch, where he raved on and on about how well his business was going in California. At one point, he opened up an attaché case he was carrying and showed me twenty thousand dollars. He kept flipping and flipping through bundles of hundred-dollar bills and then threw $3,000 at me saying, "There's more where that came from! Think of it as a bonus."

Then he said, "Dennis, why don't you come to California and work with me? I need a partner in this escort business. You could make $5,000 a week easy. I need a strongman with street smarts—some muscle I can trust to keep people from ripping me off. The way you look, nobody would even try to bother you. So, how about it, Dennis? Want to be my partner?"

Miggs explained that the escort service was really a front for prostitution, but he assured me that the service really wasn't involved. Whatever arrangement the girls worked out with the customers after they got together was their own business. "I've got the best lawyer in Beverly Hills looking over everything," said the Dog Man. "He says we're strictly legal, no problem."

I told the Dog Man that his offer was tempting but that I couldn't come to California. I was turning over a new leaf, cleaning up my act and going completely straight. And besides, I was getting married.

Miggs just grinned, and then pushed back his chair. "Okay, Dennis, if that's what you want to do, I wish you the best. But just remember—I'm out there where the money is. If you ever want to make a change, I've got a place for you."

He always was pretty wild. He'd get me in trouble for sure.

Even as I patted myself on the back for doing the right thing, a little voice was whispering in my ear, *But Dennis, did you see all that money? How else are you gonna get ahead?*

I didn't tell Anita about my meeting. I knew she wouldn't have approved of my hanging around with people like the Dog Man.

She *really* didn't understand a few weeks later, when I told her I was going to California for the weekend. "I'm going to see about a business deal with Dog Man," I told her. "Plus I can check out the gym scene and see some old buddies while I'm there." Of course, I didn't tell Anita what the "business deal" was, although I'm sure she suspected it was something illegal.

Dabbling With Evil

Miggs had called again to say he was sending me a plane ticket to come out for a couple of days. He wanted me to help him pass some counterfeit traveler's checks, and he said I'd probably make $10,000 during that one weekend. It was just too tempting...and I said "yes."

"What do you need these kind of people for?" asked Anita. "You should stay away from them. Messing with guys like this is just dabbling with evil and the devil!"

"Oh, the Dog Man's kind of crazy, but he's okay," I said. "Besides, I really need the money."

So I flew out to California. Miggs knew somebody in Hollywood who was an expert at making phony I.D.s, and we went over to Barney's Beanery, met with the guy, then went to his "office," where he put my picture on a driver's license taken from a stolen wallet. Then he gave me credit cards and membership cards that had the same name on them. That way I had two or three matching pieces of identification if anybody asked me for them.

Then we drove over to San Diego and hit the supermarkets and convenience stores up and down the main drags. I'd go in and pick up cartons of cigarettes and booze, then pay for them with bogus $100 traveler's checks. I'd take the change and the merchandise out to the car where Miggs was waiting, and we'd go on down the road to the next store.

In just a few hours, I cashed over $7,000 worth of counterfeit traveler's checks, and we had a trunk full of beer and cigarettes to sell. It was working like a charm—easy as pie! That night the Dog Man and I went out on the town to a bunch of dives where he liked to go. We had pockets full of money—and the next day we'd get even more. We were big shots on a spree—talking loud, laughing long, and flashing cash.

Miggs also used the time we spent together to tell me more about his escort service. It was a classy operation, he said. He had part-time actors driving leased cars—BMWs, Mercedes, Lincolns—to take these girls to meet the guys who wanted an escort or a massage. He assured me it was a perfectly legitimate business—his high-priced lawyer had checked it all out, and the cops couldn't touch the operation. He was paid a fee for simply making the appointment and providing transportation for the "escort" to the client. Whatever the two of them engaged in later was none of his concern.

"This business makes money like crazy," said Miggs. "You really ought to reconsider coming out here and managing it for me. You could make a bundle—maybe $3,000 a week, all legit. Plus, you'll be involved in the other businesses, and we can always add to our income with gambling."

The next day we drove back to L.A., and continued working his very *illegitimate* traveler's check scam, this time in North Hollywood. The first three or four stores I hit went smoothly. Then, as I was walking out of a supermarket with two cartons of cigarettes and a fistful of money, somebody yelled, "STOP!"

Instinctively, I turned to see what was wrong. The store manager was coming around the counter, saying, "Drop that money! This traveler's check is phony. We heard you were passing these around. I'm calling the police!"

When I heard the magic word, "police," I started running out of the store as fast as I could. I could hear the manager running after me, still yelling for me to stop. Miggs saw what was happening and pulled the car up close to the door. I jumped in, and we tore away. But the manager and another employee started chasing after us in two other cars, honking and screaming. We roared through the streets of North Hollywood at 90 miles per hour, swerving and dodging, barely avoiding one disaster after another.

We finally went over Laurel Canyon into Hollywood and lost the cars that were chasing us. But we were both pretty shook-up. It had been a close call. "I think I've had enough of this, man," I said. "I'd better grab a flight out of here."

"Yeah, probably so. If the word is out, we won't be able to cash any more of this batch of checks anyhow."

So I took my half of the money and flew back to New York. On the plane returning home, I thought, *Well, this just proves that Anita's right. Why am I messing around with this guy? He's nothing but trouble—he almost got me locked up. I need to forget this craziness and just settle down.*

I told Anita about the money I made, but I sure didn't tell her how I got it...or how close I came to getting busted. I just made up stories about winning at gambling while I was out there.

"I'm really glad to get home," I told her. "I really missed you." At least that much was the truth.

A few weeks later, Anita and I went to city hall and applied for a marriage license. On February 14, 1973, a rainy Wednesday, we were married in a small wedding at St. Paul's Catholic Church in Queens. When the priest said, "In the name of the Father, the Son, and the *Holy Spirit*, I now pronounce you man and wife," something really struck me hard. Holy Spirit. Those words, *Holy Spirit*, were powerful in a way that I hadn't experienced since I was 12 years old and heard God speak to me on the subway. It was so intense, I almost passed out.

Enjoying the "Perks"

We spent our honeymoon in Miami, Florida and enjoyed all the complimentary hospitality given to Mr. Universe and his new wife. Anita loved it there. We had beautiful rooms at the Fountainbleu Hilton on Miami Beach, dined elegantly at four-star restaurants, played on the beach in dune buggies, took rides on friends' boats, and went to see Tina Turner perform at the Playboy Club.

After our fabulous honeymoon, we moved into Anita's one-bedroom apartment in Rego Park in Lefrak City. Anita was still working at Executone, and I worked at my job at Kollsman Instrument Corporation. And, of course, we spent most of our spare time either in the gym or out on the town. With both of us working, we had a very comfortable lifestyle, but my income still felt like small potatoes—especially compared with the money I'd scammed in one day in California...or the cash James Miggs had been carrying in his attaché case when he came to New York. On the other hand, Anita had a great idea that we should save enough money to open our own health and exercise club. This way, we could continue to work together and help people develop better health and fitness.

I tried hard to settle down and be satisfied. After all, Anita seemed happy and perfectly content. Our parents were extremely proud of us, and our friends were very happy for us. And I was happy too. But lying in bed at night, staring at the ceiling until the wee hours of the morning, I kept feeling that things were moving too slow. I needed to be making something happen—something big. I couldn't shake the idea that there had to be something more to life than this. I knew I had a problem, but didn't know how to solve it. I was always striving...never at peace. It was as though I wasn't just driven, but tormented by the need to "make it big." There was no rest in my soul.

Then one day my agent called and said, "Dennis, they're making a new movie in Manhattan. How'd you like to have a part in it? It's called *Shamus*, starring Burt Reynolds as a New York detective. The part I've got for you is in a scene in a health food restaurant that will involve several bodybuilders. You'd be playing a waiter, and there's an arm wrestling scene with your friend Chris Dickerson (who was also a Mr. America and Mr. Universe). What do you think?"

What did I think? Of course, I wanted to make a movie with Burt Reynolds! But I wanted to play a tough guy, not a waiter! However, my agent said, "Listen, if you don't want to do it, I'll have to get someone else." Needless to say, I took the role, and had a lot of fun. And Anita took off from work to join me for lunch on the set. Burt was a very friendly guy, and we enjoyed meeting Dinah Shore, who was his girlfriend at the time.

Working on the film taught me more about how movies are made. It was a paid film acting class. Plus, I made friends with the director and got to shoot a few extra scenes in the film—most of which ended up on the cutting room floor. But *Shamus* was only my second film, and I was sure it would lead to other roles.

But...there weren't any other roles in movies coming in. Anita and I continued to work at our regular jobs most of the time, and I conducted a few seminars here and there which brought in some money. But a part of me was craving something with more excitement. So I told myself that I needed to make a large sum of cash in a short amount of time in order to invest in my first health club with Anita. It could happen...especially if I could move to California and make big money every week—legit—like the Dog Man had said.

Chapter Ten

CALIFORNIA, HERE I COME

I was a model husband...for about three months.

Anita and I went to work in the morning and came home at night. We'd eat dinner, talk, and hang around the apartment. On the weekends, we'd go to a movie or maybe meet with some friends. It was all very nice, very...domestic.

Anita was great. She was a super cook, making all my favorite Italian dishes, different kinds of pasta, cheesecakes, and all kinds of fabulous food. She and I both were interested in eating healthy and getting the right nutrition to be able to work out and stay in shape. And she was totally devoted to me. She did everything she could to make me happy.

But I wasn't happy. I was in love with Anita, but domestic life seemed confining. I wasn't used to regular hours and sitting around in peace and quiet. I was restless. I was always striving—never at peace, totally driven by my ambitions. I was bored.

The adjustment from single life to that of a married man was hard for me. I just didn't have the freedom I had before. And my buddies didn't seem to realize that getting married should curtail my social life. Unintentionally they tried to hold me back from being a responsible husband. Even my married friends seemed to share the idea that wives should stay at home to cook, clean, and take care of the kids, while the guys went out on the town, footloose and fancy-free.

Then, one day Anita announced she was pregnant with our first child. At first, I was ecstatic and full of joy that I was going to be a father. Soon though, the apprehensive thoughts that all first-time fathers think began rolling around in my head. How was I going to handle the responsibility of a kid? I still wasn't used to the idea of being responsible for taking care of a wife, and to be honest, I knew I really hadn't done that great a job of taking care of myself.

Thank God for family. Both sets of parents were thrilled to find out that they would soon be grandparents, and they gave us all the love and support a young couple could ever want or need, helping us to provide a safe and nurturing home for the baby.

Everyone contributed in one way or another, and Anita and I found out that close friends and family make the best support system in the world. Aunts, uncles, cousins, and even friends from the gym were always around to lend a hand or just be a good listener. Through them, I was learning to assume the responsibility of being a parent. I realized how blessed I was to have all these wonderful people around who cared about us.

All expectant couples are concerned about money, but I thought we were doing okay in that department. Anita was still working, and I continued to work at my regular job at Kollsman Instrument Corporation As well as receive an income from bodybuilding.

Then the owners at Kollsman announced they were moving their operation from Astoria to Long Island by the end of the year. I'd still have my job, but it would be a really long commute on the train, morning and evening; and I couldn't stand the thought of doing that twice a day for the next 20 years.

I'd always been a guy who imagined the grass was always greener on the other side of the fence, so I couldn't help thinking about what it must be like in California, with bright sunshine glistening off the ocean, warm breezes rustling through the palm trees, and the "beautiful people" cruising along the wide avenues of Beverly Hills in Jaguars and Maseratis.

Opportunity Knocks

Right about this time, the Dog Man called again with another hard-sell spiel about me coming to work with him. You'd think I would have learned a lesson about this guy after nearly getting busted with him in the bogus traveler's-checks scam. Even his new reason for wanting me to come should have scared me off.

"Hey, Dennis, I've got to have you out here, man," he pleaded. "I got busted for having a counterfeit hundred-dollar bill. I've been in prison and I just got out on probation. But one of the conditions of the release is that I can't go around the business for a while. You've got to come be the front for the whole operation. I'm telling you, man, you'll make a ton of dough."

I didn't see any caution flags or hear any warning bells while Miggs was talking. Instead, my ego and pride had taken over, and I was already consumed with the thoughts of being a big shot, running a successful business, making lots of money—and doing it where it was warm.

As we talked, we worked out a deal on the phone that I thought I could sell to Anita. The Dog Man would send me the money to pay the lease on our apartment in Rego Park for six months so that Anita could stay there and keep working for a while. I'd go on out to California and take over the management of Miggs' escort service on a trial basis. If I didn't like it or if it didn't work out, I'd go back to New York. We'd still have our apartment and could pick up where we had left off. If everything did work out, however, Anita could come out to the West Coast and we'd get us a place there.

So when Anita arrived home, being a couple months pregnant and exhausted from working all day, I broke the news to her with all the tact and finesse of a dump truck. "Look, Anita, we're going to move to California. I don't want to work for Kollsman Instrument anymore. I've got this great opportunity out on the West Coast."

"Dennis, what are you talking about? What in the world do you mean?"

"Well, I'm tired of New York. Things just aren't working out for us here. This is not what I want to do." And I went into the whole story Miggs and I had hatched up on the phone. I emphasized the big money I could make, but carefully left out any mention of the escort service that was a front for prostitution. I maintained that I would be involved in a successful retail business. Anita listened and didn't say a whole lot, but I could tell she wasn't convinced.

I told her that the real reason for taking the deal was to make some serious money quickly, so I could open up our own health club, just as we had talked about. After investing 15 years of my life in bodybuilding, I'd found a way to get the financial reward that I deserved, and with my own gym, I could get serious about bodybuilding and be a success at the sport all over again. In addition, I rattled on about meeting with Joe Weider to sign a contract, renewing old fitness acquaintances while I was out there, and most importantly, I could get an agent and pursue my goals and dreams of making films and being an actor.

Then I threw in the hook. "I promise California will be paradise for us *and* our new baby," I told Anita. "You'll love it out there, and we'll have everything we ever dreamed of!"

"So that's it," I said. "What do you think?"

"I don't know about this business or these people," she said. "But I love you, Dennis. If this is what you think is best for us, okay. Plus, I've always wanted to go to the Shrine Auditorium to see Katherine Kuhlman who has a miracle Christian ministry. I'm praying that you'll go with me." Anita believed we needed to be around church people and pursue God— especially with a child on the way.

When the Dog Man sent me some money the next week, I paid the apartment rent for Anita, packed my clothes, kissed my wife good-bye, and caught a plane to Los Angeles—totally unaware of the impact that this move would have on me, my wife, our family, and our future.

Risky Business

Miggs, wearing designer clothes and a Rolex watch, picked me up at the airport in a Jaguar. And I was impressed...just like he wanted me to be.

The Dog Man said we were going to celebrate, and we did just that, wining and dining and making the rounds at various exclusive clubs. He had a pocketful of cash, and he could get a table at any restaurant in Beverly Hills where the beautiful people hung out. He introduced me to some of his well-known "friends." (Later I learned that most of them were really clients.) And of course, he had women hanging all over him every place we went. The man had quite a reputation as a high roller. I thought I'd been quite an operator in New York, but this guy was amazing!

Then it was time for me to learn about the business. I first met with Roman Caldera, the attorney who handled all of Miggs' legal work. Caldera was a very prominent lawyer who represented a lot of people of wealth, power, and influence, in addition to several highly placed but shady people who—as Anita described it—"dabbled in evil."

Caldera was a man of class, highly educated, refined, respectable, and a very proper guy. Yet he seemed quite comfortable being a friend to outright criminals—people involved with organized crime. He was warm and chummy with Dog Man, the Dog Man. And he seemed to like me.

He explained how and why the businesses—there were multiple corporations—operated the way they did. Every procedure had been designed with a specific legal purpose in mind. He also carefully explained what I needed to know and do to protect myself.

After a couple of days learning the ropes and asking questions of Caldera and the Dog Man, I was on my own and had to learn the nitty-gritty details through experience.

Miggs and I were fifty-fifty partners, but all the paperwork was prepared in my name because the terms of his parole forbade him to be directly involved. We set up a new legal entity, which was the holding corporation—a sort of umbrella—for all the various companies and operations.

One of our businesses was a men's clothing store—it didn't stock much merchandise but provided a "proper" vehicle for credit card charges. The others were a massage parlor and two answering services—Princess Outcall and Dial O Service. All four of the companies operated out of a single location.

Miggs had worked out deals with most of the hotel doormen and maitre d's to give our phone number or card to guys they thought were looking for "services" like ours. They were then paid for every referral who called. Also, we ran very classy-looking ads in *The Hollywood Press*, *The Free Press*, and other local tabloids advertising out-call massages and escorts for parties, dinners, shows, etc. Businessmen from out of town would call and schedule a girl to meet them.

We'd take the client's credit card information over the phone and make a charge to the clothing store. We accepted virtually every major credit card, including the Exxon gas card. There was a base charge of $35—$25 for us, and $10 for the girl. Of course, if the client later negotiated for other services from the girl, presumably he "tipped" her directly, usually in cash.

Dial O Service and the out-call company's "legit" status was based on the premise that they provided a completely legal, bona fide service for a fair and reasonable fee. We simply assisted patrons in scheduling meetings with masseuses or companions. Any illegal activity that might later occur happened without our knowledge or involvement. Our "escorts" were licensed masseuses who worked as "independent contractors" and signed agreements with our corporation to that effect.

These "independent contractors" were pretty and well dressed, with outgoing personalities. They really knew how to charm and manipulate the customers out of their cash—and to the girls it was all business. Some of these girls were amazing entrepreneurs; they made large amounts of money, most of it in cash, and they paid other "independent contractors"—usually current or ex-bodybuilders I recruited—to be drivers and bodyguards for them.

Dog Man originally recruited the girls for the business from the massage parlors he personally frequented. Then it became a networking thing—these girls recruited other girlfriends, sisters, neighbors; or their friends knew girls who were interested. Girls looking for work would even reply to the ads directed to men. Some of our "escorts" were aspiring actresses who needed to eat; some were addicted to cocaine or pills; some were married gals who wanted to make extra money; some just did it for the excitement or to meet guys with money. We always had more applicants than positions.

The service was doing very well and handled approximately a hundred calls a night. Girls worked all over Pasadena and Orange Counties, and some customers even flew certain girls to Vegas. There was almost never a problem getting paid. Even though the business had a huge advertising budget and massive legal fees, our part of the base fees grossed tens of thousands of dollars a week. I enjoyed having lots of money, and I always kept a thick roll of bills in my pocket. When I wasn't working, I hung around with Miggs in the discos and clubs, and went with him to some of the constant parties. I soon had my own contacts and friends, and picked up the nickname "Tough Tony."

Welcome to California

After I'd been in town for several weeks and decided this new venture was going to work, I brought Anita out from New York. Miggs had started the business out of a $1,500-a-month rented house in Benedict Canyon, and we lived in that house for a few months until we found an apartment we liked in Westwood.

At first, Anita didn't know what I was doing. I told her I was working in the men's store, but that story didn't hold up very long because I was constantly gone at night—long after any store would be closed. Part of that time I was working (I soon learned there were lots of headaches in the business), but some nights I was simply out partying. And I made up a million excuses for where I was and what I was doing. I don't think my wife really believed any of them. She had no family or friends to talk to, and became very fearful and lonely in her new home.

When she finally found out about the escort service, the massage girls, and all the rest, Anita was both horrified and angry. She was also very pregnant, and she spent her days just sitting around.

Naturally, she was suspicious that I was involved with the girls who worked for the service. She had seen the ads in *The Free Press*, with photos of all kinds of women. It was true that there were always girls available if I'd wanted to get involved with them. But I was trying to follow Roman Caldera's emphatic advice to keep everything as businesslike as possible. I might play around somewhere else—but not at work.

Pretty soon, Anita had other things to worry about—telephoned death threats!

Shortly after I took over the escort service, I was contacted by a man who said he represented a group of "family" people who were moving to Los Angeles from New York. They wanted to talk about "helping" me with my business. "Hey, Dennis, you need to be working with your own people—New York Italian *family* guys you can trust. We can protect you from anyone who tries to give you a hard time. All we want to do is sit down and talk. How about it?"

I refused. My uncle had told me long ago to always be loyal to whoever was helping me make money...to not worry about being "loyal" to anybody just because of his or her ethnic background. "If they ain't puttin' money in your pocket, you don't owe them nothing," he insisted.

When I told the guy from New York I wasn't interested in meeting with his friends, he got very angry. "You're making a big mistake," he said. "You're going to be very sorry." Of course, I responded in my typically refined and tactful way—"I'll break your neck, you punk! Nobody threatens me!"

Then the calls started—muffled voices delivering graphic warnings to whoever picked up the phone. When Anita happened to answer, the callers made nasty, ugly, abusive threats. Although she had grown up in a tough city and knew all about life on the street, Anita was unnerved and frightened by the calls, which came at every hour of the day and night.

Then the girls who worked for us began reporting that strange Italian guys were coming up to them in restaurants and saying, "You're going to be working for us soon. Tough Tony and the Dog Man are finished in this town. We're taking over!"

So, one day I called Uncle G, told him what was going on, and asked him to check out these guys. He called back the next day and said, "These guys are connected, Dennis, but they're not "made men." They're just trying to horn in on your business. I know the real family in L.A. and Vegas—they're leaving you alone as a courtesy to me. If you want, I'll come out to California and straighten these guys out."

"Nah, I'll handle it. I just wanted to be sure where I stood before things got too rough."

Taking Care of Business

The next day the Dog Man (who was also getting death-threat calls) and I agreed to a meeting with the New York guys. The meet was to take place during the dinner hour at Carmine's Restaurant on Santa Monica Boulevard in West L.A. Apparently, the "wannabe" mobsters had heard that Miggs once had been a boxer and that I was a muscle man and street fighter—both too tough to handle one-on-one. So there were about eight big guys waiting when the Dog Man and I walked in.

The meeting went about the way we'd expected. The new organization wanted to provide a protection service for our business...for a fee. It was nothing but a shakedown.

One guy did most of the talking, so I listened to his spiel, pretending to be reluctantly persuaded. The Dog Man played along too, being charming and funny, putting the other guys at ease as he smoked his Cuban cigar. Finally, I said to the leader, "Okay, let's go out to the car, and I'll get you some money to get started."

He was feeling very confident as he strolled along beside me with a little smirk on his face. As soon as we got to the back of the parking lot, I turned to the guy and said, "This is my answer about you being involved in my business." Then I hit him in the face as hard as I could. I could feel his nose and cheek crunching beneath my fist. Before he could fall, I hit him with my other fist. As he staggered back, clutching his face with both hands, I kicked him in the groin. Then I started methodically working him over, beating him with my fists and feet, slapping, punching, kicking, stomping—taking out my rage and frustration on him until he slumped to the pavement, barely moving.

I drug his motionless body behind the trash dumpster and gave him one last kick. Then I walked back to the parking lot where Miggs and the others were waiting. "Let's go, Mason," I said, getting into the car.

"Hey, where's our guy?" asked one of the mobsters.

"Oh, he's out by the dumpster with the rest of the garbage," I answered, as Miggs backed out of the parking space and began pulling away. We were out of sight before they found their friend.

For a few days, the death threats and pressure got even worse, and I started carrying a gun in my car as did some of the drivers for the girls.

The Dog Man was totally paranoid. He imagined that people were following him everywhere he went. He heard noises in the night and couldn't sleep. Sometimes he'd go stay with friends because he was so shook up and afraid. In addition, we had armed guards watching the house in Benedict Canyon 24 hours a day.

A few days later, I walked into a restaurant where three of the New York guys were having lunch. I walked over and sat down at their table. "I've been doing a little checking on you guys, and I find that the 'families' don't recognize you! So I'm warning you to back off. If you're looking for trouble, you've found it. We've worked too hard for this business to back down or run from you. If we get one more threatening call or even see one of you guys around, the war's on! And I promise you'll lose."

Evidently, the message got through because they never bothered us again.

Under Investigation

After a while, we moved our business office to a plush, rented space in Beverly Hills. But despite having an elaborate, legally correct system and offices in an upscale, elite area, we certainly hadn't fooled the police. They knew exactly what we were doing. The bottom line was that we were operating one of the biggest stables of "working girls" on the entire West Coast, no matter how "legit" and clean we said we were.

The police had heard rumors that a Mob war was brewing and that New York underworld characters were trying to move in and take over. So, they began a surveillance operation, keeping a watch on my house and my office.

The police already knew all about the Dog Man. They'd investigated several of his scams but hadn't been able to pin anything on him until they caught him with the counterfeit money.

Then I showed up. They soon figured out that I was Miggs' link to the business while he was on parole, and they started putting together a dossier on me. They knew I was a bodybuilder, a former Mr. America and

Mr. Universe, and officers even showed up at Bill Pearl's gym, asking questions. They figured I must be connected in some way to alleged Mob operations in southern California and Las Vegas, and thinking they might be on to something really big, they kept working on my "case," trying to put together all the pieces of the puzzle.

The reputation I was building around town with the party crowd didn't help my cause either. If there really were police detectives following me, they certainly got their ears full. I was a high-rolling, big-spending, tough-talking show-off, making the rounds at all the popular restaurants, bars, and clubs. My friends liked to tell stories about my exploits in New York, and I liked the Tough Tony nickname and the admiring whispers of the "beautiful people."

I was invited to all the biggest parties in town where I met the top names in the entertainment business—the who's who of directors, producers, agents, stars, and has-beens, plus big-name sports figures and TV people. The California scene was even wilder than the New York circuit—more money, more fancy homes, more people seeking a thrill a minute and looking for life in the fast lane.

Miggs and I both did some pretty serious gambling too. It was nothing for us to bet between $5,000 and $10,000 a day on horse races, football, or baseball games—whatever was going on. We learned how to work the point spreads, playing one bookmaker against another. We might lose $5,000 with one guy, but we'd win $5,500 with the other.

Miggs and I didn't know what the cops had on us at the time, but we knew if we were to keep operating, we needed to diversify into some other businesses that would appear more legitimate. Meanwhile, the police continued to harass and intimidate our people, and were constantly arresting the girls, pulling over the drivers to check their registrations and licenses, and writing tickets for the slightest offense. Officers often just "dropped in" at the office, hoping to find something illegal going down.

Some of the cops respected me for my bodybuilding achievements and tried to give me some good advice. "You've got to quit this stuff, Dennis. Eventually you're going to get busted and go away for life. Get out while you can and go back to the fitness business."

I found out later that at times the police had people following me 24 hours a day. They even put surveillance devices called bumper-beepers on my car and tapped my phones at the office and at home. My attorney said what they were doing was probably illegal, but by then I was in so much trouble I didn't have the time, money, or energy to fight it.

In addition to the police harassment and unending "personnel management" matters, I also had to handle advertising, accounting, writing checks, paying utility bills—all the regular details any business has to tend to. And I wasn't particularly good at these kinds of details.

I wanted out, but by now I was in so deep, I didn't have a clue how to even begin finding my way back where I belonged.

Getting in Deeper

I started feeling really frazzled. I was running all the time, and when I did try to go home to rest for a while, Anita would lambaste me for never spending any time with her and for putting myself at risk. "I worry every day that you'll either get arrested or killed," she said. Many times when I was home, somebody would call with a problem and I'd have to leave.

I'll never forget when it was time for Anita to go to the hospital to give birth to our first child, Tara. I got her there okay and did the waiting father routine, pacing the halls, looking through old magazines in the waiting room.

When our daughter was born, I felt an indescribable thrill. Holding tiny Tara for the first time was a joy-filled moment. She was so beautiful, and I felt closer to Anita then than ever before. Yet, as I held her, the questions were raging in my mind. *What future can I give my daughter? What kind of father will I be, involved in this seedy business?*

A half hour later, I received a page at the hospital. There was an emergency at the office, and I had to go—immediately. I never did get back to the hospital. Three days later, I told Anita to call a cab to take her and Tara to our apartment in Westwood near UCLA. I just couldn't get away. That's how bound I was to my lifestyle.

Things didn't get much better after Tara was born. I tried to spend some time with her every day, but something always dragged me away. I would get home very late, after Anita and the baby were both sleeping. Then I'd grab a few hours of sleep myself, and when I woke up, I'd take off again. Anita never saw me more than a few hours a week, and my only day off was Sunday. She sat at home alone, with a brand-new baby, no friends, no relatives, and no husband. She knew a few people who worked for the service, but they were working almost as much as I was. She got no help, no encouragement, no social contact, and no adult conversation. I honestly don't know how she kept her sanity.

Meanwhile, the Dog Man and I just kept getting into deeper trouble. We actually started running a shylocking operation. Because we had lots of money coming in, certain high-risk people wanted to borrow from us, and we'd oblige them...at extremely high interest rates. When our loans were repaid, we made a tremendous profit. But sometimes our customers were slow to pay, and so we established a "collection department" to deal with them.

I used some of my bodybuilding contacts to work collections for me. When a couple of these big bruisers would go "warn" a guy, he'd usually find a way to pay up. Otherwise, he might have an "accident" and break an arm or leg. Our collection methods were crude but effective.

Once my "collection department" was set up and operating, I began using it to collect past due accounts for other "lenders." We were paid a percentage of what we collected, so we became very persistent. We found intimidation and fear to be very effective. Of course, the threats, holstered guns, and baseball bats might have had an impact as well.

Before long, we had earned a well-deserved reputation for being mean and rough. Actually, the Tough Tony reputation made my job easier. Lots of times all I had to do was make a phone call to get quick action.

The police harassment then became so persistent in Beverly Hills that we moved the operation to the Exxon Building on Santa Monica Boulevard, right in the heart of Hollywood. By this time, Hollywood was filled with weird people doing every kind of far-out thing imaginable. We thought that maybe we wouldn't be such a target for the police in a neighborhood filled with drug dealers, scam artists, struggling actors and actresses, eastern religious cult members, and curious tourists.

But the cops kept up the pressure wherever we were and whatever we did.

In the meantime, the escort service business never ran smoothly for more than a few months. Then some new headache would pop up. At one point, we started getting complaints from the girls that a certain guy was calling them to his apartment and then taking all their money. If they resisted, he'd slap them around. This happened several times.

One night I got a call from Dixie, one of our best escorts, and she was really upset. She'd been called to this guy's apartment, and when she arrived, he took all her money, mauled her, and threatened to kill her. The bodybuilder who was her driver and bodyguard burst into the room with a gun and got her out. "If he hadn't been there, Tony, I don't know what would have happened to me. What are we going to do?"

"Don't worry, Dixie," I told her. "That's why you're working with us. We'll take care of this guy for you. In fact, when we do it, I'll let you wait in the car and watch."

This kind of thing was very bad for business, so I decided to make an example out of this guy. I wanted the word out on the street that nobody could mess with our girls and get away with it.

Less than a week later, the guy called again. As soon as he gave his address, we recognized him. We told the caller, "Look, we've been having some problems inside some of the apartment buildings. We need you to meet the girl out front so you can be sure she gets inside safely."

As soon as he hung up, our phone scheduler called Dixie and told her and her driver to pick me up, and he called to let me know they were coming.

When we drove over to the guy's apartment, he was standing out front. Dixie and her driver, Vick, both recognized him from the trouble they'd had before.

We drove on past and stopped down the block. Then I got out and walked back to where the guy was waiting. I asked him for a light for my cigarette, and he popped off some smart reply. I grabbed him by the shirt and said, "What's your problem, buddy? Who do you think you are? I don't like your attitude, punk!"

Then I started beating him up. Vick came running from the car, carrying a rubber hose, and he started hitting the guy. Right out in broad daylight on Hollywood Boulevard, we gave this guy a savage beating. We took the money out of his pockets, ripped his shirt off, and kicked him in the groin and in the face.

Before leaving, I gave him a warning to never mess with our girls again.

Police Crackdown

But instead of learning a lesson, this guy called the police. He told them that he'd called our service for a masseuse, but instead, two strong-arm guys had come out and beat him up. Later that night, I looked out the peephole of the office to see his black, blue, and puffy face...with two cops in the background. Before they could even ring the bell, I had crawled out the office window and gone over the roof to my car. I thought if I just disappeared for a couple of days, it would all blow over.

The police came to both my office and my house, but they didn't find me. The Public Utilities Commission then shut down our office with some mumbo jumbo about "probable cause to believe the business was being used for illegal purposes."

Less than a week later, we opened up again under a new name in a new location, directly across from the famous Graumann's Chinese Theater. Soon, the cops showed up to shut us down again. Naturally, we had our own expensive lawyers working to stop them. We then moved to another place on La Cienega. Again, the cops had the Utilities Commission close us down. Then we moved to still another place, this one back on Santa Monica Boulevard. By this time I was getting really sick of the escort business, and my goal was to get out as quickly as I could.

So I started trying to distance myself from the operation. But there was one problem—everything was still in my name even though we hired some new people to operate the business. In fact, we hired the editor of one of the tabloids to be the manager. I also brought in some guys I could trust to work part-time—people who don't like their names mentioned in books.

Unraveling

I knew I had to make some changes because my life was unraveling in all directions. I was a nervous wreck from all the turmoil and police harassment, my blood pressure zoomed, and I had a very bad duodenal ulcer. I was trying to work out a couple of hours a day in the gym while still making the party scene three or four nights a week, and Anita and I were constantly at each other's throats.

"Why do you always leave me here alone?" she demanded. "Are you out cheating on me, going around with other women? You never spend any time with Tara. You think I don't know what you're doing? I heard you on the phone. You're going to the Playboy Mansion and then to Wilt Chamberlain's house to party! These people are not your friends. I hope you lose everything you've got. Maybe then you'll come to your senses!"

"I'm out of here. I've got to do what I've got to do. Leave me alone!" I shouted.

In rage and total frustration, she replied, "Then I'll show you. It's over. You're never going to see your daughter again. I'll fix you good!"

"Don't ever say that to me!" I yelled. And we started pushing and shoving each other in the hallway, actually having a tug-of-war with our baby daughter. And, to my shame, I wound up slugging my wife in the face. This wasn't the first time I'd hit her. I'd bruised her lower lip one time before when her father was out for a visit.

I shouldn't have done that. Then she kicked me, breaking my right floating rib and ran into the kitchen and grabbed the biggest knife she could find. When I followed her, she tried to slash me. It was a tense, emotion-charged scene. It was a miracle that neither of us remembered the guns we had stashed around the house.

Finally, I backed away and started to leave. Anita grabbed a piece of trim on my expensive leather coat and ripped it off. Then I stood out in front of the house, cursing and screaming, "I hate you!" Anita yelled back, "Oh, yeah! Well, you're a lousy husband, and those people you hang out with are losers! You need to be a father to your daughter."

I went to the party, but I didn't have a good time. I ended up getting high on marijuana and God knows what else. When I finally started home at dawn, I ended up getting lost in my own neighborhood. It took me three hours to find my own apartment. At last, I finally pulled into my driveway, hitting the gas instead of the brake pedal and smashing my Lincoln Mark IV through the garage door.

Anita flew out of the house screaming, "What is wrong with you? Why did you come home?" Pretending to be totally unconcerned as the neighbors came out to stare at the spectacle, I shouted back, "To eat breakfast. What else!"

That's when I knew I had to change.

I convinced the Dog Man that we had to start some truly legitimate businesses. Because we had hired some capable guys to run the escort service, we could now concentrate on becoming respectable businessmen. After all, if we were as smart as we thought we were, surely we could be successful in anything we tried.

Going "Legit"

Anita came up with a brilliant idea and suggested that we use our money to buy an apartment building in Santa Monica and eliminate the escort business from our lives. Like a fool, however, I overrode her in this business decision, and our first venture instead was a company that marketed speaker systems—high-quality installations for auditoriums, movie theaters, and discotheque clubs. And at last, we had a legitimate business. We hired an engineer who was a near genius, and with him on board, we were able to create systems like no others in the country. We started wholesaling speakers to retail stores and, through our contacts, gained contracts from New York and Beverly Hills for disco systems that sold for $20,000 to $30,000 each.

We then went to the Electronic Consumers Show in Las Vegas to display all our products, and we signed up some major new accounts that placed sizable orders. Our company even received an award for the most innovative new development!

Thrilled with our success, we also started a specialized cleaning service. We bought three mobile trucks with high-pressure hoses that could clean the exterior walls of businesses, washing away graffiti and grime. It was a good operation, and we kept our equipment busy. We were making money legitimately, and it felt great.

Anita and I then started to get along a little better. She felt much better about what I was doing, now that I was working with respectable companies. And she liked our new home—we'd moved to a nice four-bedroom home in the San Fernando Valley.

Although I was still the corporate head of the escort service, I tried to maintain minimal contact with the operation. I made sure the money was deposited in the bank, and I looked over the books to be sure the operating expenses were in line. However, I was no longer handling the details or making decisions about the day-to-day problems.

Maybe the lurid career of Tough Tony could finally come to an end. Just maybe you *could* teach an old dog new tricks. Maybe the nightmare of crime and violence was really over, and my long-forsaken hopes and dreams could be born again.

Chapter Eleven

DREAMS AND DISAPPOINTMENTS

SOME of the happiest hours of my life have been spent in gyms, working out, lifting weights, and conditioning my body, training for competition.

One of the reasons I like it so much is that during the time I'm working out, nothing else matters. I focus completely on making my body perform to its limit. There's really not even any competition—except with yourself, to give all you have to achieve your goals. The weights and machines are both adversary and benefactor because you must overcome their opposition to perfect your physique. There's no time to think about politics, money, business, or what's going on in the news. You must bring to the gym a positive mental attitude and a visualization of what you want your physique to become.

The gym for me was not a place of recreation or a place to socialize or escape. I was a palette of clay and the gym was my sculpting tool. When I first started bodybuilding, I was an idealist—a physical culturist in pursuit of overall fitness, a strong body, mind, and spirit. The Spartan existence demanded by bodybuilding helped develop a purity of discipline that became my strict way of life. I made a vow that if I became a

Dennis with Idol Reg Park

champion, I would give dignity to the title by staying fit even when I wasn't competing. I'm grateful and humbled to have walked through the many doors that being a champion opened for me. The title projected me as a larger-than-life hero. These accomplishments demanded a standard of fitness for my peers and fans.

I also am indebted to the legacy of former champions who paved the way for me—Charles Atlas, Sig Klein, Jack LaLanne, Gordon Scott, Mark Forest, Larry Scott, Lou Degni, Steve Reeves, Bill Pearl, Reg Park, Joe Abbenda, Tom Sansone, Vince Gironda, and numerous others who influenced me through publications and physique contests. The benefits I received were strength, health, energy and longevity, self-preservation and relief from physical and emotional stress, which released a natural high.

Certainly, this helps explain why I never stopped going to the gym—never stopped working out—through all the twists and turns of my life and career.

———>❖<———

In 1975, after being in California a little over a year, I wanted to leave the escort service, related businesses, and everyone involved with it. Soon, I found myself wanting to regenerate my dreams of being a competitor at the championship level. Consequently, I stepped up my daily workouts into a full-blown training program.

Living in California gave me the opportunity to fulfill my dream by meeting famous people who were knowledgeable in the sport of body-building. I wanted to meet the athletes who had fueled my passion as a teenager starting out in Brooklyn, New York, where I had read articles and seen pictures in magazines, and ordered courses through the mail.

One afternoon, I decided to visit Vince Gironda's gym in North Hollywood. As a beginner, I had read his articles in *Iron Man* magazine and purchased his courses, which laid a foundation for me. He was nick-named the Iron Guru and was a pioneer who created the methods of training and diet that are the foundation of all fitness and bodybuilding today. He loved dedication and hard training, hated steroids, and was an expert on hitting the muscles from different angles. His small, no frills hard-core gym was outfitted with his custom-designed machines. He coached many champions, including Larry Scott, Don Howorth, and Arnold Schwarzenegger. Even Lou Ferrigno trained there while filming "The Incredible Hulk." Dozens of major movie stars and actors trans-formed their body through his efforts. All you had to do was be willing to submit to his methods.

One afternoon while training there, I heard Vince say, "Hey, Dennis, you look good enough to win the IFBB Mr. Universe contest that's coming up. What do you think? If you train hard, you could win, you dumb Italian." He continued, "I'll help you with your posing. Do you have the guts to enter, Dennis?"

"Of course, Vince," I said. "I'm already the winner." Vince's challenge got me on track and gave me a goal to obtain—Mr. Universe.

The 1975 competition was to be held in Los Angeles, and I was determined to win my first IFBB Pro Mr. Universe title. My partner decided he could take a more active role in our two companies, which freed up more of my time to spend in the gym. Everyone, including me, was astonished to see how fast my body responded.

My longtime mentor and friend, Bill Pearl, had been invited to be one of the judges at the competition, as had another bodybuilding friend, Zabo Koszewski. I knew that with them judging, the best man would win, and I was confident that I could get a fair decision.

I also knew that one of the favored entrants was a guy named Bob Birdsong who was said to be a great bodybuilder, but I didn't know much about him. And I'd heard rumors that Franco Columbu, the show's promoter, might compete.

My application to enter the competition was accepted and approved. By show time, I was very confident and went into the competition in tremendous shape, and I believed that I would have favor with the audience and judges.

The rumors about Columbu's competing in the show turned out to be true! Supposedly, he was getting ready for another event—the Mr. Olympia competition—that was to be held in South Africa later in the year. It was the "Super Bowl" of bodybuilding competitions, open only to the winners of major professional championship titles. Apparently, his

Dennis posing at the 1980 Mr. Olympia contest, Sydney Australia

strategy was to use the Mr. Universe contest in Los Angeles to set up his participation in the Sixth Mr. Olympia event. But I more or less ignored all the discussions and furor over Franco being both promoter and contestant.

During the prejudging, I enjoyed myself to the hilt and poured all my energy and effort into my posing routine. In a pose-down with Franco Columbu and Bob Birdsong, I could heard the chants of screaming fans yelling out, "Tinerino you're the winner. You're ripped to the bone." Based on my past experience, I felt I was the crowd favorite to win.

After the afternoon prejudging, there was a lot of speculation by the crowd, other contestants, and the media about whether or not Columbu had created a conflict of interest by participating. Rumor had it that Franco had checked with some of his friends on the panel of judges and discovered that his scoring wasn't very good in the prejudging. Other reports said the judges had challenged his involvement.

At any rate, Columbu withdrew from the event before the evening competition. This left the sports commentators and bodybuilding fans scrambling to pick the new favorites to win. Everyone was pretty much in agreement that the two top contenders were Bob Birdsong and Dennis Tinerino.

Several of my friends and acquaintances showed up at the evening competition, including some of the girls and drivers from the escort service-massage parlor businesses. Anita was embarrassed to see them there because they were very vocal and demonstrative in cheering me on. She'd been trying hard to build me a new image as a respectable businessman and to sever all connections with my former associates.

But there they were—the who's who of Sunset Boulevard—attracting lots of attention and yelling, "Hey, Tony! You look great. You're the best!" Anita was so upset; it's a wonder she didn't walk out!

The evening competition went smoothly. Then it was time for the announcer to reveal the second-place winner—Bob Birdsong.

I drew in my breath in excitement, and the announcer made it official—"Ladies and Gentlemen, the 1975 IFBB Mr. Universe...DENNIS TINERINO!" It was a great thrill to win, and I was presented with a beautiful trophy and a check for $5,000.

A Contender Again

Winning the IFBB top championship was a really big deal to me. After meeting with Joe Weider in New York years before and making the decision not to work with his organization, I'd been sort of standing along the sidelines, while Arnold Schwarzenegger had become the unquestioned leader of the sport, winning five Mr. Olympia competitions.

Now that I had become an IFBB winner, I envisioned winning Mr. Olympia and other contests. As 1975's Mr. Universe, I had renewed confidence and was eligible to participate in my first Mr. Olympia competition—to compete with the best of the best. And once again, I'd have the opportunity of going head-to-head with Arnold. In addition, being a current Mr. Universe winner would automatically give me coverage in all the bodybuilding magazines. I'd even be able to book posing exhibitions, fitness seminars, establish a mail order business and a new health club. My vision for reestablishing myself in the fitness business was coming to pass. Then came even more exciting news. Charles Gaines and George Butler were planning to film a documentary about the 1975 Mr. Olympia competition in South Africa, which would be called *Pumping Iron*. The film would highlight each individual's training routine, lifestyle, and the interaction between the competitors. This would be the first ever event to be filmed. In my heart, I knew this movie would take the sport and competition of bodybuilding to a new level of worldwide recognition and exposure which would translate into media success, movie careers, and big money for the competitors showcased.

Just imagine—Arnold Schwarzenegger would compete against Franco Columbu, Serge Nubret, Kenny Waller, Paul Grant, Robbie Robinson, Mike Katz, and a new youngster who was an absolute giant, Lou Ferrigno, and me. Lou Ferrigno was a huge man—six feet four and about 270 pounds. His big claim to fame would come later when he played the Incredible Hulk who turned green on the TV series based on the comic book hero. We had been close friends in Brooklyn, and we'd worked out at the R & J Gym. We also competed together in the NABBA Mr. Universe Contest. This friendship continued when we both relocated to the West Coast.

Most of the Mr. Olympia contestants attended their first meeting with the producers at Schwarzenegger's house to talk about the documentary movie project. One of the producer's staff started talking about the theme of the movie and how to formulate the story line. "We could build it around Arnold, the veteran champ, and this big, new challenger, Lou Ferrigno, and the tension between them as the competition goes along," he said. The previous year, Lou had placed second to Arnold. "Can Louie dethrone him this year?"

"Hey, wait a minute," I said. "I'm the current Mr. Universe winner. Why not showcase me against Arnold training to win his sixth Mr. Olympia title, and Lou, my friend the gentle giant, the challenger?"

"Yeah, that would work too," said the producer. "And we could do some vignettes of Columbu, Mike Katz, Serge Nubret, the champion from France, and Waller and Grant."

There was more discussion, including how much we were going to be paid. We'd already heard that George Butler had a contract with Arnold. Winning five Mr. Olympia titles and international exposure through *Muscle & Fitness* magazine, he became the number-one recognized body-builder in the world.

So Arnold jumped in and said, "Well, we really shouldn't be concerned with what the pay is because this movie will promote our sport. It will be good for bodybuilding, and that will help everybody."

Paul Grant and I seemed to be the spokesmen for the rest of the group. "Well, that's true, and we all want the movie to be a success. But there must be some money in the budget to help cover the time and energy we'll all be putting into it."

Finally, the producer said, "Next time we meet, we'll talk about everyone's participation in the film and your payment. After all, what would the movie be without us? Everybody was really excited about the next meeting with the co-director George Butler, the movie, and the upcoming Mr. Olympia competition. We all started training like crazy, working out day and night, and dieting, to get ready for the trip to South Africa.

I made sure I got my entry form completed and submitted well before the deadline. I was ready!

Booby-trapped!

In a few days, I received a letter back from the IFBB. I opened it with a smile, expecting a confirmation of my entry. Instead, the letter said I was disqualified from the IFBB and was being stripped of my Mr. Universe title. I would be allowed to keep the $5,000 prize and the trophy, but since I was no longer an IFBB member and did not have a valid professional Mr. Universe title, I was not eligible to enter the Mr. Olympia competition. And naturally, because I wouldn't be competing in the Mr. Olympia contest, I wouldn't be appearing in the *Pumping Iron* movie.

The reason given for taking away my title—I had violated IFBB rules by competing in a NABBA Mr. Universe championship years earlier and had therefore been ineligible to participate in the IFBB Los Angeles competition.

I felt that my world was coming to an end. How could this be? Schwarzenegger, Paul Grant, Serge Nubret, and several other guys had participated in previous NABBA contests, but they weren't being disqualified. Even Franco Columbu, the promoter of the 1975 IFBB Mr. Universe competition, was a former NABBA Mr. Universe winner! The whole thing was absolutely preposterous.

All my friends were outraged. They told me to get a lawyer and file a million-dollar lawsuit. I was a professional bodybuilder, and was being deprived of earning a living!

I called Joe and Ben Weider, who headed the IFBB, but they didn't respond immediately. I wrote a furious letter of protest but got no reply. I

Dennis and "Master Blaster" Joe Weider backstage

called everyone I could think of who might have some influence with the organization. They were sympathetic but could do nothing. Tom Minichiello, an IFBB promoter and official, tried to help me, but to no avail. He was disgusted and angry over what had happened, as were virtually all the other bodybuilders I knew. It was the talk of every gym.

I asked my friend Bill Pearl what he thought. He felt I was being treated unfairly, but said there was probably nothing I could do about it. "This can be a dirty sport, Dennis. In this case, there's a lot going on behind the scenes that we're not even aware of. It's obvious there are some people who don't want you around because you're a threat. They don't want you in the

Mr. Olympia contest because if you are in it, you'd have to be in the *Pumping Iron* movie—and that's the problem. Don't you understand? You don't fit in to the script they've already written! You hadn't competed in any IFBB shows before, and then the first one you enter, you win. You came out of nowhere."

"This is crazy!" I cried. "This is supposed to be an open and fair competition. Many other people told me the same thing. My good friend Pete Samra, a veteran bodybuilder who was very close to some of the IFBB insiders, later said, "Dennis Tinerino was feared! He was in such good shape that year—and certain other individuals *weren't*—that if he'd been allowed to compete in the Mr. Olympia contest, he could have won. That would have messed everything up. They simply couldn't allow that to happen. That's why Dennis was axed."

Whatever the reason, I was crushed. I had my heart set on competing in South Africa. And I really wanted to be in the *Pumping Iron* documentary. I felt this film could have been a vehicle to express my personality, my training philosophy, and my physique through the media. For no valid and legal reason, I was out!

I told my wife, "There's more corruption in bodybuilding than there is in the underworld! What do I need this sport for?" I was so full of bitterness and hurt. My wife said, "Can't you see the handwriting on the wall? You just don't fit in. You have to find something else to do with your talents and not be beholden to anybody. You're wasting your energy and your life on this sport."

After the movie was released, Arnold arranged to get me reinstated in the IFBB. He came up to me at World Gym where we were both working out and started talking to me. "It's terrible what they did to you, Dennis. I didn't know anything about it until it was too late. I had absolutely nothing to do with it, and I felt awful about it."

Then he said, "You're still a champion. You're strong, you're in shape, and you look fantastic. Why don't you let me talk to Joe Weider and his brother Ben? I think they feel bad about what happened too, but it was just one of those things. If we can work this out, you'll be back in the IFBB and you can get involved in competing again. I'm promoting the 1977 Mr. Olympia."

All I could say was that I'd think about it. I certainly knew the IFBB was currently the only game in town for championship bodybuilding. Besides, Arnold was holding out the "olive branch of peace," and I knew it would be foolish of me not to accept it.

Not long after that, I got a call from Bill Reynolds, a well-known writer on bodybuilding. He wanted to do a series of articles about me for *Muscle and Fitness* magazine. I put him off for a month to give me time to fine-tune my body for the photos he wanted. Then we scheduled the interviews and photo shoots. The articles he wrote about my career and training techniques appeared in several issues.

Then I got a call from Joe Weider, who was the publisher of *Muscle and Fitness*, as well as the head of the IFBB. He wanted us to get together for a meeting and I agreed to it. Weider offered me a contract for future articles and my endorsement of part of his product line. I also would get a full-page ad in the magazine each month to advertise my training booklets and to book exhibitions and appearances. I immediately established my Natural Champion line of products, *and part of the deal included my participation in the 1977 Mr. Olympia competition.* So, I signed and instantaneously I was a member in good standing with the IFBB.

My family and I then moved from Santa Monica to our new home in Northridge. Our life was on an upswing. The businesses were running well, and my vision to achieve success in the fitness game was in high gear. We showed our hospitality by having a stream of house warming parties, which included such guests as Bill Pearl, Lou Ferrigno, Joe Weider, Dave

The pose that won Dennis many contests

Draper, Sergio Olivia, Bill Reynolds, Pete Samra, Greg DeFerro, Paul Grant, and others. Some of the best times we had were eating Anita's non-Atkin's gourmet meals, throwing each other in the pool, and scheduling photo shoots. The neighborhood paparazzi were literally trying to jump over the walls to catch a glimpse of big Lou and other modern-day goliaths. Bill Pearl helped me with my contest strategies, and Joe Weider planned upcoming articles for his magazine. This was a great year of excitement, unity, and peace for my family. There was also a great amount of productive activity unleashed as I pursued my goals. The phone was ringing off the hook with requests for photo shoots, seminars, trade shows, personal appearances, and gym openings. My new agent was busy getting me commercials, auditions for movies such as *Stay Hungry*, print ads, and magazine covers. It was also at this time that Anita launched her posing suit line "Heavenly Bodies" while representing and booking several bodybuilders for fitness promotions. We were expanding our fitness business contacts and able to make a living at bodybuilding. My transition from the previous situations was almost complete.

Before we knew it, we were in Columbus, Ohio at the 1977 Mr. Olympia contest, where I placed third in the over 200-pound class, and Frank Zane was the overall winner. I was overwhelmed by the audience's response and acceptance.

My entire family was in attendance, and friends and other relatives came from New York to cheer me on. At the party after the contest, Anita enjoyed dancing with Joe Weider while we basked in the glow of compliments from judges and fans. All agreed that I was fulfilling my calling as a successful bodybuilder. As I left Columbus, I was satisfied that I had competed, but I knew that I had unfinished business. I could see myself in the winner's circle next year.

Chapter Twelve

ALL FALL DOWN

IT was the white buckskin shoes—they didn't belong in a place like this. I saw his reflection in the mirror while doing barbell curls, and I recognized him right away...

His name was Pat Boone.

He stood out from everybody else in the gym like a sore thumb. He was quiet, mannerly, and modest; and about him was a presence that spoke of goodness, innocence, and decency. Those were rare commodities—especially in Beverly Hills, and particularly in this gym! Here was a world-renowned celebrity, a great singer known for his Christian faith standing right behind me, and I felt...uneasy.

I had heard about the Shelton Health Club in Beverly Hills. It was the place where all the high rollers met and more deals were made in the steam room than in corporate offices. When I started working out there, I immediately became friends with the owner—a former New Yorker who knew how to relate to everyone who walked in the door. His clientele covered a broad spectrum of personalities and occupations—from celebrities and the wealthy to business executives and wise guys. It was a health club with a swimming pool, steam room, sauna, and the back room, which seemed to have more action than the gym! This cigar-filled room provided a space for big money card games, bookmaking on any sport you could think of, and more. Most conversations were laced with profanity and anger. Men boasted about their sexual exploits, talked about how to make big money quick, and how to beat the odds in Vegas. Miggs and I fit right in! And right away we saw the opportunities for meeting new people and expanding our "business endeavors."

Working out with famous actors like Bert Young and Jimmy Caan was great. Kenny Norton, the heavyweight boxing champ who broke Muhammad Ali's jaw, was also a member, and we became good friends. I even bought the same car and custom jewelry as he did. I enjoyed sharing health tips, training, and socializing with him. And then...there was Pat Boone.

At first, I resented the guy. He looked so happy, so calm, so squeaky-clean. Frankly, I was jealous of Pat Boone and his loving family. His lifestyle convicted me. I was beginning to have problems with all my businesses, and here he was—a happy-go-lucky guy.

One day I said to Amos Hoyt, a semi-retired boxing trainer and the gym's locker room attendant, "I can't stand that guy."

"Who's that you don't like, Dennis?"

"Pat Boone. He thinks he's so special. He's a goody-two-shoes kind of guy. I saw his wife and Debbie and the other daughters picking him up in a Rolls Royce the other day—they were saying, 'Hi, Honey...Hello, Daddy! We love you!' Nobody's that perfect."

"Hey, man, don't be talking like that," said Amos. "Pat Boone's all right. He helped change my life!"

"What do you mean?"

Dennis & Pat Boone

"See this watch?" He was wearing a gold watch with the words, "Jesus Saves" on the face. "Pat Boone gave this to me after he prayed with me for Jesus Christ to come into my life. The reason you can't stand him, Dennis, is because you're serving the devil and he's serving God!"

I didn't say any more about Pat, but I found myself watching him whenever he was around. One day Amos brought Pat over and introduced us to each other. After a few words of greeting, Pat said, "Dennis, you're a great bodybuilder and a true champion. God has really given you a great gift. Think about it. How many people get to be Mr. America and Mr. Universe?"

I didn't know what to say except "Thanks." Then he asked, "Do you have any pictures of yourself...any books or magazines with articles about you? I'd really like to have an autographed copy of one."

"Well, sure. I'll bring you anything you want," I said. "I'll give you an autograph if you'll give me one."

Pat smiled, then looked very serious for a moment. "You know, Dennis, God has a plan for your life. Jesus loves you. If you'll use the talent and good looks He's given you for good, and take care of your family, the Lord will help you stay on track. I used to be a party guy with lots of problems. I was caught up in the whole Hollywood party scene. There is so much evil in this town, but the short road to success is often the longest road. Then, one day Jesus changed me—and my life has turned around. I've found that the only thing that's really important is to serve Christ." Putting his hand on my shoulder, Pat looked me straight in the eye and said, "Dennis, God will do the same thing for you! All you have to do is call on Him. He's waiting to hear from you."

I didn't know what to say. "Yeah, sure, that's right. Thanks a lot, man." As he walked away, Pat said, "I'll be praying for you."

I'll be praying for you. As I continued my workout, those words were spinning in my head. Why would a guy like him be praying for a guy like me?

When my 1975 Mr. Universe title had been rescinded and I was cut out of the *Pumping Iron* movie, I didn't think life could get any worse. I thought wrong.

There were now serious, long-term problems with our custom speaker system manufacturing business. The overhead costs for a huge factory with 35 to 40 employees were staggering, and the development and engineering costs for new product configurations we had working were high. In addition to our upscale home systems, we had been putting together high-performance installations for nightclubs and theaters. Our engineers were developing a theater sound system that used some cardboard components that vibrated—actually shook big-time—at certain low-frequency signals. We were anxious to market this new technology, which we called "Vibrasound."

Although the company's sales had been excellent, some of our big-business clients were very slow to pay. For example, we had a contract for $35,000 speaker installations in several discos. After getting a modest down payment, we did all the work and installed all the equipment, but the corporations didn't pay us the balance for five months!

Several clients owed us to the tune of several hundred thousand dollars! We didn't want to get too aggressive in our collection efforts because we needed the business so badly. Yet, we couldn't afford to carry such large accounts receivable.

The cleaning business had its own headaches. The high-pressure mobile equipment broke down all the time; there was a constant turnover of the employees; and the operation required a constant, aggressive, ongoing sales program to keep the trucks busy. Nobody seemed to be able to sell the way I could, but I was simply too overloaded to devote full-time to it.

In addition, all of our businesses were demanding more and more money from us. The more we invested into them, the more they needed. We were taking money from the escort service just to keep the other businesses going. Our financial situation was rapidly deteriorating.

Our Family Grows

Anita was pregnant with our second child, and we were absolutely overjoyed! We both loved children, and were looking forward to another addition to the Tinerino household.

"Well, Dennis, God must think this is the right time for us to have a new baby," Anita mused as we talked about her pregnancy. "He knows the future, and He must know we will be able to take care of this child."

"Yeah, I guess so, but I'd sure feel better about it if we just had medical insurance to cover the doctor and hospital bills when the baby is born."

"I know," she said. "Maybe we'll find the money to pay for the baby in a special way."

So, I started looking for that "special" income source. A few months later, at Al Hines Health Club in Westwood, California—there it was! I saw a flyer about an upcoming bodybuilding championship promoted by an ex-NABBA Mr. Universe, Chet Yorton. The event was to be held at the Tropicana Hotel in Las Vegas and would be the first Natural Mr. America competition, stressing a drug-free contest—no steroids or drugs of any kind. Each contestant would have to submit to a blood test to prove he was drug-free before being allowed to compete. The winner, the first Natural Mr. America, would be awarded a cash prize of $5,000.

The contest was coming up in just a couple of months, so I had very little time to get ready. Fortunately, I'd been working out regularly and was in excellent shape. All I had to do was switch back to my pre-contest nutrition program and training regimen. I had done it before, and I could do it again. I felt excited about competing again, and I was glad to be part of the first event that tested for and rejected the use of illegal drugs—particularly the dangerous anabolic steroids like Dianabol. When I started competing, there was little or no steroid use that I can recall. But by the late '60s and early '70s, I saw a paradigm shift. Virtually all leading contenders used drugs, and one of my former training partners was found dead with a bottle of Dianabol and other drugs nearby.

I went into the Natural Mr. America competition feeling and looking like a champion. Although the field of entrants was not as strong as the Mr. Universe contests, there were some excellent bodybuilders competing. The event was a first-rate, professionally run contest, and it attracted tremendous media attention because of its drug-free emphasis.

I knew after the prejudging session that I was doing very well. So, while I was not really surprised, I was still honored and thrilled to win the competition. Ralph Kroger came in second, and Anabel Lopez placed third. I made history by being the first Natural Mr. America!

I gave Anita my $5,000 check to deposit into the savings account, and when our second daughter, Marissa Denise, was born on March 13, 1978, we had the money to pay the doctor and the hospital!

Training With Champions

About this time, I started working out at Joe Gold's new World Gym in Santa Monica—the bodybuilding Mecca of the world. Joe had built the best equipment, and his gym attracted some of the top bodybuilders in the world. I'd get up early every morning to drive from Northridge to Santa Monica, where Arnold Schwarzenegger trained, along with guys like Mike Mentzner, Lou Ferrigno, Dave Draper, Kenny Waller, Franco Columbu, Robbie Robinson, Frank Zane, Eddie Guiliani, and Zabo Koszewski. An old competitor friend from England, Paul Grant, had moved to California, and he and I became training partners, along with a guy named Doug Beaver. It was a high-energy, sparks-flying, all-out competitive atmosphere. I don't know how Joe Gold tolerated our rowdy exuberance or our inflated egos!

I can't adequately describe the "rush" and the thrill of training and being an inner-circle participant in this elite group, to "belong" and thrive in this adrenaline-packed atmosphere. Bodybuilding fans literally flew in from all over the country and from all over the world to watch "the best of the best" pump iron. Every day we were surrounded by flocks of fans with cameras in hand. I was happy, and training offered an oasis for my disturbing business situations. It was my anchor of hope.

In fact, some nights I couldn't sleep in anticipation of working out in Santa Monica. The World Gym was within walking distance from the beach, and you could feel the freshness of the sea air whether you were pumping iron inside or outside on the sundeck. The variation of training added enthusiasm and excitement to my already grueling three to four-hour sessions, six days a week. No music played on the radio. Sometimes all you heard was a cacophony of sound, created by steel plates and weights with the clanging of selector machines and Olympic bars.

Joe Gold would yell, "Don't drop the 150-pound dumbbells, you crazy Italian so-and-so! I'll throw you out of the gym!" Pete Samra, my friend and spotter would call out, "Do one more rep!" challenging me to pump my chest to the max. Sweat dripping from my body, I would look into the mirror, flex my chest, feel satisfied, and then do it again. The adrenaline rush forced me to push my body beyond its limits. I would concentrate with each rep and visualize my body being formed into a bigger and better me. I did this with every body part, year in and year out. After a workout, Anita and I would go eat lunch on the beach with our children, take a swim, and get a tan. This was my paradise, my Canaan Land.

Back to the Platform

In preparation for the 1978 Mr. Olympia contest, it took sacrifice, dedication, and great strength to endure all the rigorous hours of training, dieting, and posing. But I realized that I needed supernatural strength mentally and emotionally to deal with all the personal and business problems that came upon me. On top of that, nagging at the back of my mind was the possibility that I could lose everything and go to jail besides. This would be the ultimate humiliation because over the years I had tried to maintain a good image and a spotless reputation. It felt good to be back in Columbus again. I was relaxed and competent. This was my world, and I knew I was at the top of my game.

The competition was big-time show business with a carnival atmosphere and was the most spectacular Mr. Olympia contest ever. There were disco dancers, slide shows, guest posers, loud music, five thousand screaming fans, and lavish pageantry staged for the television cameras. For the first time in bodybuilding history, the contest was being covered by ABC on their top-rated Wide World of Sports. Bodybuilding had come out of the gym and into the limelight!

The contestants for Mr. Olympia included 13 world-class bodybuilders—all champions. The staging of the contest was very professional, with Arnold Schwarzenegger serving as color commentator for the ESPN telecast. Everything was great—except the judging! From the first ranking by the judges in the initial prejudging event, there was controversy. Virtually everybody in the building—spectators, contestants, trainers, even people involved in staging the competition—felt that the judges were watching a totally different event than the rest of us. Almost every decision the official panel made was controversial...and unpopular.

I went into Columbus in top shape, and was the unofficial pick for the most muscular man in the competition. However, I placed second in the heavyweight class, which was won by Mike Mentzner. The competition was tough. Every man on stage was a champion—a legend in the golden age of the sport of bodybuilding.

The final winners were Frank Zane, Robby Robinson, Roy Callender, Boyer Coe, Kal Szkalak, and Dennis Tinerino. When the results were announced, Szkalak was livid with rage. As the cameras rolled, he extended his arms and put one foot on top of the other, assuming the bodily position of a crucifix—communicating his outrage and opinion that he'd been maliciously wronged—"nailed to the cross!"

The crowd went wild—a large segment angrily erupted in jeers and catcalls to express their displeasure at the decision of the judges.

As the cameras focused on his limp "crucifix," Szkalak suddenly broke into bold, strong, bodybuilding poses, angrily flaunting his body as a defiant challenge to the newly crowned Mr. Olympia. Instinctively, all other contestants followed. This created the most loud, excited bodybuilding audience I can ever remember. Even though there was one winner, all competitors were hungry for the cheers of the audience. When I heard screaming fans call out my name and give approval, I hit my favorite poses, and it gave me great satisfaction, which overshadowed my disappointment of not being number one. I think that to this day, more people remember Kal's sacrilegious posturing than Frank Zane's victory.

The Beginning of the End

Meanwhile, our business problems continued to worsen. Although he was a brilliant PR man, Dog Man was a lousy businessman. He was always trying to find shortcuts to success, and his management and customer relations tactics were the same as his street hustling style—high pressure and heavy-handed intimidation.

This led to a growing hostility between Miggs and our English-born engineer, John Vidal, who had merged his business with ours. When I was in the office, I managed to keep things relatively calm. But during the time I was away, concentrating on bodybuilding, things started to unravel.

Distrusting the Dog Man's management—probably rightly so—Vidal started to make plans to get out and go on his own. Specifically, he began building up a private inventory of speakers and equipment. Fortunately, Mason found out about it and called it to my attention. No matter how legitimate his grievances may have been, what Vidal was doing was dead wrong. But he refused to even discuss the matter with us.

So, Miggs and I took trucks down to the factory—which originally had belonged to Vidal's company before we had merged—and cleaned it out, wall to wall. Someone called the police and told them we were robbing the place. As we arrived at our new warehouse, the SWAT team surrounded the building and aimed high-powered scope rifles at us. Then they ordered us to lay facedown on the pavement in the pouring rain. Somehow we managed to convince the investigating officers that we were the owners and were just moving stock from one warehouse to another. We then hauled everything to a warehouse we controlled and locked it up. The next morning, when John saw what we'd done, he was livid. And he immediately filed a lawsuit against us.

To keep the business going, we formed another company and set up a new manufacturing facility to continue producing speaker equipment. Because we had controlled the marketing and sales for the old company, we knew all the customers and had knowledge of the orders, so we were back in business relatively quickly.

We had made good contacts in Hollywood for the new vibrating sound system we were trying to develop and market to theaters, and eventually one of our prospects came through—a fellow New Yorker who was associated with Dino de Laurentis, a revered movie producer who was very interested in the new technology we had developed. He then produced two major movies, *King Kong* and *Midway*, a World War II story, which incorporated our new technology. By using our Vibrasound speakers in addition to the regular sound system in selected theaters, the two de Laurentis films added a new dimension to the movie. When King Kong walked, the extra speakers vibrated and shook the seats, creating the sensation that the gigantic ape was inside the theater. When bombs went off in the war picture, viewers could *feel* as well as see the concussion of the blasts.

Working on these movies was a fantastic experience. As we attended a private screening in Beverly Hills with three thousand theatre owners and celebrities, producers, and directors, we knew we had made it. People were calling us inventors and pioneers in the industry, competing with other major products such as Sensurround.

Consequently, all this publicity enabled us to begin working out a contract to install our vibrating speakers in hundreds of theaters across America. In fact, we had de Laurentis' endorsement for our system, and authorization for our company to use an inflatable King Kong on top of our speakers at the various trade shows and in promotional photographs!

Unfortunately, our company had one major problem—the operators—an estranged electronic engineer, an ex-boxer con artist, and a streetwise playboy-bodybuilder—who had virtually no business experience amongst them. In addition, we were woefully undercapitalized to be able to take advantage of our once-in-a-lifetime opportunity.

After struggling along and wrestling unsuccessfully with these problems for several months, our lawyer started warning us that we were approaching bankruptcy. Several suppliers and short-term lenders we had borrowed from were threatening to sue, and we were behind on employee benefit and tax payments.

And so, although I'd been desperate to get out of the escort business altogether, I realized it was the only thing that was keeping us going. At one time, we controlled eighty percent of the out-call services in California. It was a big operation, and we had to have the cash flow it generated every week to keep the other businesses afloat. Unfortunately, things weren't going well there either.

Paulie, my friend from New York who was helping run the operation, was causing havoc. He was smoking marijuana and doing coke with some of the girls, even getting sexually involved with them. There were fights with girlfriends, and he even beat up a coworker in the office! Then he skipped town with several thousand dollars. I soon found out why— Paulie had been placing bets on sporting events over the phone with a friend in Arizona. He had also been bragging to his friends—again on the phone—about his New York Mafia connections. Because the police had my phones tapped, I was arrested for interstate bookmaking, and, in handcuffs, had to go to Arizona with my lawyer to face the charges— another $15,000 in legal fees piled up on that trip alone!

My life was becoming a nightmare. Every waking moment was filled with pressure and problems, and I couldn't sleep. And because of all the stress, Anita and I were constantly fighting.

She had finally snapped when I was arrested. Her fear about what was going to happen to our family and me was ruling her every thought. She'd been telling me for years that I was going to end up in jail if I stayed involved with "evil" people like Miggs, and she begged me repeatedly to break all ties with Miggs and focus on our original vision for our lives. She also constantly reminded me that bodybuilding was a challenging business that would never pay off unless I concentrated on it alone. She had endured enough. One night she even told me, "You know what? I'm *glad* you're going to jail! Maybe now the girls and I can have a normal life!"

Those words cut me like a knife. But as much as I hated to admit it, Anita had been right on all counts. Nevertheless, I kept telling her that I couldn't just walk away from everything. I was so caught up in the web of trouble I'd helped spin that I couldn't break free.

Tragedy!

One day, the new guy we'd hired to manage the escort service came to see Miggs and me at our other office, and he was very upset. "Hey, guys, I don't understand what's going on. I think I lost one of the girls!"

He told us he'd gotten a call from a customer who said, "Thanks for sending Carol over to the house. You don't have to worry about her any-more—I fixed that whore for good! She's dead!"

The girl had told him earlier that she was afraid of her ex-boyfriend. She'd left him to come to work for our service, and she was worried that he would track her down. Apparently, he did.

The police found her body in Pasadena. She'd been brutalized and tortured. Everybody was scared and shocked.

Two months later, another of our girls died. She overdosed on drugs, went swimming, and drowned! As soon as this incident hit the news, our escort service manager said, "Dennis, I'm out of here. I can't take this any-more." I then decided it was time to find someone else to handle the office because I didn't want to be associated with the business any more than I had to. So, I hired a guy I thought was a friend to take over.

After he started working for us, I would check up on things just every couple of weeks. I'd look at the books, answer any questions, and then get out of there.

What I didn't know was that this new manager had some problems of his own with the police—they'd caught him using and selling drugs. So they pressured him into setting me up. One day, when I called and told him I'd be coming over at a certain time, he tipped the cops that I was coming. "If you want to see Tony, he'll be here. You can get him."

I hadn't been at the office long when there was a knock on the door. "Open up—it's the police." Looking out the windows, we could see that not only were several police cars outside, there were also all kinds of media people, including reporters with TV cameras and microphones. When we didn't unlock the door right away, the police broke it down—and they had a search warrant.

As soon as I heard them, I called my attorney. He said, "Don't say anything! They don't have anything on you. It's only a search warrant. Just walk out of the office."

Before I followed his advice, I decided to make a quick call to Miggs to let him know what was going down. "This place is swarming with cops!" I told him. "And they've got TV cameras all over the place."

"Don't worry about it," he said. "Talk to them! It's no big thing. We'll just get lots of free publicity out of this."

Then the police were inside, shutting down the phones and ransacking the place, searching through all the desk drawers and file cabinets. And I decided to get out of there.

But when I stuck my head out the front door, I was instantly surrounded by a mob of reporters. There were bright lights shining, cameras grinding, microphones being jammed in my face, and reporters yelling questions at me.

"Are you Dennis Tinerino, the owner of one of the biggest escort operations in the history of southern California?"

"Why are the police after you—a former Mr. America and Mr. Universe?"

"Do you know anything about the girl who was killed?"

"Can you confirm that your escort service and massage parlor does ten million dollars' worth of business a year?"

I couldn't even understand all the questions they were yelling. I simply said, "I'm just a businessman. I don't know what the police are doing here. I don't know anything about this." Finally, I was able to get to my car and leave. *How can this be happening?* I thought as I sped away. *Maybe this will all die down in a few days. I need some time to think!*

That night, my voice and my picture were on every major radio and TV news show in the state. Then it hit the wire services—"Dennis Tinerino, former Mr. America and Mr. Universe, accused of involvement in the largest escort business in the history of Los Angeles. It is also rumored that Mr. Tinerino is deeply involved in organized crime."

The newspapers did their thing, speculating that I would be charged with prostitution, pimping, pandering, and all sorts of other allegations. I got more publicity in one day than I had received in 20 years of bodybuilding...but this publicity was extremely destructive.

The media made it sound as if I was public enemy number one. People drove by and pointed at my house. My daughter Tara had just started school that year, and she came home crying. "Daddy, people are saying terrible things about you. Are they true?"

I didn't know what to tell her. I just wanted to crawl in a hole somewhere and disappear.

No Place to Hide

The continuing publicity was a nightmare for my family—for Anita and my children, and for my folks back in New York. There was a big furor, and everybody was embarrassed and upset.

Curiously enough, it was no big thing to my social contacts, my circle of fair-weather friends. They still invited me to all the parties and welcomed me in the discos and clubs. The attitude seemed to be, *Fame or notoriety—what's the difference. As long as he's making big money and spending it—who cares!*

As much as we needed to shut it down, we had to keep the escort service going—it was our only source of income now because the other businesses were sinking fast. And if we were going to pay the rent, keep the fancy cars, use the charge accounts, and eat at the swanky restaurants, we had to have the cash flow.

Throughout all this, Miggs and I were trying desperately to salvage the speaker business. We knew it had enormous potential, but we weren't getting along with each other at that point. I was very critical of some of his decisions, which had turned out to be major mistakes and blunders, and we were facing lawsuits from a dozen different people. Moreover, because my name was on all the legal paperwork as president of the companies, every one of the lawsuits named me. In addition, we constantly had to check our phones and cars for police monitors because we were under 24-hour surveillance.

Also, there were rumors that Miggs thought I was ripping off the escort service and not sharing the money equally with him. And he was paranoid that if I actually was arrested, I would implicate him as my partner. Two or three different people warned me to watch my back...that Miggs had put a contract on me!

In the meantime, the bodybuilding community had heard about my involvement with the escort services, and rumors raged about my activities and alleged involvement in organized crime. My all-American image had definitely been tarnished! When I went to the gym, everybody was wary of me. I felt as though people were thinking, *Watch yourself with Tinerino. He's a rough guy!* I even heard one person say, "You'll find him dead in an alley sooner than you think!"

My attorney then called and said, "Dennis, I've just found out that the police are building a big case against you. They've subpoenaed all the corporation's records, and they've arrested a bunch of the girls who are willing to appear in court and say you were very much a part of the prostitution end of the business. They'll make a deal and say anything to save their own necks. The cops are working with the district attorney, and this case is going to the grand jury. Vice have spent a fortune tailing you and watching your operation, and as much as you've done and gotten away with, they're now going to do everything they can to nail you.

"If they put all of this together, there's a very good chance you'll lose this case. I honestly believe they'll convict you and you'll get at least five years. If they can't make this stick, they'll try again on robbery, money laundering, and loan-sharking charges. You've been involved in many bad things, Dennis, and as close as they've been watching, they're bound to catch you in some mistake. One slip is all it takes to bring the whole house of cards down. The best advice I can give you is to 'cop a plea.' Let me see if I can work out a deal for a minimum sentence and some probation. It's over for you, Dennis. You're going to have to serve some time and clean up your act. You'd better lay low or get out of town until I can make the arrangements."

As if to confirm my attorney's fears, a gym owner friend then called to say LAPD had been by the gym and were putting together a file on me.

I knew I couldn't go home or show up at any of my usual spots without being picked up. So, I started calling some of my buddies, trying to find a place where I could "go on the lamb" for a few days. But the word was out that I was about to go down, and none of my so-called friends wanted me around. Amazingly, all of my *gumbas* had disappeared in a matter of days! Feeling like an outcast, I got into my car, drove to Las Vegas, and checked into a hotel for a couple of days.

Sure enough, the police showed up at my house and office, with an arrest warrant charging me with pimping and pandering. Not finding me, they ended up talking with my attorney. He told them I was out of town, but that he was sure I'd cooperate with them when I returned. He learned that the recommended bail for the charges was $250,000 and that if convicted, I faced three to five years in prison, with five years probation. He went to work immediately, trying to get my bail lowered and to negotiate a deal for a shorter sentence.

In a matter of hours, my attorney worked out a deal that would allow me to go before a judge and plead guilty in exchange for a reduced sentence of one year in prison, with three years probation and a $25,000 fine. I would be released on my own recognizance for 60 days before I had to turn myself in and start serving my sentence.

When I called him from my hotel room, he told me the news and recommended I take the deal before they changed their mind. "The prosecutors are screaming about this one, Dennis. They don't want a plea bargain. They think you might get sent away for a long time because of the girl who was killed. This is the best deal you can hope for. Do your time, stay clean during probation...and find a new way to make a living!"

I met my lawyer at the courthouse the next day and turned myself in. The judge agreed to the deal my lawyer and the district attorney had worked out. Then he told me that starting that day, I could not associate with anybody involved in organized crime or be involved with anybody

I'd worked with in the massage parlor or escort service business. Then, after I finished my sentence, I'd have to do some community work, and the court would be watching me during my three years of probation. If I slipped just once, warned the judge, the deal was off, and I'd serve the maximum sentence.

Paying the $25,000 fine took all the cash I could scrape together. At the moment I walked out of the courthouse, I was flat broke. I was afraid to contact the escort service office to get some cash, so I decided to withdraw some from my personal bank account. To my astonishment, the bank teller told me that my account had been closed...the Internal Revenue Service had seized it!

Devastation

At home, I found Anita totally crushed and confused. After the humiliation and shame of my arrest and prison sentence, now she had to deal with the IRS! They claimed that I was responsible for more than $800,000 in back taxes. Although they determined, after completing an audit, that the businesses owed most of the taxes, as the president of the corporations, I was being held personally responsible for all the taxes.

Virtually overnight, our businesses were, to all intents and purposes, shut down, and all of our corporate assets were seized. With no cash flow, the only measure of protection available was to file Chapter 13 (Bankruptcy). So by the time I had to turn myself in to the authorities to begin serving my sentence, we would be totally bankrupt and facing more than a dozen lawsuits from creditors and others we'd done business with for the past three years. I just couldn't face bankruptcy, even though I was told it was our only way out. I just knew there had to be another way.

Once again, the media trumpeted the news about former Mr. America-Mr. Universe Dennis Tinerino's conviction on pimping and pandering charges for operating the largest out-call service in the history of California. The newspapers gave the story bold headlines, and TV and radio news reports made it their lead story.

The ongoing public humiliation was the last straw for Anita. Tara was subjected to taunts and snubs at school, and wherever my wife went, people stared at her and whispered behind her back. Curiosity seekers cruised past our home, hoping for a glimpse of the notorious crime king or his family.

We were destitute, and my wife was at the breaking point emotionally. She needed reassurance and support in a less-threatening environment, so I flew Anita and the girls back to New York to stay with her family for a while.

Desperate for cash to live on, I tried to get in touch with my "buddies" again, but nobody wanted to talk to me. Those I did find said they couldn't help me. I was out in the cold...alone.

I didn't know what to do or where to turn. How was I supposed to take care of my wife and daughters while I was in jail? Who would pay the rent, buy groceries, and provide medical care? I started trying to get in touch with all the guys I'd ever done favors for, asking them to help me now. Many of these guys genuinely had nothing to give me, and all of them claimed they couldn't help. When I pleaded with my family to do what they could for Anita while I was locked up, they were sympathetic and concerned, but they were barely making it themselves. And so, I had no guarantee that my family would be cared for.

By this time, it was starting to hit me that, like the prodigal son, I'd gone to a far country and wasted all I had on riotous living. All my party-time friends who had been glad to help me spend my money were suddenly hard to find when I got in trouble. At the time, I really didn't know the rest of the Bible story—but I could identify with the *despair*.

Down to my last few dollars, I made the circuit of some of the places where I'd hung out with my friends, just to see if I could find anyone who could help me. Sure enough, I bumped into one of my old New York buddies, Joey, a guy who'd worked with me on some local strong-arm jobs I'd done for some Chicago people. He had a reputation for being well connected, as well as absolutely cold and vicious, but he was also known as a no-nonsense, stand-up kind of guy. Plus, at that moment, he was the only friend I had.

"I'm out of money, Joey. I've got to have some cash for my wife and kids to live on while I'm in jail. Nobody will loan me anything—I need a big score!"

"Yeah, well, I might know a job we can do. I've been watching this business, and I know how the manager operates. After a long weekend, he'll have $40,000 in cash, easy. He opens at the same time, closes at the same time, drives home and parks his car in the same place—he's like a machine. All we have to do is grab him and make him take us back to his place and give us the money. Then we'll tie him up and leave. Simple deal."

That should have been my cue to walk away...nothing like this is ever simple. Instead, I stalled for time.

"I don't know, Joey. I'm in a lot of trouble already...."

"So, what have you got to lose? Besides, you don't have any other great ideas, do you?"

I didn't. So, we decided to do the robbery the next night—Sunday night—so we could grab all the weekend receipts. Joey would be waiting when the restaurant manager got home from work and then pull up to his parking place. Then he would pull a gun and force him to drive back to the restaurant. I would follow in another car.

When the restaurant manager arrived home, opened his car door, and looked up into the barrel of a gun, he panicked and went to pieces. "Oh, my God, you're going to kill me!" he screamed. "Don't shoot me—I haven't got anything you want!"

"Shut up or you're dead!" Joey yelled, but the guy kept screaming.

"All right, that's it! I'm going to blow you away right here. Say your prayers."

As I watched from my car, I broke out in a cold sweat. I knew Joey would kill the guy at the drop of a hat, without a second thought...and there was nothing I could do.

The shaken victim somehow managed to get control of himself...it probably saved his life.

At the restaurant, things went smoothly. The manager opened the door, turned off the alarm, and took us inside. "All right, good, now give us the money," I demanded. The guy went to the register and opened the cash drawer. There was a few thousand dollars in small bills. Nothing else. I felt like I was back with the "gang that couldn't shoot straight"!

"Where's the rest of it?" asked Joey, pulling out his revolver again.

The guy stammered, "This is all there is—the rest is already in the safe. I don't know the combination—you've got to believe me! The owner comes and opens the safe and takes the money to the bank. I'm telling you the truth. Don't shoot me, man."

Not knowing what else to do, we tied the guy to a chair and taped his mouth shut. Then we tried to figure out other options. We were both convinced that the manager didn't know the combination—he was too scared to lie. Besides, we'd already tried threats and intimidation, and he still stuck with his story.

"I can't believe we went to all this trouble for a few lousy bucks, Joey. Let's just get out of here."

"Yeah, I guess so. But first I'd better waste this manager guy. I don't want to leave no witnesses, man, because he can identify us. I'll just shoot him in the back of the head!"

"No, man, no killing! It's not worth it. Let's just leave the guy tied up and go. They'll never find us. But if you kill this guy, they'll start a major manhunt. Forget it!"

Somehow I managed to persuade my trigger-happy friend not to shoot the restaurant manager who was so terrorized he was about to pass out. When we got in my car, Joey cursed angrily as he shut the door. I eased around the corner and pulled up to the stop sign. Just as I turned onto the next street, two police cars, lights flashing and sirens wailing, slowed to turn and make their way to the restaurant parking lot. If they had arrived 15 seconds earlier, they would have caught us in the parking lot.

By the time the police got inside and found the manager tied up, we were long gone.

I was so relieved that we hadn't been caught. However, that had been my last chance to get my hands on any significant amount of money, and I was more discouraged than ever. Joey knew where to get in touch with a couple of street guys we'd worked with before, and one of them gave me a couple thousand dollars to leave for Anita saying, "It's okay, Tony. I know you're good for it when you get out of jail."

A few days later, Anita flew back to California. She was still very bitter and angry with me, but was much calmer than before. I turned over the money I'd been able to scrape together—about $2,500—and told her I'd asked my friends to get more to her later.

Then it was time for a few hugs and kisses as I told my wife and little girls good-bye. It was time to start serving my sentence at the Los Angeles County Jail.

Chapter Thirteen

GOING TO JAIL

THE hours seem endless when you're in prison. Days crawl by. Nights seem like an eternity. The boredom is stifling. You get up when they tell you. You go to bed when they say. You take a shower when they let you. You wear what they give you. You eat what they offer...when they have it ready. They set the schedule—you follow it.

Part of the punishment of incarceration is the vast amount of time you have to think. Your body is going nowhere, but your mind races, working overtime. *Why...? Suppose... What if...? Next time....*

You think about all the things you could be doing if you were out. Little things like getting the car washed or going out for a hamburger seem like grand adventures. You wonder what your wife and kids are doing. I remembered how little time I had spent with my family...how I'd mistreated and abused Anita.

After what seemed like a lifetime of thinking, worrying, fretting, fuming, despairing...another day went by. *Oh, man, I've got a whole year to spend in here! How am I going to make it? I can't stand this!* And I wondered about guys who were doing sentences of ten years, twenty or thirty years...or life! No wonder these inmates were so hard. No wonder they were ready to fight over even trivial matters. No wonder they acted as if a human life had little meaning or value to them—without hope it doesn't!

Despite the critics' label of being a "country club" facility devoted to coddling criminals, I found the Los Angeles County Jail to be every bit as unpleasant as I'd expected it to be. Hearing the heavy metal door clang shut behind me as I walked in was a chilling experience. And being strip-searched to be sure I was not carrying drugs in any body cavity was completely degrading and humiliating.

The officers who processed me into the jail made it quite clear how much they loathed and despised me—to them I was nothing but a pimp. Many of the inmates seemed to know of my reputation and were eager to get a look at me. "Hey, Tough Tony's here. Check it out!" The word spread that I was a big *Mafioso* dude, in charge of the Mob's ladies, making big money, and that I had heavy-duty connections. Many of these guys were impressed by my criminal notoriety and wanted to be my buddy. Others knew me from my bodybuilding career and couldn't wait to work out with me in the jail's primitive rooftop "Tar City" gym. Another group resented me, and their jeers, insults, and threatening comments as I was led through the passageway to my cell was completely unsettling.

I soon learned that the jail really was full of bad people. There were gang members, drug addicts, homosexuals, transvestites, and guys who were just plain mean and ugly. Virtually all the inmates felt that they were locked up unjustly...and most of them were already planning more illegal or criminal activities when they got out, just like me!

There were all kinds of scams and deals constantly going on in the L.A. County Jail. There was one fellow who must have been making more money behind bars than he'd ever made outside. Somehow he was smuggling in women's underwear and selling them to the transvestites for $50 a pair. He had all styles and colors!

Just about every kind of pill or drug imaginable was available if you had either money or something to trade. A single marijuana joint cost $10 inside the jail. Guys who were allowed to leave during the day on the work-furlough program smuggled in drugs. They'd put pills, marijuana, cocaine—all kinds of dope—inside balloons and swallow them. When the balloons came through their digestive tracts, they'd retrieve the drugs and sell them.

Even the nights in jail brought little rest. Sometimes it seemed the noise never stopped. The guy in the cell across from mine was on the edge of a nervous collapse and pounded on the walls, yelling, talking, and screaming until he collapsed from exhaustion. Down the line, guys were arguing...laughing...cursing. Some nights men would cry; others would moan and groan in their sleep.

The guy who was in the cell with me stayed half-stoned all the time, and he'd keep me awake at night, mumbling and groaning, and was rancid. After several nights of sleeplessness, I broke the chains that supported the lower bunk so the guards would move the guy out. They were angry with me for damaging the bunk and confronted me with accusations and threats. "I don't know what you're talking about. The guy just fell down on his bunk and it broke—why are you blaming me?"

My plan worked, though. They never got around to repairing the broken bunk, so I had the cell to myself the rest of the time I was there.

Learning to Live Locked Up

I discovered that the guy in the cell next to me was something of a national "celebrity." Evel Knievel was a daredevil and motorcycle stunt rider who'd once jumped his bike over 13 Greyhound buses. At Caesar's Palace in Las Vegas, he'd missed a jump over several parked cars, crashed, and was unconscious for 29 days. Perhaps his most famous exploit was attempting to hurdle California's Snake River Canyon as TV news cameras recorded his perilous—and again near fatal—exploit.

Knievel was a nice guy who'd been convicted of charges relating to assault and battery on his agent. He offered a few words of encouragement to me. "Don't get involved with the guys in here, Dennis. They're nothing but trouble. Just keep quiet, lay low, and do your time. Once you're out, be sure you don't ever have to come back."

Every day I'd go up to the rooftop gym and work out. This was not a well-equipped gym, but I found inventive ways to get a workout. I became friends with some of the lifters and shared routines and diets. Many of the inmates had never seen a professional bodybuilder's physique before, and they were highly impressed. The word went out that Tinerino really was a strong man and to treat me with respect. On the other hand, the serious lifters in jail couldn't understand why a world champion like me would wind up in a place like this. Many said they would give up anything to accomplish what I had achieved in my career.

As a result, I often found myself as the middleman in disputes, breaking up fights between rival gang members. The Mexicans and blacks always seemed to be at each others' throats. Little did I realize that each time I laid a hand on one of these toughs, I was literally putting my life in jeopardy. Fortunately, I was never seriously hurt.

One night a bunch of guys were talking about what they planned to do when they got out of jail. Nobody wanted to get a job and earn a living—they all had grand schemes on how they could pull a robbery, cheat somebody, or find some way to score big and live on easy street. After a while, someone asked me what I planned to do.

Half-joking, I outlined a wildly impractical scheme about setting up a party boat with booze and girls and taking it out just beyond the "three-mile limit" so I'd be out of the reach of any law enforcement agency. "I'll sit out there and let guys bring their money to me. I'll get rich and nobody will be able to touch me."

As I talked, I watched the faces of the guys around me. They were all laughing, enjoying my idea of doing something illegal just out of reach of the cops but close enough to flaunt it. Except one guy! He was listening carefully and wearing a forced smile on his face. But there was something about the look in his eyes that instantly put me on guard.

It later turned out that there were some police informers in jail who'd been assigned to find out as much as they could about me and my future plans. My attorney and some friends told me that the authorities had agreed to give me a reduced sentence on the hope that they could later set me up and nail me on something more serious that would put me away for several years—if not for life.

I caught on immediately. Never again did I participate in that kind of talk or allow anyone else to say that I planned to do anything illegal in the future.

Another Seed Planted

After eating dinner in prison one day, I was headed back to my cell when I suddenly heard music and singing and loud shouting. I looked into the room and saw a big buffed black preacher conducting a church meeting with a hundred inmates. He was preaching to a captive audience, saying that the wages of sin was death, that you reap what you sow, and that Jesus could set you free. The inmates responded, "Praise God...Amen...Preach it, brother...." "What a loud and enthusiastic group," I said to myself. I had never been to this type of meeting or heard this kind of preaching before and felt drawn to what I observed. I continued to stand outside and listen while the preacher continued talking about his life before he got saved. As I listened to him speak, I thought, This guy has a lot in common with me. He was from the New York projects and we had done similar things. He continued on, "I had many dreams and visions. God gave me many gifts, but I got involved with the wrong people and made wrong choices. I was caught up in a life of crime, robbing, cheating, and stealing. This was my old way of life, and many of my friends were murdered or ended up in prison. Yes! The devil came to steal and destroy, but Jesus came to give life and give it more abundantly! You see, I was destined to fry in the electric chair or rot in a prison cell. But, hallelujah! A man told me about Jesus! All it took, brothers, was one prayer. Yes! Just one prayer, and He set me free. Hallelujah! Let Him set you free from your prison of sin...just open up your heart and pray! Yes! Pray, my brothers. If you pray to Him, you will be saved. You will be born again!"

Born again. Where had I heard those words before? As I listened to the preacher, it came to me...Pat Boone and my wife's friend Mildred! That's who had told me about being born again! Suddenly, the preacher turned and pointed to me. "And there's Mr. Universe, someone who I followed in the bodybuilding world—Tinerino. He achieved worldwide recognition and many honors and much fame, which should have fulfilled him. There's a void in his life and in your life that cannot be filled by anything in this world. That void can only be filled by repenting of your sins and asking Jesus to become your Savior. He thinks he's tough, but Jesus already has His hand on him! The Holy Spirit has a plan for his life, and God is gonna use him in a mighty way!"

As I stared at him in amazement, the preacher asked those who wanted to accept Jesus as their Lord and Savior to come forward. I then noticed one member of the "congregation," a low-life creep whom I had seen being booked into jail for being involved in a male prostitution ring on Sunset Boulevard.

"Wait a minute, Reverend. I'd like to know one thing."

"What's that, Mr. Universe? What do you want to know?"

"This guy was arrested for male prostitution on Sunset Boulevard, trying to get kids—young boys—in the hustling scene. Now he's trying to get religion. This guy's a hypocrite...a phony! He knows he doesn't want to change. I saw people praying for him in a cell—then in the chow line he's hitting on some young guys. Why are you allowing him to keep operating?"

"Don't worry, Tinerino. God's gonna get him if he keeps comin' around. Remember, if you point the finger at others, three more are pointing at you. Before you cast the first stone, you need to repent of your own evil and sinful ways, and ask forgiveness for all the wretched deeds you have done in your life. And I'm prayin' that the Holy Spirit will remove your hardened heart. Remember, Tough Tony—you can run, but you can't hide from Jesus!"

"I don't want nothing to do with you guys," I yelled. "You're all a bunch of phonies. This is a crock of bull!"

"We're prayin' for you, Tony. Your life is a mess, and the devil's got you in his grip. What did you get for serving the devil? A jail cell—that's what. You're still filled with so much pride and anger you can't even see it. But Jesus loves you, He really does. I bind the power of satan over you and release you in Jesus' name to be set free!"

I shook my head, snorted in disgust, and stomped out.

Getting a Break!

Slowly, prison life settled into its own sluggish, tedious routine. I tried to let myself go numb so I could deal with it...so I wouldn't feel it so much. A week went by...a month...three months...four.

"TINERINO! You've got a phone call."

My attorney was waiting on the line. "Dennis, I've got some good news for you! I think I can get you on the work-furlough program. If we can find you a job, they'll let you out of jail in the morning to go to work. Then you go back to jail at night to sleep. I don't understand why they're allowing this, but things are really going your way."

"Well, I don't know if I want that deal or not!"

"Dennis, what are you talking about? You're out, man. You just do time from 7 P.M. to 7 A.M. and on the weekends."

"You know what, man—I'd rather stay in here, because once I get out, there's no way in the world I want to come back to jail at night!"

"You'd better think again, man. You're going to have to do at least nine months of your year, even with good behavior. And I'm telling you right now the cops aren't finished with you."

"What do you mean? What can they do if I serve my time?"

"Look, Dennis, you've got 15 lawsuits piled up. Your businesses are bankrupt. The local cops would still like to nail you for some of the jobs you guys pulled—they're still working on it. And your big worry is dealing with the IRS. If they send you away on tax evasion, you're going to do some hard time in a federal pen. You need to be out on the street so we can be working on your case. It's better to meet for lunch than to sit in the visiting room at L.A. County Jail!"

"Yeah, I guess you're right. How soon can you work it out?"

"Don't go anywhere—I'll get back to you."

As it turned out, not one of my former friends or associates would help get me a job, and the only way I could be on the work-furlough program was to get a job. But my attorney couldn't find anyone to put me on the payroll. Finally, I suggested that Anita contact one of my former body-building training partners, a guy named Doug Beaver. He'd worked as a manager for Win Paris, one of the founders of the Jack LaLanne gyms, who also owned a vitamin/supplement company called Super Fitness. Doug told him about my situation and asked if he could put me to work. Paris agreed to make a place for me as a telemarketer, calling various gyms and signing them up as retail outlets for Super Fitness products.

Doug then completed all the paperwork with the court so that I could enter the work-furlough program. I was released from jail at 7 each morning to drive to Redondo Beach for work, and each evening I'd leave work at 6 P.M. and drive back to the jail for the night.

My paycheck was sent directly to the work-furlough office. And from my earnings of $1,000 a month, the furlough program gave my wife $600 a month, gave me about $50 a week for lunches and gasoline, and kept a percentage for administration costs. Basically, I saw no money.

Being able to earn a little money for my family was a big help though. By this time my wife had used up what little cash I'd left her to live on. My grandparents were helping her a little financially, and occasionally one of my buddies would send her a couple hundred dollars. For the most part, things were very tough and stressful for Anita.

Although I'm not the world's greatest salesman, I was willing to try anything. So I'd stay on the phone for three or four hours in the morning, then Doug Beaver and I would go work out at a local health club on our lunch hour. He tried to be my friend and encourage me, and provided lists of prospects to call, while coaching me on my selling spiel. I'd make more calls and write up my orders in the afternoon until it was time to start back to jail.

Rosemary's Prayers

My very first day on the job, I noticed a woman across the room gazing at me. It made me feel uncomfortable because it felt as though her eyes were penetrating my soul! Finally, she came over to my desk and asked, "What is your name?"

I introduced myself to her and explained that I was now working as a phone salesman for Super Fitness. "My name is Rosemary Bix," she responded. "It's nice to have you here."

As she turned to walk away, I noticed there were tears in her eyes. "What's the matter—is anything wrong?" I asked.

She hesitated for a moment. Then she said, "I'm a born-again Christian, and Jesus is showing me that you've been caught up in a sinful life and the devil has you in his grip. The Lord wants me to pray for you because your soul is at stake."

"Aw, come on, Ms. Bix—what are you talking about? What Lord do you mean—the landlord?" I joked. Everything was a joke to me. "I see that you also have a mocking spirit," she said. "I want to pray for you, Dennis."

"Okay, great! Hey, that's wonderful. Throw a blessing on me—what can it hurt?" I spoke facetiously, not knowing exactly how I was supposed to react. After all, besides Pat Boone, Mildred, and the black preacher in jail, she was one of the few born-again Christians I remember meeting.

Rosemary was a very small lady, and I was bulked up to about 230 pounds at the time. She reached up and put her hands on my face and head. As she started to pray, I felt weak in my knees, and I had no control over the strange but peaceful presence I felt engulfing me. The next thing I knew, I was on the floor. I couldn't believe it. "Oh, heavenly Father," prayed Rosemary, "in the name of Jesus, set this man free. I can see that he's bound by the powers of darkness. I bind you, satan, in the name of Jesus. I come against the spirit of anger, the spirit of death, the spirits of confusion and oppression. I command you to go and leave him right now, in Jesus' name. This man is called by God."

Suddenly, Rosemary jumped up and down and started speaking in a strange language—almost like the Latin that I remember hearing as a young boy in the Catholic Church. "What are you saying? What language are you speaking?"

"Dennis, I'm a Spirit-filled Christian, and I'm praying in my heavenly language to receive wisdom and knowledge from God concerning you. Praying in tongues is a gift of the Holy Spirit. There's a spiritual battle being waged for your eternal destiny. I'm also praying for your salvation and deliverance from demonic spirits."

Even though I wasn't aware of the spiritual things she was talking about, I couldn't deny how real it was. "I see that God called you when you were a boy; I see you on a train, listening to the voice of God."

"Huh? What did you just say?"

Others workers who had been led to the Lord by Rosemary came out of their offices and started praying for me as well. They were telling me about God's love, speaking in tongues, and commanding the devil to come out of me. Others were crying out to God to save my soul. Meanwhile, I was in total disbelief that I was still on the floor, looking up at seven people who were praying and crying over me. I was trying to stand up, but was unable to move!

"Hey! Which one of you guys pushed me down?" I asked in frustration.

"Wait a minute, Dennis. I'm seeing a vision about you. I see you driving in your car. You're being tormented and controlled by demonic forces of anger, rage, murder, paranoia, and fear. You can't sleep at night. I hear the devil saying, 'Kill him, kill him!' I see you arguing with your wife; she doesn't want you to leave. She sees you're up to no good. You leave anyway. The devil has planned a death trap for you and another person. I see you're looking to do harm to somebody. I see a woman and others praying for you, and because of their prayers God has stopped this death plan. Now you're down by the ocean...wait...you've got a gun and you're throwing it out into the ocean. Thank you, Holy Spirit, for showing me this in a vision. Does this mean anything to you, Dennis?"

A little voice inside me was screaming, *Stay away from this woman. She's with the FBI or the cops. She's a police informer. How else would she know about that gun?* I discovered later that what I had just heard was the voice of the devil!

As she was talking, I immediately saw myself sitting next to my dad on the BMT subway telling him that the Holy Spirit spoke to me and has a plan for my life.

When Rosemary said, "I see a woman and others praying for you," immediately I realized who that woman was. "The woman's name is Mildred." She was a seamstress who I met at my house one week prior to the encounter that I almost had with my associate. She said that she and others would be praying for me. She also told me, "You will never have peace until you are born again." I knew in my heart that her prayers had caused my associate to get a flat tire so I wouldn't be able to meet him.

Months before, someone had told me that my partner, Dog Man, the Dog Man, had put a "contract" out on me. After arguing with my wife, I left my house with a loaded revolver. I decided to get him first. I was having tormenting nightmares and was driven by voices saying, "Kill him, kill him!" I actually drove over to where he lived inside a gated community. But before I'd figured out how to get inside without being recognized, a security guard spotted me looking suspicious and asked what I was up to. I told him I wanted to see the Dog Man. The security guard said that he had just had a flat, and that he was on his way to help him. Realizing that I wouldn't have the opportunity to confront him that night, I decided to take a drive to the Santa Monica pier and started smoking a joint. On my way there, the police pulled me over and tested me for alcohol and drugs. Amazingly, they let me go. Once again, I avoided arrest. I escaped just as Rosemary had said. I then threw the gun as far out into the ocean as I could—but nobody had seen me. And I had never told anybody what happened. Only God, the devil, and I knew about that night. So, how could this woman have known about these things?

As I stood up, totally shaken and moved by the experience, I looked at Rosemary and shook my head. "How could you possibly know about this? Are you a psychic?"

"I told you before, Dennis. I'm a Spirit-filled believer, and the Holy Spirit is showing me these things so you can see the power of Christ and understand that He's real. You don't have to serve the devil anymore. God knows everything that you've ever done and still loves you. You've been seeking fame, money, publicity, and power in order to fill the empty void in your life. But only accepting Christ can fill that void—nothing else but Him."

Then she smiled and walked away. After my encounter with Rosemary and friends, I realized that even though I had physical strength and power, Rosemary had a spiritual power from Heaven's arsenal to deal with eternal spiritual forces that I didn't know existed. She had the ability to go into the archives of Heaven and receive information about the good and bad in my life. I was experiencing a miraculous manifestation of God's grace and power.

My first day's work orientation came to an end, and all I could think about was the incredible and miraculous meeting with Rosemary.

Then it was time to go back to jail.

When I arrived at work the next morning, there was Rosemary waiting for me, smiling. "I didn't mean to upset you, Dennis. I just really care about you. Tell me about your wife. Do you have children? Where do you come from? I want to know all about you!"

"I don't want to talk about it right now."

"That's okay, I understand. Be encouraged. And I'm putting your name on the prayer list at church too. Someone is going to be praying for you all the time." After she left, I thought, *Why didn't I tell her that everything she saw in a vision was what I experienced?*

Soul-searching

I tried to focus on doing my job. Making cold sales calls on the phone was really challenging, and many gym owners I spoke to would ask me about my legal problems...but people were praying!

Then I received an update from my attorney...and it wasn't good. He said that not only was I going to end up losing everything I'd worked for, it looked like I was going to be saddled with judgments against me totaling hundreds of thousands of dollars...but people were praying!

My relationship with my wife was really shaky too. She'd been hurt too often, too deeply. In addition to the neglect and abuse she'd suffered at my hands, the embarrassment and humiliation from the publicity of my arrest and conviction had left deep scars. And after growing accustomed to having plenty of money for fine restaurants and expensive clothes, it was a shock for Anita to not have enough money to pay the bills and keep food on the table. Plus, she had to endure the pressure of calls from collection agencies and an avalanche of threatening letters and legal documents through the mail.

"I don't know what to do, Dennis. How can we keep on living like this? We're losing everything—it's all being taken away."

So many times I felt like telling my wife, "Honey, I love you, and I'm sorry I've made such a mess of our lives. Why don't you forget me and go back to New York and try to start over?"...but people were praying!

Instead, I would encourage her to hang on and be tough, that somehow we'd get through all this mess. I don't know if she believed those heartening words or not—most of the time I didn't!

In any case, she and the girls stayed in California, and in order to have some time to spend with Anita, Tara, and Marissa, I told the work-furlough people that I now had to work six days a week because my sales were low. I really didn't have to work on Saturday, of course; instead, I would complete a full workout at the gym in the morning and then go home to spend the afternoon with my family.

I'd park the car away from our house, jump over a cinder-block wall, and enter through the back door. If the phone rang while I was there, Anita would answer it. We were both almost paranoid—afraid to let anyone know I was there. And we were always wondering if the police would check up on me some Saturday to see if I was at work. If they realized I wasn't at work, I'd have to go back and serve my full year of jail time all over again, and possibly even part of my probation. I was taking a big risk, so I could never totally relax.

One Saturday, we planned a birthday party for our daughter Tara and invited a few friends over, cautioning them not to mention to anybody that I'd be there. It was nice to be around some regular people, to hear laughter, and to be with friends I could trust.

All of a sudden, there was a knock on the door. Anita looked out and gasped, "Oh, my God, it's the police!"

I dashed out the back door, vaulted over the wall, and ran to my car. I drove away from the neighborhood and carefully doubled back, but I never did see any police cars or any sign of trouble. Finding a pay phone nearby, I called home.

"Oh, Dennis, I can't believe it. It was the Federal Express man—he was wearing a uniform. Your father sent a birthday gift to Tara. Come on back."

By this time, I was doing some serious thinking and soul-searching. What did I have to show for my life? Only wasted years and ruined dreams. Was there any hope? How could I even start to pick up the pieces of my life and put them together again?

Despite all the money I'd made through scams and strong-arm tactics, I'd never managed to hang on to any of it. All my attempts to be successful as a legitimate businessman had ended in failure, and the bankruptcies and lawsuits pending against me threatened to cripple my earning potential for the rest of my life.

Any fame or prestige I might have gained had been totally discredited by my arrest and conviction. I was a jailbird. And even when I got out—if I could stay out—for the rest of my life I would be labeled an ex-con.

Besides all these things, I had been an unfaithful, abusive husband and an absent, negligent father.

Thinking about all my problems, I was reminded of a little Chinese finger-trap toy someone had given my daughter. Playing with this toy, you put one finger of each hand into the toy's web of tightly woven bamboo. Then the harder you tug against the web, the tighter it squeezes to trap your fingers. That was the way my problems felt to me. The more I struggled, the more pressure I felt. There seemed to be no way out. I was totally confused and disheartened, and I didn't know what to do.

I decided to turn back to bodybuilding and told Anita that I'd decided to start training again very seriously. "I've got to get a pair of posing briefs to wear in case I get the chance to do some exhibitions or enter a competition."

"Well, I have a friend who is a fantastic seamstress. She can make you a pair that will be better than anything you could buy. Let me call and see if she can come over."

The woman's name was Mildred, and when she showed up at the house to take my measurements, she said, "Oh, Dennis, Anita has told me all about you, and I've been praying for you for months now. I can see that you really need Jesus in your life."

I was startled. Here was another Christian who was praying for me. Almost every day at work Rosemary Bix came over to pray for me or to remind me that she was praying. Now this Mildred lady was praying too.

"Why do you feel so strongly about praying for me?" I asked her. "Why don't you go pray for someone else?"

"Don't you understand—the things that have happened in your life were not just accidents. There's a spiritual battle going on...spiritual warfare is being waged over you. I believe God has big plans for your life, and the devil doesn't want to give you up. That's why I've been so burdened for you. You need to be born again so you can enter the Kingdom of God."

"Born again?" I interrupted. "I didn't know I ever died!"

Mildred just nodded her head patiently and said, "The day will come when you will open your life to God. When you surrender yourself and let Jesus become your Savior and the Lord of your life—that's the day you'll finally be free."

I just shook my head in bewilderment. I couldn't relate to all this spiritual stuff. All I could think about was getting finished with jail—and the work-furlough program—so I could get on with straightening out the mess I'd made of my life.

Chapter Fourteen

LIGHT IN THE DARKNESS

ONE morning at work, the door opened and Pete Samra walked in. I was glad to see Pete. I'd known him for a long time and considered him to be a good friend. He was always gregarious, positive, and encouraging, and had a constant smile on his face whether we were training or socializing. He was a former Mr. South Africa and Mr. Natural USA bodybuilding champ, and had been the manager of Gold's Gym in southern California for several years.

"What brings you to Super Fitness, Pete?"

"Well, Dennis, our old buddy Doug Beaver is helping me out with a job, just like he is with you. I told him I was a good salesman and really needed the work, so he arranged it with Win Paris."

"What happened? I thought you were managing Gold's Gym."

Pete had fallen on tough times. He told me an amazing story of one stroke of bad luck after another. One afternoon, as he was working at Gold's Gym in Santa Monica, he confronted a member who was creating problems and told the guy to take it outside. Words were exchanged, then as tempers flared, a fight ensued. The troublemaker pulled out a knife and stabbed Pete. He was stabbed so severely that he heard the ambulance drivers say, "This guy's bleeding to death. He's not going to make it." Pete remembered his mother telling him, "Whenever you're in trouble, call on Jesus," and Pete began praying to Jesus to save him, then passed out. When he woke up in the hospital, the doctors told him it was a miracle that he survived.

After a long and painful recovery, Pete was ready to go back to work and expected the gym to praise and reward him for his heroic actions. Instead, when he recovered, Gold's rewarded him for his bravery by firing him. If that wasn't enough, his wife left him, taking everything they owned with her!

Most men would have been devastated by a chain of events like these, but Pete had the joy of knowing that Jesus had performed a miracle—saving his life—and he refused to be discouraged.

So, Pete Samra became a supplement salesman too, and started going with Doug and me to the gym to work out during the lunch hour. We used our time together to have a positive influence on each other, as we both were starting over trying to rediscover our goals and rekindle our vision.

One day, Pete received a phone call at the office from a guy named Ray McCauley. I knew that name—Ray was a bodybuilder, a former Mr. South Africa, and he'd also been a Mr. Universe contestant during one of the same years I had competed.

I'd sort of kept up with his career through the fitness magazines and from friends' reports. He had once worked with the legendary Reg Park, trained with another bodybuilding superstar Frank Zane, as well as with Arnold Schwarzenegger. Much of his life had been like mine—he'd auditioned for commercials, played some bit parts in movies, chased girls, worked as a nightclub bouncer, owned his own gyms—he'd done it all. So I was interested in finding out where Ray was and what he was doing when Pete finished his conversation with him and handed the phone to me.

Ray got right to the point. "Hey, Dennis, is what I'm hearing about you true? You're selling vitamins to get out of jail on a work-furlough program? What's happened to you, man?"

In just a few moments, I found myself spilling my guts to Ray, telling him all about my misfortunes. I ended up saying, "But, I guess everything will turn out okay. Things don't always go the way you think, but you've just got to keep pushing."

Ray was quiet for a few seconds. "Sometimes just pushing by yourself isn't enough. Do you know what I'm doing right now, Dennis?"

"No, man, I was wondering."

"Well, I had two gyms and a nice house in South Africa. I left them— gave them up. I'm at Rhema Bible Training Center in Tulsa, Oklahoma. I'm studying to become a pastor of a church."

"You mean, you're going to be a preacher, Ray? Why in the world do you want to do that? By the way, do you have anything to do with a lady named Rosemary over here? All she talks about is Jesus, Jesus, Jesus. She prays for me every day. She just won't let up. She puts tracts in my lunch box and in the bathroom. They say, 'You must be born again.'

"What's with all this born-again stuff anyhow? Pat Boone says he's born again. I go to prison, and there's this black preacher telling everybody about Jesus. Are all these people religious fanatics or just plain lunatics?"

A Message of Hope

"Dennis, let me ask you a question. In your whole life, have you ever had true peace? Were you ever really happy? Did you ever stop to consider what life's really about?"

"Well, I guess so. Winning Mr. America and Mr. Universe made me happy. I liked being famous, having a chance to make some big money."

"Nah, Dennis, that's not what I mean. I had a little of that kind of success, but it never gave me true peace. And you're sure not doing too well right now, are you?"

He had me there. I had just told him how screwed up my life was, so he knew how I was feeling. "What's happening with your wife now? How's Anita holding up?"

I wanted to give an upbeat answer, but I couldn't. "Not good, Ray. She's had a really rough time. I don't know if we're going to make it. To tell you the truth, I don't know what I'm going to do with my life."

Once I got started, all my fears, despair, and apprehension came pouring out like floodwater rushing through a broken dam. "When I get off this work-furlough program, I've got three years of probation. My lawyer says the cops will be watching me like a hawk. My businesses are closed, and there are about 15 lawsuits pending against me. The IRS says I owe $800,000 in taxes, and they've confiscated every asset I had. I have no income and no marketable talent or skills to make a living. I'm probably even through as a bodybuilder—I've been written up in the bodybuilding magazines as a criminal who headed up the biggest escort service in California history."

"Yeah, Dennis, I've seen the articles," Ray interjected.

"There's just not much hope. I've never been a pessimist, but things are pretty bad. Sometimes I think the best thing I could do is just drive away in my car and never come back."

"Believe me, Dennis, I know exactly how you feel. I did lots of the same things you've done. So I understand. But here's what you need to know right now. You don't know where you're going or which way to turn. You're just stumbling in the dark. But when you realize that...when you can admit that you're in the dark...that's when you're going to find the light of the world!"

He was quiet for a moment, waiting for that to sink in, I guess. And I took the bait. "Well, what is the light of the world?"

"It's not what, Dennis; it's who. Jesus is the Light of the world! And that's what you need. He loves you. He can turn your life around and put your feet on solid ground."

"I don't know, Ray. I don't know much about this religion business. But I do know I've done some real bad things."

"Well, listen, Dennis. We'll talk again soon. I've got a lot more to share with you. But I just want you to know I'm going to be praying for you, and I'll ask the other five hundred students here at Rhema to pray for you too. I'll be talking to you later. Bye for now."

Later that day at our regular noontime workout, I asked Pete why McCauley was calling him. "Oh, he's been my buddy for a lot of years, you know. We're both from South Africa. He heard about my problems, and he's been calling to try to cheer me up. He's really into this Christianity stuff. He says I need to get God in my life."

"Yeah, that's what he told me too."

Ray called several more times during the next couple of weeks. He'd talk with Pete Samra, then he'd talk with me, quoting lots of Bible verses and explaining what they meant. One verse really hit home—"*...a man's life does not consist in the abundance of his possessions*" (Luke 12:15 NIV). Over and over he emphasized that God was my friend, that Jesus loved me, and that there was hope for me and a way out of my trouble.

The Pressure Builds

I really needed Ray's encouragement because everything else in my life was getting even worse. My attorney was starting to hassle me about my unpaid legal bills, but I had no money to pay him—I didn't even know what to promise. It was just more pressure.

A couple of times in the evenings after I went back to jail, guards would show up at my cell with a German Shepherd dog that was trained to sniff out drugs. They'd go through my clothes and my few possessions. I'm sure they meant to scare me and shake me up, but I never had any drugs. So after a few checks, they gave up.

Then sometime later, at three o'clock one morning, the police guards shook me awake in my prison cell and said, "Get up and come with us, Dennis." They took me to an interrogation room and started asking me lots of questions while showing me pictures of various people.

"Do you know this girl?"

"Yeah, I've seen her around. I believe she used to work for my escort service and some others."

"Well, somebody killed her. She was strangled!"

"It wasn't me, man. You know where I've been!"

"What about this girl...and this one?"

"Yeah, both of them worked for different escort services—they free-lanced."

"They're dead too."

"Oh, no! What's going on? Who's killing all these girls?"

A serial killer the press had dubbed "The Hillside Strangler" was stalking prostitutes on Sunset Boulevard and killing them one by one. The entire city was worried and upset, and the cops were going crazy trying to nab the killer. Although they knew I wasn't involved, they thought I might have some information that would help.

I kept seeing the faces of the murder victims in my mind long after the guards took me back to my cell. I knew that those gals had gotten sucked into a way of life they couldn't get out of—chasing glamour and fame, riches and stardom. Most of them became addicted to drugs and alcohol and ended up selling their bodies and souls for one more fix, one more shot. And now they were dead. I remembered one of the Scripture verses Ray McCauley had quoted on the telephone: *"The wages of sin is death"* (Rom. 6:23a NIV). Did I deserve to die for all the bad things I'd done?

I was still awake, filled with guilt and condemnation, tormented by my thoughts, when it was time to get up and go to work. All day long I thought about those dead girls—what they had done was no worse than my behavior. No matter how I tried, I couldn't get them off my mind. I felt like I was trapped in a Western movie where the settlers have circled the wagons and the Indians are riding in from every direction. I was in a fight for survival against insurmountable odds...and I was wearing down fast!

A Radical Change

A couple of days later, I looked up to see Pete Samra walk out of his office. He didn't say a word, but the change in him was dramatic. *My God, what happened to this guy?* I thought to myself. His face looked different, and there was an indefinable difference in his whole manner and appearance.

"Pete, what's going on? You look fantastic, man! What happened to you?"

"Dennis, I don't know if you really want to hear about it, but something tremendous just took place on the phone."

"Tell me, Pete. I want to know."

"I was talking to McCauley, and he told me it was time for me to pray. He read John 3:16 to me again, where it says, *"For God so loved the world that He gave His only begotten Son, that whoever believes in Him should not perish but have everlasting life"* (NKJV). He said if I committed my life to Christ, I would be a brand-new creation, that all the old things would pass away and all things would become new."

"Yeah, he's told me that too."

"Well, Dennis, I made the most important decision of my life today. I surrendered my life to Jesus Christ. I've been so miserable I couldn't stand it anymore. I wanted to get even with my wife for leaving me, get even with Gold's Gym for firing me, and get even with the guy who stabbed me. I was so full of bitterness and hatred that it was eating me up inside."

Pete turned away for a second, and I could see him wiping his eyes. His face was wet with tears. I'd never seen a tough guy cry like this. In fact, this was beyond emotional; it was spiritual, and I had never dealt with anything of this magnitude before. Whatever had happened to him penetrated his heart on the deepest level. "Let me tell you something, Dennis." Pete turned back and looked me straight in the eyes. "I prayed with Ray—I said just what he said, word for word. And it worked, man, it worked! All of a sudden, something started happening—something in here!" Pete jabbed at his chest with his finger. Tears were pouring down his cheeks, but he didn't try to hide them.

"I can't explain what happened, but I feel so different now. It's like a one-ton barbell has been lifted off my shoulders. I can breathe, man. I'm not hurting in my heart. It feels so good, Dennis! I didn't know I could feel so good. I feel like Jesus really is making me all new inside. I feel like a new man.

"I'm forgiving everybody who has ever hurt me. From this moment on, I'm going to have a new life and a new way of living. This is a new beginning for me."

Pete smiled at me through his tears, and he just lit up. It was like there was a light emanating from him. I knew by this presence that Pete had an encounter with the Lord. There was an anointing, a kind of glow, that was tangible. It was amazing.

There was a lump in my throat so big I could hardly swallow. And I felt like hugging the guy, but I was afraid to. So I just cleared my throat and said, "I'm glad for you, Pete. I can tell something good has happened."

Pete didn't say a lot more. He didn't make a big scene about his experience. But I saw Rosemary hug his neck, and a couple of other people who were Christians talk to him; and they were all smiling. Every time I saw Pete simply walk across the room, I could see the change in him.

The next day Ray McCauley called me. "Did you see what happened to Pete?"

Rev. Ray McCauley - Led me to the Lord

"Yeah, Ray, he looks good. Something really happened to him. He's happy about it."

"The same thing can happen to you."

"I don't know, man. I'm not ready for that. I've still got a lot of desires and lusts in me. I'm a first-class sinner—a tough case. I don't think I could ever give up all my vices and become a saint. But I'm happy for Pete. It's good for him."

"Listen to me, Dennis. You'll never be able to straighten up your life by yourself, by your own will. Nobody can. You can't break the power of sin and overcome evil desires and temptations by your own ability. There's a spiritual battle waging for your soul. Look at the death and destruction all around you. That's why you need the Lord Jesus Christ. He can change you by His power, through His Holy Spirit. Jesus said, *"Most assuredly, I say to you, unless one is born again, he cannot see the kingdom of God"* (John 3:3 NKJV).

Then he prayed, "God, open up Dennis' eyes to see Your Kingdom."

"Just remember, Dennis, God loves you. He wants to help you and get you out of that turmoil and mess you're in. But it's got to start with you choosing Him. You could have been dead, but still you aren't grateful for anything. I'm praying for you, and a lot of the people here are praying for you that God would remove your hard and stony heart. Open up your heart and let Christ in, Dennis. He's knocking. How long are you going to let Him stand out there?"

Immediately after I hung up with Ray, I received another phone call. An old friend unexpectedly phoned to say, "I felt led to send you a Bible." This was beyond coincidence, and my mind was reeling! I felt shell-shocked.

All week long I thought about what had happened to Pete. I knew what bad shape he'd been in since he'd come to work at Super Fitness, and I could see a dramatic change in him. He was so different, so lit up, so happy! I also thought about what McCauley had told me during our last phone conversation. I knew he was right about me not being able to change myself—I'd tried and failed lots of times. But was it really possible that God could change me and "fix" all the messes I was in? How could saying a few words in a prayer give you a new heart? It sounded too easy—too good to be true. Besides, maybe I really didn't want to change. Maybe all I really wanted was just to get out of trouble.

Time to Pray!

One evening the following week, the phone rang just as I was getting ready to leave work. I had to be back at the jail by seven o'clock, and I didn't want to be late. So I was a little antsy when I heard Ray's voice because sometimes he talked for a long time.

"Listen, man, I was just leaving. I've got to get back to jail for the night before they get shook-up. I've only got a minute."

"That's all right—I understand. As I was praying for you, I felt impressed to tell you this—I think you're concerned about your old friends and buddies. You're wondering if you'll ever belong or be accepted again. But what you need to ask yourself is, where are your friends right now? Who is taking care of your wife and kids? You've been too concerned about your so-called friends, but they're really not your friends. They only hung around you because of your money. They only loved you 'if' and 'because'—*if* you'd do something for them or because you were somebody."

I wasn't expecting that kind of challenge from Ray, and it got to me. Inwardly, I was bitter that none of my buddies and friends had lifted a finger to help me when I was in such desperate need. I'd helped lots of them—I'd bailed guys out of jail, lent others money that I knew I'd never get back, and picked up the tab for guys while we were hanging out. Yet when I needed help, they looked the other way.

Still, I really hadn't expected anything from the "beautiful people" I'd partied with, even though some of them were conspicuously wealthy. Long ago, I'd discovered that many celebrities are selfish—they love to live high as long as someone else is paying for it. They're all masters at knowing how to disappear just before it's time to pay the check. I'd found that many big-name actors and sports stars were totally self-centered, never thinking of anybody else or doing anything for others...unless they could get some publicity out of it.

So there was an edge of bitterness in my tone when I responded to Ray's comment. "You know what, you're absolutely right. You can't depend on anybody. The sooner you learn that, the better off you are."

"It doesn't matter, Dennis. They're really just fly-by-night friends. But there is a Friend who sticks closer than a brother who will never leave you or forsake you, no matter what. His name is Jesus, and He wants to be your best Friend and have a personal relationship with you. All you have to do is invite Him into your life. Ask Him to forgive you of your sins and failures. He'll change you and make you a new creation."

Somehow, I had forgotten about the time, and getting back to the jail was no longer a top priority. Instead, I felt compelled to keep listening to what Ray was talking about, but I just couldn't bring myself to take what seemed to be a drastic step.

Suddenly, a very loud voice spoke to me, *Don't listen to this man! Hang up the phone!* In my heart, I knew it was the devil's voice...there was a spiritual battle waging.

"Gee," I mused, half to myself, "if I got born again, what would people think about me? 'Mr. America gets religion.' I wonder how that would go over in Beverly Hills?"

"That's just pride talking, Dennis. ... I bind you, spirit of pride!" he said authoritatively.

"Wait a minute. Maybe this is not what I want."

"That's ego—edging God out. ... I bind you, ego! Get out of his mind now, you lying devil! Go! Right now!"

Strange sensations were traveling all over my body. I felt like I was weaving in and out of the twilight zone. "Ray, something is happening to me. I feel strange. What is this?" I started to weep uncontrollably. I knew that I wanted God to come into my life more than I wanted life itself! I realized that I was a sinner.

"Get him, Holy Spirit, get him!" Ray exclaimed. Then he said, "It's time to pray, Dennis. Let's do it right now—but you've got to mean it with all your heart. Just repeat this sinner's prayer after me.

Lord Jesus, I believe You are the Son of God. I believe that You died on the cross so my sins could be forgiven and I could receive eternal life. I'm sorry for all my sins and evil deeds. Forgive me and wash my heart as white as snow. Take away my sinful appetites and desires. Make me a new creation, a new man. Help me to be like You—pure and filled with the power of God. I believe that You receive me into the family of God right now. Thank You, Jesus. Amen.

I repeated the words and phrases after Ray, all the way through. I still felt eerily disconnected from reality, but there were no other feelings or emotions. I didn't understand.

When I said, "Amen," Ray began to say, "Hallelujah! Praise You, Jesus!" Then he spoke a little bit in what sounded like another language, just like Rosemary Bix had done the first day I met her. It all seemed very bizarre to me.

"Okay, Dennis, I know you're running late. I know you have to go. But I'm prophesying that something is going to happen to you tonight. God will manifest His presence to you, and you'll know when it happens. I'll call you later."

Click—the phone went dead. Ray's words had reminded me that I had to hurry. But as I turned to go, I felt something come over me. It made me twitch my shoulders and shake my head. What was it? Then it dawned on me—I felt this tremendous sense of peace, joy, and happiness! I couldn't ever remember feeling that way before.

Take a Ride on Heaven's Side

Moments later I was in my car, pulling onto the Santa Monica Freeway. The road was jammed with traffic, bumper to bumper, but I didn't feel uptight or nervous about it. And I was aware of a divine presence in the car with me.

Then, in an instant, I started seeing scenes from my life—I was having an open vision. They appeared around me in living color and three-dimensional detail, like I was viewing them on a movie screen or TV set. It was like a stream of consciousness unfolding out of my inner man, only bigger, clearer, and more distinct.

I saw myself in my parents' arms as an infant. Their care and adoration for me released love and joy to me, which was my lifeline. My hunger for life grew as I absorbed the wonders of God's creation. My inquisitiveness released excitement and joy for life. Years flashed by in a second. I saw every spectrum of emotion—crying and laughing, joyfulness and sadness, and so on.

I then saw myself at 12 years of age with my proud parents, the sound of church bells ringing in the background. Suddenly, I saw myself sitting on the train beside my father, saying, "Hey, Dad, I heard the sound of God's voice. He said, 'Life will pass but knowing Christ and serving Him is the only thing that will last.'" God's love for me and my pursuit of Him manifested His destiny for me. I also saw a wound in my heart that I had received because I had not been shown how to overcome sin and temptation by those in spiritual authority.

School yard fights, working out with weights, playing baseball—I saw God's angels encamped around me as a youth. There were times I could have been stabbed, maimed, or blinded. Facing and overcoming challenges until they became accomplishments, standing in the winner's circle, saying my marriage vows, the birth of my children.

There was no purgatory in this vision, only Heaven or hell, God's angelic host or satan's demons. The awesomeness of God and His majestic Kingdom and the despair of hell's hopelessness. The battle was in the spirit realm, a tug-of-war for my eternal destiny. The scenes kept unfolding, moving at a lightning-fast pace, yet with no sense of rush or disorientation.

I then saw the direction of my life starting to veer into darkness. I saw myself lying, cheating, stealing. I saw the fights, the scams, the compromises. I saw the temptations, desires, lusts, and seductions. And everything was happening right before my eyes.

I became aware that the mistakes my character was making in the unfolding drama before me were not entirely my own. There was also a shadowy figure in the picture, setting traps, camouflaging areas of quicksand, placing people in positions who were enticing me with money, fame, recognition, and women who were attempting to seduce me.

"*Watch out!*" I called out to the Dennis on the screen. "*Why are you doing that? Can't you see those people are deceiving you? Be careful—don't go that way!*" Wait a minute—that is me I am talking to. I am trying to change my own behavior, my own history, my own destiny!

But it didn't help. The me on-screen continued to make poor choices that led to other bad choices. I even saw the shameful things I'd managed to forget—there they were, even more loathsome than I'd remembered. I felt ashamed—there I was engulfed in evil.

No wonder my life had ended up in such a wreck. I could see every development that had led to such despair and hopelessness. *Oh, no!* I saw all the times I'd been so nasty and mean to my wife, Anita. There we were, screaming and yelling at each other. What was I doing? Waving a gun in her face, threatening her, shoving her, terrorizing her! Oh, my God, don't make me look. How could I have hit her, smacking her face with my hand? She even had a bruised and swollen face when her father was there for a visit!

I could see my parents sacrificing so much to help me achieve my goals. They were pushing themselves, giving all they could, holding me up, and encouraging me. They were so proud of me. There I was, full of potential and promise. How could I have thrown it all away and brought shame and grief upon their heads? Why did I do it?

Wait a minute! Look! After all these mistakes and failures, there's a way out. If this Dennis will just make a turn, Someone is waiting to pull him up. But no, he's going the wrong way. He's turning his back on the answer. He's slipping away—straight toward the evil one. There's nothing but death and destruction ahead. *"Go back! Turn around!"*

The scene changed. Then in my open vision, I could see a panoramic shot—a wide landscape. On one side there were dark clouds on the horizon, and a fast-moving storm was building. There was wind and lightning. And as the storm moved closer, the picture started growing darker and darker. Wait—there in the foreground was Dennis, watching the storm move in. The clouds moved closer...and closer...and closer. The wind was howling. Thunder rumbled and growled. The lightning ripped the sky with jagged, angry bursts of violent energy.

He knew—and I knew as I watched—that if the clouds engulfed him entirely—if he was swept up into the heart of the storm—he would be lost forever...for all eternity. He drew back in terror, shrinking away from the onslaught. *"Run, Dennis, run! Get away from the darkness. Find shelter! Get help! Don't let the storm take you down!"*

Dennis was spinning around, looking from side to side, up and down, back and forth. Wait! On the far horizon...just on the edge of the shadows...what is that? Oh, my God! It's a light. It's a light! That's what I've been looking for—*the Light of the world.* And it's moving this way. It's getting brighter. It's coming for me. *"Come on, Light! I need You, Light. It's so dark around me. It's almost too late. Come, Light! Save me, Light!"*

Suddenly, I was gripping the steering wheel of the car so tightly that I could feel my fingernails cutting into the palms of my hands. And I was screaming at the top of my lungs—"Oh, God, help me! Help me, Jesus! Save me, Jesus!" I felt like a drowning man gasping for one last breath before slipping beneath the ocean waves for the third time. I was crying for help! There may have been people in the cars all around, watching me, thinking I was crazy, but I didn't care. For me this was a matter of life or death! It was now or never.

Each time I cried out to Jesus, the light in the tableau before me got brighter and moved closer. And as the light got brighter, the dark clouds moved back. And suddenly, I understood! It all made sense to me. I could see what was happening.

In an instant, I was praying. There was no hesitance, no awkwardness. The words gushed up out of my belly, through my chest, and out of my mouth—rushing, lifting, soaring straight up to Heaven!

"Jesus, I give all my life to You. I'll live for You from this moment on. Take away every trace of sin; remove everything from my life that has ever stood between You and me. I repent of every transgression, every evil. Forgive me for sinning against You, the King of the universe, the Lord of all."

And then I heard the voice of Jesus. It was a quiet voice, barely a whisper, but it sounded like a bell ringing in my heart. "Dennis!"

"Somebody is speaking to me! Who's calling me?"

"Dennis, My son, don't look back and grieve over your past from this moment on. Don't look back in regret. I don't see that life anymore—I can never see those things again. Today, at this very moment, you are a new creation. Old things have passed away; behold, all things have become new! Behold the glory of My presence!"

On the screen before me, the Light suddenly grew so bright that I couldn't stand to look. And when I looked back an instant later, the dark clouds were gone! Then the screen disappeared—but the Light didn't. It moved to the top of my head, stayed there a moment, then started moving down my body. The Light was shining on me, but it was also in me at the same time. And as it moved down, I could feel the darkness inside of me breaking up and melting away! It moved through my head, then into my chest, then down to my belly, into my legs, through my knees, my ankles, and shot out the bottom of my feet!

"My God," I gasped. "I must be dying. That's it—I'm going to Heaven. I must be in Heaven right now!" I wasn't aware of my body. I wasn't aware of my car. Yet I was driving, moving safely along the highway.

I was having a supernatural visitation with Jesus of Nazareth, with the Holy Spirit, and with God the Father, all in One, all at once. His divine presence had totally engulfed me...and saved me...and changed me. If I multiplied everything I had ever experienced in my lifetime by a million—no thrill, no joy, or no happiness could compare with how I felt when the power of God came into my life.

This is what I had been looking for. Why hadn't somebody told me? Bodybuilding didn't satisfy. Being Mr. America and Mr. Universe didn't satisfy. Fame and money didn't satisfy. Relationships with beautiful models and movie stars didn't satisfy.

The only true satisfaction—the only thing that matters in life—is having an intimate and personal relationship with the King of kings.

I felt free and completely fulfilled.

At that moment, I pulled my car into the parking lot of the Los Angeles County Jail. It was way past time for me to check in. I was already supposed to be back in my cell.

I got out of the car and started for the door of the work-furlough station. The guards would be waiting for me.

Chapter Fifteen

Out of the Darkness, Into the Light

THE old life is over; a new life begins!

As I walked across the parking lot to the work-release entrance of L.A. County Jail, the presence of God was so real and powerful that I felt invaded and overwhelmed. It seemed as if the sky above me had opened and Heaven had poured out huge vats of liquid glory that saturated my entire being.

I could feel a burning force inside me—crushing and breaking the ropes, chains, and bonds of sin that had squeezed my chest until I could barely breathe and that had kept my stomach tied in knots. When a new wave of this liquid fire hit me, my whole body shuddered. My legs got so weak and shaky I couldn't stand up! Three times I actually sank to my knees and fell over—weak, helpless, almost paralyzed.

Two other work-furlough inmates returning to jail saw me staggering and falling on the parking lot and ran over to me. They grabbed my arms and tried to pull me up. "Hey, man, what have you been taking? Get it together, Dude. If they find you doped up or drunk, they'll put you back in straight time." Then they half-carried, half-led me inside.

The officer who checked me in and made me change from street clothes to my prison uniform kept looking at me strangely. I could tell he sensed the difference in me too. But he didn't know what I knew; I was fully aware that I had experienced God's loving presence—something dramatic and earth-shattering. I felt different inside—changed, clean...forgiven!

As I started down the long corridor toward my cell block, I was suddenly aware that there was another realm behind the ugly, grimy, physical realm that surrounded me. It was as though someone had flipped a switch and turned off the scrambler device on a cable television channel. What was once a jumbled mass of vibrating lines and jumbled colors clicked into a clear, vivid picture. The invisible realm became visible; the unseen, seen; the inaudible became audible.

Through this new "eye of the Spirit," I could see the dark, sinister, evil forces manipulating and controlling the people around me—inmates and jailers alike.

I passed a cell that held two men—one convicted of embezzlement and the other serving time for armed robbery. Behind these men was a dark spirit of greed and selfishness, accompanied by another spirit of violence.

Farther down the hallway, past the first turn, was the transvestite who called himself "Rhonda." In the spirit realm, I was "seeing" how a dark, twisted force had perverted this man's mind, body, and spirit, making him burn with an unnatural attraction for men.

Looking into cells of murderers, rapists, and other men who had committed violent crimes, I could see that these men were controlled and literally inhabited with evil forces so ugly and dark that I knew they must be demonic.

No wonder the world I lived in was so full of misery and pain! No wonder I had felt driven to wallow in such dirty and degrading activities, and constantly battled such inner turmoil and confusion. Any goodness or decency within me was under relentless attack by the dark forces that surrounded me. Like the men imprisoned around me, I was a victim of my own choices—a casualty of the unending spiritual warfare raging in the unseen but very real spirit world around me, and I had been unable to struggle with the powers and principalities that attacked me.

The intensity of the revelation I was seeing was overwhelming. I covered my eyes with my hands for a moment, just to make sure I wasn't hallucinating. As I looked again, I realized that the Holy Spirit was revealing two kingdoms to me with such deep power—God's Kingdom, overflowing with majestic splendor and immense goodness, and satan's kingdom, filled with immense evil. What I was seeing and experiencing as I saw both kingdoms, showed me that as a born-again believer, Christ had given me the power and authority to live victoriously over and above the invisible powers of darkness. He had defeated the devil; He had already paid the price for my sins at the cross. I had been delivered from the kingdom of darkness into the Kingdom of the Son of God; the power of the evil one had been dissected from me on God's operating table.

I stayed in my cell the rest of the night and didn't talk to anybody. I was so overwhelmed and overjoyed at the same time that I needed to just sit and absorb it all. I felt so humbly grateful to God for setting me free. Still, I wondered how I was going to escape from the deep pit I had dug for my family and myself. I was trapped in a twisted, tangled web of personal, professional and legal situations; and there was no way I could get out of it on my own. Yet as all these concerns raced through my mind, I was filled with confidence, faith, peace, and joy! The Lord had taken all my cares upon Him, clearing my mind of worry and allowing me to think clearly.

The first obstacle was to get out of jail. Christ had touched me super-naturally when I gave my heart to Him. Therefore, I knew that as long as I walked with my heavenly Father, He would restore and provide for my family and me. I knew I was able to trust the Lord, and I knew that He would do it in a miraculous way.

Testifying!

As I drove to work the next morning, I was still weeping and singing for joy. The Santa Monica Freeway was still jammed with traffic, but I saw only the beauty all around me. I could hardly wait to get to the office. I wanted to tell Rosemary and Pete about my salvation experience, and I had to call Ray McCauley in Tulsa.

When I opened the door to the workplace, I yelled, "Rosemary, Rosemary, you're right! I found what I was looking for. Jesus set me free. I'm saved, born again...I'm free!" Rosemary was thrilled but not surprised. "I knew the Lord was going to save you, Dennis. He had already shown me that. God has big plans for you! So many people are going to be helped by hearing your testimony—you will preach to multitudes! This is just the beginning."

When I phoned Ray McCauley at his part-time job at the Century Health Club in Tulsa, he was ecstatic. "Thank You, Jesus, for saving Dennis. Hallelujah!"

I related what had happened after he had hung up the phone the night before. He kept interrupting my story with joyous shouts and praises to God. "I'm so happy for you, Dennis. Thank You, God, for answering prayer. What a wonderful testimony!"

"Ray, I want you to know how much I appreciate all you've done for me. I never would have known that I needed to cry out to God if you hadn't told me. I don't know what's going to happen to me now, but if God can touch me in such a real way like He did last night, I know He'll help me put the pieces of my life back together."

Suddenly, Ray began praising God again, speaking in another language—in the "tongues" that he later explained to me was the language of the Holy Spirit. Then, in English, he dropped a new bombshell into my lap—"Thus saith the Lord, you're going to get out of jail...this week! God's going to cut your sentence short! This is part of His perfect plan for your life. So, Dennis, you need to get into the Word of God."

"Ray, are you sure? How am I going to get out of jail? What is this 'plan' God has for me? And how do I get 'into' the Word?" I was hearing an entire new group of words and phrases that I didn't understand.

"I don't know the exact details, Dennis, but I know in my spirit that you're going to be released from jail *this week*. God is going to work out His plan for your life—it's already starting. Stay close to Him in prayer. In addition, just as soon as you can, start reading and learning from His Word. Find a Bible study group that can help you understand the Scriptures so you can start living for Him. Start with the Gospels— Matthew, Mark, Luke, and John. They'll tell you all about the life of Jesus.

"Now, listen to this. You have to tell people what's happening to you. The Bible says if you confess Jesus before men, He will confess you before the Father. Just tell them what you're experiencing—what you know about God. And the first person you need to talk to is your wife."

"Ray, my wife isn't going to believe me. I've hit her with every kind of scam, every story, every con you can imagine. When I wasn't trying to deceive her, I was attempting to sell her on some harebrained scheme that never worked out. She doesn't have much confidence in anything I say."

"Well, Anita needs Jesus too, Dennis. And how did she put up with you all these years without Jesus, anyway? Your wife must have been a saint and didn't even know it!

"If God could reach you, He can touch Anita. I'll get my friends here at Rhema to pray with me for her. You pray too, and witness to her as soon as you can. In the meantime, I'm so happy for you, Dennis. We'll talk again soon."

When I hung up the phone, I thought to myself, *Well, I guess I'm going to get out of jail.* It didn't seem possible to me, but I wasn't going to bet against McCauley. He seemed to have a hot line to Heaven.

Nothing was any different when I went back to jail that night...except me! Instead of talking and hanging out with the other inmates as I usually did, all I wanted to do was spend some quiet time in my cell—just God and me. I managed to get my hands on a Bible and read a little bit before bedtime. I tried hard to keep reading and be inspired by it, but the language it was difficult to understand. After skipping around several places, I finally gave up for the night.

Getting Out!

I hadn't been at my desk for more than five minutes the next morning when the phone rang. "Dennis, this is Richard Caballero." *What could my attorney want?* I wondered. "I've got some good news and some bad news."

"Well, hit me with the good news, man."

"I don't understand it, Dennis, but I just found out you're going to be released from jail."

"Released from jail! Wait a minute, Richard. Do you know a guy in Oklahoma named Ray McCauley, a former Mr. South Africa?"

"What are you talking about? I never heard of him."

"Well, this guy is a friend of mine—he's studying to be a preacher. He told me on the phone last night that I was going to get out of jail this week. Did you tell anybody?"

"I just found out myself. Who would I tell? What's going on, Dennis? Are you okay? You're acting very strange."

"Richard, I know how it happened. It was God!"

"What's God got to do with it?"

"I had a supernatural experience with God two days ago. I asked God to forgive me of my sins, and He did. I'm born again—saved! I'm a new person."

"Yeah, Dennis...sure. I've seen a lot of guys get jailhouse religion. They try to straighten up for a few days, and then they're right back where they started from. I hope whatever you've got is real and it sticks. But I'll have to see it to believe it. You've been too good a customer for too long for me to expect you to change now."

"Yeah, I've kept you busy while I've tried to be an upstanding citizen! Now, if the good news is I'm going to get out of jail, what's the bad news?"

"I need to file some more briefs and motions, and go before the judge for you to get all this worked out. You're going to owe me another $15,000 on top of all you already owe."

"Don't worry about it, Ritchie...you know I'm good for it. When I get out, I'll pay you every cent, just like always."

"Yeah...sure, Dennis...fine. Now, listen, Dennis, I think I might have figured out why this is happening. The other day I bumped into the district attorney, and he asked about you. He told me his office was considering releasing you with the stipulation that you have absolutely no contact with anybody involved in organized crime or anybody who has anything at all to do with the escort service business. I said, 'Fine, great. Let's do it!'

"But remember when you were blowing off your mouth about setting up that boat with girls out past the three-mile limit? I think they're letting you out because they think you're planning to be involved with underworld people again. The police will be watching, and the minute you meet with these people, they'll nail you with a sentence that will put you away for years."

"Yeah, well, that ain't going to happen. I'm through with that kind of life."

"Just remember to watch yourself, Dennis."

"When am I going to be released?"

"Just as soon as I can file the papers and everything goes through the computers. While I'm at it, I'm going to see if we can get your whole record expunged—at least it's worth a try. I'll be back in touch as soon as I know something definite."

Two nights later, back in jail, the guys at the guard station got a call just before midnight. "Roll up, Dennis Tinerino. He's out of here!" The word spread like wildfire. Some of the other inmates knew about it before I did.

The work-furlough cell block hadn't been locked down yet, and a bunch of guys came around to see me.

"I can't believe you're getting out so soon, Tinerino."

"Yeah, all you Mafia 'wise guys' have got connections. But you'll be back in here soon enough."

"Hey, Tinerino, pose for us one last time! And don't forget about us."
I started posing, flexing, giving a spontaneous bodybuilding show while
my cell mates laughed and cheered. Then I started handing out some of
my muscle shirts, shoes, and other personal items.

The guards had to put their two cents in as well.

"I've never seen this happen before!"

"Tinerino, you must know somebody that's pretty influential to get
you sprung like this!"

Finally, the guards had me clean everything out of my cell and go up
to the desk. The officer there said, "I don't understand why they're letting
you out. This doesn't make any sense. You don't even have a rap sheet left
in the computer! All you have to do is check in with a parole officer once
a month."

The guy let me come around and look at the screen. He and I both
knew that my New York bust as a teenager and my arrest by the Arizona
authorities had been on my record, along with my California run-in with
the law. Now there was nothing!

I felt a surge of excitement inside my chest. Not only had God
cleansed me of all my sins and washed away every stain, He had caused my
criminal record to be erased. My release papers simply noted that I was
under the supervision of a parole officer for the next three years.

Going Home!

Five minutes later, I walked out of jail a free man and started for my
car. I could go home! But what was I going to tell Anita? She didn't even
know I had been released.

I hadn't told Anita about my conversion, either. I knew she wouldn't understand. Her heart was filled with bitterness and anger toward me—and with good reason.

She had lived in fear for three years. She was afraid some of my old business contacts would come around. And she knew I'd kept guns everywhere—one in the armrest of my car, another over the door in the entryway of the house. There was a shotgun under the bed, and a revolver hidden in the backyard. Some of my paranoia had rubbed off on her.

So I wasn't too sure how Anita would react when I showed up at one o'clock in the morning. But I didn't have anywhere else to go. I knocked on the door, and kept calling out, "Anita! Anita!" She didn't answer, but I sensed she was there, listening. "It's me—Dennis. Let me in."

"What are you doing here in the middle of the night? Go away! Leave! Don't you know this is the first place they'll look for you when they find out you've escaped from jail?"

"No, Anita, I didn't escape. They let me out—I'm free!"

"I don't believe you. You're crazy! I've got enough to deal with already—now you have to do this. Get away from me."

I could hear her crying hysterically. Getting my release papers out of the car, I slipped them under the door. "Look at this, Anita. I'm not lying to you. They released me—all legal and proper. I'm out!" Laughing and jubilant, I added, "You're supposed to be happy...I'm home!"

In a few moments, the door opened. Anita was holding the papers in her hand, shaking her head in bewilderment. Then she threw them at me in anger. "Why did they let you out of jail? Why didn't you tell me you were getting out?"

Then my little daughters came running in. "Daddy, Daddy! Daddy's home!" With tears running down my face, I held them and cuddled them for a little while before we put them back to bed. By this time Anita had calmed down, but she was still very angry and upset with me.

I started to explain about Ray McCauley and the influence he'd had on me in the last few months. But the minute I said he was a former Mr. South Africa, Anita exploded. "Oh, another of your worthless bodybuilding friends. I can use the fingers on one hand to count how many of those guys have any value at all. Most of them are just steroid freaks, playboys, and parasites. They care only about themselves. They're totally self-centered and egotistical."

Then my wife dragged me over to the desk in our den. Anita pointed to the mail and legal documents that had piled up all over the desk—some of the stacks were at least a foot high!

"This is what we're getting in the mail. This is the mess you've gotten us into. There's lawsuits here, bankruptcies, collection notices.... The IRS says you owe them $800,000—they've already seized almost everything we had! Why didn't you listen to me and not get us into all this? What in the world are we going to do now? Call up some of your old buddies so they can come drag you back down into the sewer? Maybe they've got some new scams and wild ideas so you can wipe out all these bills in a week!"

"Well, I was starting to tell you about Ray McCauley. He's been helping me."

"This is the ex-bodybuilder? What's he done for you?"

"Well, he's going to be a preacher now. He's been calling me on the phone and praying with me for months. I've accepted Christ as my Lord and Savior—I'm a born-again Christian now. Ray says I can't get out of this mess without God's help, but the Lord can deliver us!"

"Give me a break, Dennis!" Sarcasm and derision dripped from Anita's words. "You've tried some low-down tricks, but you can't stoop any lower than this. How dare you try to use religion to make me think you've changed! I've heard everything now.

"If I were you, I wouldn't think about getting too comfortable here. Maybe the best thing we can do is pack up and leave, probation or not. Who's going to give you a job out here? What are you going to do to earn a living? How in the world can you possibly earn enough money legitimately to pay off all these demands and judgments?"

Suddenly, my shoulders slumped, and I was very tired. "I don't know, Anita. I just got out of jail tonight. I don't know what I'm going to do. All I know to do is take it one day at a time and trust in God." I felt deflated, empty, broken, disgusted.

All I could do was shake my head in frustration. Only a few short days earlier I'd experienced such a tremendous spiritual cleansing and uplifting that I thought I could never be discouraged again. Now, I realized that my battle to live a godly life had only just begun. "Anita, if anyone ever had a reason to be upset and angry, it's you. I'm sorry I messed up our lives so bad. I don't have the answers. I don't know what's going to happen. All I can tell you is that with God's help, we're going to get through all this. No matter how we feel right now, He'll make a way out of this hopeless situation.

"Right now, I'm too tired to even think. Let's both get some rest, and leave it in God's hands, okay?"

When my little girls woke up the next morning, they were so excited that I was still there. Tara said, "Are you going to be home for a while, Daddy? We really missed you. You don't have to leave again, do you? Please don't go."

"Daddy's not going anywhere ever again, Tara. I love you, honey. Daddy wants to make up for all the time he's been away."

Crying, I went out in the backyard by myself and started to pray the best I knew how. "Jesus, I know You're real. I know what You've already done in my life. You spoke to me in my car on the way back to jail. You spoke to me through Rosemary and through Ray McCauley. But right now, I don't know what to do next. I'm facing some big problems, and I don't know where to turn. Help me, Lord."

As I waited, I felt His presence around me, and thoughts came to my mind as clearly as if a voice had spoken them. *Call your friend Ray, and he'll pray with you and Anita. Your wife is going to forgive you, Dennis, and accept Me also.* When I looked up, I felt calm; the ripples of panic I'd felt before were gone. And I knew exactly what I was supposed to do.

Ray Prays With Anita

"Oh, Dennis, I'm glad you called. We've been praying for you and Anita. How's it going?" I told Ray how Anita was reacting to me.

"I thought this could happen. Remember, pal, you weren't the best husband and father. You did some terrible things. There's a lot of hurt in Anita—lots of wounds and scars to be healed. You're going to have to be really gentle...and patient. The most important thing is that your wife accepts the Lord. Have you told Anita what happened to you?"

"Yeah, I tried, but she didn't believe it. All it did was make her mad. She thought I was lying to her again."

"Do you think she would talk with me? I'd really like to try and help her understand."

"Hold on, Ray. I'll try to get her on the phone."

I went into the kitchen and found Anita cleaning up the breakfast dishes. "Anita, I've got Ray McCauley on the phone. He's the guy I was telling you about—Mr. South Africa. He's in Tulsa now, studying to be a pastor. And he would really like to talk to you."

"What am I supposed to say to this man? He doesn't know me. What could he possibly say that would change our situation?"

"Please, Anita, just talk to him. I'm not lying to you. Ray says the Lord will help us get our lives straightened out—that God will forgive us and change us. Come on, Anita. What could it hurt to just talk to the guy? He's got connections in high places. Listen, he prophesied that I would get out of jail early, and I did...right? I'm here...aren't I?"

At last, Anita was persuaded to get on the phone with Ray. Pretty soon she started asking questions. "What do you mean, 'born again'? Are you some kind of 'Elmer Gantry'? What kind of Bible do you use? Are you a Mormon, Jehovah's Witness, or what? We're Catholics, you know."

I couldn't stand the suspense. After a while I went into another room and got on the other phone so I could hear their conversation. Ray was telling Anita many of the same things he'd told me—that she needed Jesus in her life and that He wanted to take over and help her find solutions and answers that would see her through any trial or circumstance.

"Anita, I can sense in my spirit how wounded you are. I understand that Dennis has really hurt you with his lifestyle—the all-night parties, not coming home for days on end, the gambling and illegal business deals, the years of leaving you alone most of the time, not spending time with your daughters. He was a bad influence on you...a bad influence on them. All the money and expensive things didn't satisfy you, did they? Because that's not what you wanted. Now you're afraid it's too late—that there's no hope. Well, you might be right! I don't think there is any hope for you and Dennis!"

"What are you saying?" she gasped. "What do you mean?"

"Well, the Dennis you knew—the Dennis who hurt you so bad—that Dennis is dead. He has now become a new creation, a new man, changed and made over by the power of God. And you can never have a real relationship with this new Dennis as long as you're still bitter about the bad things the old Dennis did to you—the involvements and relationships you feared so much, the shame and humiliation he brought upon your head. You see, he's changed now, but you haven't. And that conflict will destroy any chance the two of you have to make it together."

Anita was crying—great wracking sobs shaking her shoulders. I could see her from where I was listening on the phone in the next room. And I was crying too.

Tara and Marissa hugged Anita's legs, looking up at her tear-streaked face. "Mommy, Mommy, what's wrong? Why are you crying?" She couldn't even answer them for the sobs.

"Isn't there anything I can do?" she managed to choke out. "Is it just over?"

"Anita, the only answer is for you to die to the past and lay down all your pain, hurt, and cares at the feet of Jesus...and leave them there. And then, you've got to let Christ Jesus give you a new life and make you a new person. Only a new Anita can ever make it with the new Dennis. Are you willing to let God change you and give you a new life?"

"Yes! Oh, yes!" she cried. "I can't stand the way I've been living any longer."

Ray prayed the sinner's prayer with her, leading her phrase by phrase through her confession of sin and affirmation of faith in the Lord Jesus

Christ. Anita prayed with him, and somewhere during that prayer, her sobs changed from despair and desperation to the joyous cries of a newborn soul, born again into the family of God.

As soon as Ray said, "Amen," I let him know I was listening on the other phone. "Good," he said. "Dennis, the two of you have suffered some really deep hurts in the past. Go to Anita right now and tell her you're sorry for what you did to her in the past."

I stretched the phone cord as far as it would go so I could see Anita. "I'm so sorry for all I did. Please forgive me."

"I do," she said. "I'm sorry for what I did back to you. Forgive me." And then I forgave her, with gladness in my heart.

Ray then counseled us both a little bit about spending time in prayer, reading the Bible together, and getting into a Bible study so we could learn more about the Word of God.

Getting Out of Debt

Before we hung up, Anita brought up the problems we were facing. "Ray, what are we going to do? We owe about $2,000,000 in debts. The IRS says we owe them about $800,000. Dennis is just out of jail. It looks impossible."

"All things are possible if you will believe, Anita. In the natural, your situation is overwhelming. But I tell you, it's no problem! Hallelujah. Jesus is *Jehovah Jireh*—that means He's the God who will supply every need. Go to your Bible and underline this verse—Philippians 4:19. It says, *'And my God shall supply all your need according to His riches in glory by Christ Jesus'* (NKJV).

"No matter how impossible your condition may seem, God is the answer. Stand on the Word of God...confess the Word of God...believe the Word of God!"

Then Ray asked Anita and me to put our hands together on the stacks of bills on the desk and pray with him. "Dennis, the Bible says, '...*if two of you shall agree on earth as touching any thing that they shall ask, it shall be done for them of My Father which is in heaven*' (Matt. 18:19 KJV). Let's come into agreement right now that your finances are loosed and that poverty, lack, and debt are bound in the name of Jesus." Then Ray led us in praying to that effect.

"Listen to me now," he said. "What's bound in Heaven is now bound on earth. What's loosed in Heaven is now loosed on earth. What you need to do now is hang up your disco shoes and get yourself to work. You can have the faith of a mustard seed and speak to the mountain of your need—the Bible teaches that. But if you don't put your faith to work, it's dead."

"Ray, what work? I don't know what to do. I just got out of jail, and you're asking me to work out of over a million dollars worth of debt?"

"That's right, Dennis. God's not going to drop manna out of Heaven for you. You're going to have to put your hands to the plow and earn your living by the sweat of your brow. But I can tell you this—if you'll do what you can, God will bless you, and everything your hands touch will prosper!"

"Okay, Ray. I'll get busy."

"Anything else, Anita?"

"Yeah, but I don't want Dennis to listen to this." I took the hint, said good-bye, and got off the line. I found out later that Anita was concerned that my old friends and buddies would be calling to celebrate my early

Dennis & Anita being baptized

release and would end up dragging me back to the old life. Ray suggested that we change our phone number and start making some new Christian friends. He also said he'd send us some Christian books and tapes to help us get started studying the Word.

Our family started attending the Chatsworth Foursquare Church. The pastor, Carl Burns, counseled us and taught us the Word, and at the "New Beginners" class we learned the fundamentals of faith. We then started to associate with other Christians, who offered us fellowship and friendship. Hearing my daughters quote Bible verses, and being able to pray with my family made me feel like a real father at last. Finally, I was experiencing true family life, and it was a joy! We were on fire for God...as a family. We were even baptized together one Sunday by Pastor Burns. And as I came up out of the water, I actually heard church bells ringing!

Even before I was out of jail, the marketing program at Super Fitness was discontinued; and so, now I had to learn to exercise my faith and totally depend on the Lord to provide for my family.

I started bodybuilding workouts, hoping to schedule some exhibitions and seminars. And I met a fellow at our church who was also a bodybuilder. Bob Rossi was originally from Chicago, where he had been involved in selling cocaine and living life in the fast lane. Now he was a Christian and was enthusiastic about reading and studying the Bible and praying. I called him "Born-again Bob." He became a great friend, someone to help me grow and mature in my Christian faith. He also became my training partner and helped me get in competition shape again.

Meanwhile, Ray stayed in touch by phone, encouraging both Anita and me, offering good counsel, and praying with and for us. Without question, God used this godly man to save my life and help me begin the long road back from evil (see Job 8:7; Joel 2:25-26).

Getting All God Has for Us

Ray phoned one day and asked, "Dennis, have you been baptized in the Holy Spirit with the evidence of speaking in other tongues?"

"No, I haven't. I don't even understand it."

"Well, I think you need to come to Tulsa and receive the baptism. The Bible says you will receive power after the Holy Ghost comes upon you (see Acts 1:8). That's what you need—spiritual power."

"What if I arranged a plane ticket for you and set up a bodybuilding seminar at the health club where I work? They would pay you a fee. Would you come?"

"Are you kidding me, Ray? This is what I've been wanting to do! I'd have to see if I can get permission from my parole officer. I can't leave the state unless he says it's okay. But I'll talk to him. Pray that God gives me favor with the man."

After I got off the phone, I told Anita about the seminar, and that Ray said I needed to come to Tulsa to get baptized in the Holy Spirit with the evidence of speaking in other tongues. She was openly skeptical. "I don't know about this speaking in other tongues business," she said. "I don't think Catholics do that."

So, Anita tracked down an old friend of ours, Father Stephan Wagman, a former U.S. Army chaplain in Brooklyn who was now a parish priest in Fargo, North Dakota. She related part of our story to him and asked his opinion about the speaking in tongues issue.

"Well, all I can tell you, Anita, is that there is a strong Catholic charismatic movement that has started at Notre Dame, and Pope Paul has endorsed the movement. There are charismatic Catholic services all over the country, including southern California. If you're uncomfortable at the church you're attending, you might want to check out these meetings."

This seemed to allay Anita's concerns. She said, "If the Pope goes along with it, there must be something to it. Maybe you should go to Tulsa, Dennis. Let's get all that God has for us."

I went to see my probation officer at his office on Sherman Way in Van Nuys. He listened with interest as I told him my story, including my conversion experience. Then I told him I'd been invited to do a bodybuilding seminar at a health club in Tulsa that would pay me a fee of $1,000 and also include round-trip airfare.

"You show me a letter from the health club that confirms what you've told me, and I'll give you permission to go," he said. "You also have to show me the check when you get back."

With all the legalities out of the way, we made arrangements for me to go to Tulsa. Ray was excited about getting me to Rhema Bible Training Center. He had arranged for me to meet Kenneth Hagin and his son, and to attend some of their services at the school.

"I believe this is going to be a life-changing experience for you, Dennis," Ray told me. "My wife and I will meet you at the airport. Come expecting God to do something really special for you."

Chapter Sixteen

You Shall Receive Power

THEY looked like saints to me.

The minute I walked off the plane, I recognized Ray and walked directly over to him. He stood out from the crowd, and I could immediately sense the anointing of God on his life.

Not that he would not have recognized me. I'd been training hard for weeks, and was wearing my best jacket, Gucci shoes, a gold Rolex watch, and a gold chain with a gold-and-diamond-studded lion's head from Jeffrey's of Beverly Hills—all relics of a past that no longer mattered to me.

As we walked through the airport concourse toward the baggage claim area, Ray said, "Dennis, you're going to be staying with us tonight. We're renting a house not far from the Rhema campus in Broken Arrow, just east of Tulsa."

"That's great, just fine. I really do love and appreciate all you're doing for me."

"This is going to be a great weekend, Dennis," said Ray, putting his hand on my shoulder as we walked along. We're really blessed tonight. Ken Hagin, Jr. and his wife, Lynette, are taking us out to dinner. I've been telling them all about you. You'll really like them."

An hour later, the Hagins drove us to a very nice hotel dining room in south Tulsa for dinner. Ken Hagin, Jr. was a down-to-earth, fun-loving man who still talked with an east Texas drawl of his boyhood. His wife, Lynette, was a charming and gracious lady with a disarming smile. Like Ray and Lyndie, they made me feel at ease, as if we'd been friends for ages.

I was struck by the fact that both couples talked about God, the Bible, and spiritual things as comfortably and matter-of-factly as most people talk about the weather. Even though I had been going to church since I accepted the Lord, I'd never been around people like them who related, in a completely natural and unremarkable tone of voice, how God spoke to them and gave them guidance and direction.

After a while, I said, "Tell me more about this baptism in the Holy Spirit that Ray's been talking about. I'm not sure I understand its purpose or even what it is, especially the speaking in tongues part."

They proceeded to give me the scriptural foundation for the baptism experience, reading from the second chapter of Acts in the New Testament. The more they expounded, the greater the witness I felt inside me. I was hungry and thirsty for the fullness of the power that God had for me from on high.

"How can I receive this blessing?" I asked. "What do I have to do to get this?"

"Well, Dennis," drawled Ken, Jr., "my dad feels that the Lord wants him to pray for you. Many times when Dad prays for someone who is seeking the infilling, the Holy Ghost fills him almost immediately."

"I'm ready," I said. "This is what I've been needing. I want all God has to offer!"

On the way back to Ray's house, I said, "Ken, I'd also like to learn more about the healing ministry. Is there a special meeting or service being held that I could go to?"

"That must be God speaking to you, Dennis. There is a healing service at the school tonight, and Dad will be praying for the sick. We hadn't mentioned it to you, so you're really hearing from the Lord. Sure, we'll take you over there."

When we pulled into the parking lot, I noticed a van with a motorized lift. A woman in a wheelchair was being lowered from the van to the ground. I spoke to her and asked how she was doing. "Oh, wonderful," she said. "I'm getting healed tonight. I've got my faith out, and I'm going to be totally healed in Jesus' name."

"God bless you, sister," said Ray. "We'll be believing with you for a miracle!"

When we walked into the auditorium, I was amazed to see that there were thousands of people packed inside. I saw children with braces, men on crutches, ladies in wheelchairs. But from my front-row seat, the thing that caught my attention was the total involvement and sincerity of the crowd as they joined each other in singing, praising, and worshiping God. There were people of all shapes, sizes, ages, and colors, raising their hands, enthusiastically participating in the praise and worship service.

Ray kept pointing out people to me, even taking me over to shake hands with some individuals. "This is Dennis Tinerino," he'd tell them. "Oh, I'm glad to meet you, Dennis. We've been praying for you!" Ray had told me on the phone that he had hundreds of Rhema students praying with him, but I was amazed to see that so many of them had taken it seriously and were thrilled to know I was now a Christian.

God Wants to Heal You!

In a little while, Kenneth Hagin stood up and in a gentle, unassuming way, quietly began teaching about healing. He quoted verse after verse about faith and healing, stressing that the devil was out to kill, steal, and destroy, but Jesus came to give life more abundantly (see John 10:10). He said that it was God's will for people to be well, and he quoted Third John 2: *"Beloved, I wish above all things that thou mayest prosper and be in health, even as thy soul prospereth"* (KJV). He also quoted Mark 16:18 about laying hands on the sick to heal them.

I noticed right away that Brother Hagin was not trying to impress anybody. His tone of voice was almost conversational—like one friend talking to another. When he opened up his Bible, he read with sincerity and authority, yet he himself remained humble. As he taught, Brother Hagin kept stressing that Jesus was the Healer, not him. He quoted First Peter 2:24, illustrating that because Jesus died on the cross, we could now be healed by His stripes. Brother Hagin again emphasized that his role was to simply be a point of contact and to agree with people in faith. Utilizing stories from the Bible, he illustrated the healing ministry of Jesus, saying, "He healed people 2000 years ago, and He is still healing people today. He is the same, yesterday, today, and forever."

Then he called for all those who wanted prayer for healing to come forward. There was a tremendous response, with people of every description going toward the platform. I saw people going forward who looked completely normal, others who obviously were suffering from incurable diseases, many in great pain. As I watched, the lady I'd seen on the parking lot went by—someone was pushing her wheelchair to the front.

I closed my eyes and said, "Oh, God, please heal this lady."

Suddenly, I realized that Brother Hagin was already praying for people. He wasn't being dramatic or directing attention to each individual. He was just moving along the line of people, touching his hand to the forehead of each person. When he got closer to where I was sitting, I could hear him saying quietly, "In the name of Jesus...in the name of Jesus...in the name of Jesus."

Brother Hagin touched a woman who was standing almost directly in front of me. As soon as he touched her, she began speaking in tongues. I felt a powerful anointing emanating from her and realized that the Holy Spirit touching her was also the same presence I had felt in my car in Los Angeles when the Lord manifested His glory and Jesus spoke to me.

In a moment, I spotted the lady in the wheelchair at the edge of the aisle. Brother Hagin was moving in her direction. Under my breath I said again, "Oh, Lord, get that lady out of that wheelchair."

Brother Hagin stepped over to the wheelchair and put his hand on the lady's head. "In the name of Jesus, be healed!" he commanded.

The instant he said, "be healed," the woman's hands shot up and she screamed. Then she started trembling all over. In just a few seconds, her legs snapped out straight, then her feet hit the floor! In a flash, she was running down the aisle, shrieking as she went.

The lady's husband, who had pushed her wheelchair, just came unglued! He was crying and jumping for joy. "She was paralyzed and hasn't been able to walk in years!" he cried. "Thank You, Jesus. Thank You, Jesus. Thank God for this miracle!"

Brother Hagin just watched the woman go and chuckled. "Well, I guess you'd run too, if you'd been stuck in a wheelchair for years. Get out of her way and let her go."

People all across the auditorium were on their feet—hands lifted, crying, shouting, worshiping, and praising God. I had never seen any church service like it before in my life. I could sense the Holy Spirit moving on these people—healing, delivering, refreshing, meeting needs, and answering prayers.

I was weeping for joy and completely speechless, totally in awe of the miracles I was witnessing and overwhelmed by the tremendous presence of God in this place. Ray came over and prayed for me at the end of the service. He said, "Oh, Holy Spirit, I pray that You will finish the work you have started in Dennis' life. Use him, touch him, and bless him, I pray."

I didn't want to leave the meeting. I had never experienced such peace and contentment. The presence of God was so contagious that I wanted to sleep there! But because that wasn't an option, we went back to the house. I could hardly sleep that night for thinking about all I had seen. I remembered when I had been so critical of preachers and people who believe in the power of faith and prayer. I even mocked a woman named Kathryn Kuhlman who had been on television, denouncing her as a fool and a fake. Yet what I had seen in the Kenneth Hagin meeting wasn't at all what I'd always supposed healing services were like. What I witnessed and felt that night could never be denied! Everything that was said and done there was completely biblical. How could anyone argue with the transforming power of Jesus that was present in that auditorium?

———⟫●⟪———

The next morning, I conducted my bodybuilding seminar at the Century Health Club. There was a capacity turnout, and I was pleased to see the large crowd of bodybuilders who were in the Tulsa area. Many of them knew who I was, and said they had followed my career over the years.

Kenneth E. Hagen Sr., Dennis, and Kenneth Hagen Jr.

I gave a posing exhibition and demonstrated the training techniques for each muscle group in the body. Another part of the seminar was a question and answer segment. I really enjoyed sharing my years of experience and knowledge, which made me a champion, with people who wanted to improve their bodies.

When the seminar was over, I agreed to an interview with a newspaper reporter. In addition to boosting the local health club, I was given an opportunity to testify about how I'd recently been transformed, and how Jesus was really making a difference in my life. The reporter did a good job writing the story, and the photo that ran with the article attracted many readers. I was so excited to be doing what I loved again.

The manager of the health club was very pleased with the seminar and said he wanted me to come back soon. The success of this seminar gave me new confidence and confirmed that this was God's direction for my life.

Afterward, Ray and I grabbed a bite of lunch, then headed out to Rhema to meet with Brother Hagin.

At the meeting was Ken Jr., pastor of Rhema Church, Billye Brim, and a Rhema student named Mike Dalton. After a few minutes of visiting, Brother Hagin asked me to sit in a chair near his. Then he began reading to me from the Book of Acts, stopping to explain each part of the passage to me. He got very intense with his explanation, but he never raised the volume of his voice.

After the Bible lesson, he began explaining to me what it meant to receive the baptism of the Holy Spirit with the evidence of speaking in other tongues. He told me that it was God's plan for me to receive it, and that I would! He explained what was going to happen to me. He said that once I became filled with the Spirit, I would have spiritual power to overcome the enemy and live a victorious life. He also said the baptism would activate the gifts of the Spirit in my life and give me power to witness boldly and evangelize.

I was drinking in every utterance of this teaching, soaking up every word like a sponge. The more Brother Hagin talked, the more I wanted to be filled with the Spirit, and the greater my faith grew that I *would* receive it.

"I'm going to come over and lay my hands on you, Dennis. When I do, the power of the Holy Ghost is going to come on you, and you will speak in tongues as the Spirit gives utterance. Are you ready?"

Receiving the Baptism of the Holy Spirit

I simply nodded, too focused and intent on what was happening to speak. Brother Hagin stood up, and I raised my hands in expectation.

Somehow, I knew what he was going to say: "In the name of Jesus, receive the baptism of the Holy Spirit." He stretched out his hands, and I whispered, "Lord, I want all that You have for me." Then Brother Hagin said, "In the name of Jesus..."

Immediately, inwardly in my spirit, I saw the face of Jesus with a crown of thorns on His head, bloody and marred, reminiscent of the crucifixion scene from Mel Gibson's movie *The Passion of the Christ*. Then suddenly, a mighty, rushing power hit me in the back of the head! It was not violent, yet the force was so tremendous that my whole body flew five feet into the air and hurtled from one end of the room to the other. This surge of power swept through my body, shaking me like a rag doll; yet, I knew I would not be harmed.

Then I heard a strange voice singing. It was a song I'd never heard before, and the voice was worshiping and praising in another language. The song was joyful, refreshing and triumphant, with a spirit of celebration and full of the sounds of liberty and freedom. Then I heard this same voice speaking in this curious language, and somehow I understood what was being said. The voice was praising and thanking God, saying beautiful and wonderful things that simply could not be expressed in English or any other earthly language. It was miraculous, supernatural, divine!

I listened in fascination to the voice. How fluent it was! How expressive and full of joy! How strong and sure and confident it sounded. Then I noticed that the voice sounded familiar. There was a certain quality, a timbre that could not be disguised.

The voice was mine! The singer was me! The new language was coming out of my mouth! I was so excited and happy that I could hardly breathe. It suddenly dawned on me that I hadn't gotten the Holy Spirit—He had me! I could sense the distinct sensation of a mighty, gushing flow, pouring out of my belly, coming out of my spirit. It was literally uncontrollable! Out of my heart flowed "rivers of living water," just like it says in John 7:38.

I don't know how long I continued speaking in my new heavenly language, but I never did get tired. All I wanted to do was keep praising and crying out to God. Finally, Ken and Ray helped me up and led me outside. Although temperatures were below freezing, I started running all over the grounds of Rhema Bible Training Center, singing and speaking in other tongues, leaping and jumping for joy, and praising God as I sprinted across the campus and back.

My friends just stood there laughing at my joy and exuberance. "Man, the Holy Ghost sure got hold of him," they said. After a while they persuaded me to get in the car. Even then, I couldn't stop singing and praying in other tongues.

I had a wonderful evening of fellowship with Ray. Every now and then I'd break out into tongues again! I even stood up in bed most of the night, still praying in the Spirit, and when I finally laid down, I had a wonderful night's sleep, resting in the Holy Spirit.

The next day, Ray took me to the airport to fly back to California. I boarded the plane carrying two big shopping bags full of tapes and books—a complete two-year study course—a gift from Brother Hagin and Rhema. On the flight home, I spoke to numerous people about their need for Jesus, and led many of them to Christ. No one could shut me up about Jesus, not even the man on the plane who said I was an "unlikely looking preacher!"

As I left LAX, I felt compelled to stop at the World Gym before going home. Full of boldness from the indwelling of the Holy Ghost, I shared the glory, the wonder, and the majesty of Jesus with Arnold, Joe Gold, Franco, Lou Ferrigno, and other bodybuilding friends. Arnold said I had been "brainwashed" and had been spending too much time hanging out with ladies with big eyelashes and carrying tambourines. I replied that my mind had been filthy and needed to be washed. Furthermore, I told them that my sins were washed away by the blood of the Jesus at the cross of Calvary.

I continued to share God's love and plan of salvation with all who would listen. Many laughed and mocked me. Some said I wouldn't have fun anymore; others said I was using Jesus to get a new image. In spite of that, I continued to tell them how Jesus had changed my life, and that He wanted to change their lives too. They couldn't relate to the new Dennis and wanted the old Dennis back. But they didn't realize that the old Dennis was dead!

As they shouted that I sounded like a religious fanatic, and thought I was involved in a cult, I left the gym with a sad heart but a clear conscience. I lost many of my longtime worldly friends that day, but I had gained the Friend who would never leave me or forsake me.

When I got home, Anita was waiting for me at the door. Ray had already called to tell her what had happened to me. "Dennis is different," Ray declared. "He is filled with the Holy Spirit."

I showed her all the tapes, teaching books, and praise and worship music I'd brought back, then I explained as best I could what had happened. "I want to receive the Holy Spirit too," Anita exclaimed. "I want to have everything God has for me, just like you." I prayed with her for a while, but nothing seemed to happen.

Finally, I went to bed. Anita couldn't sleep, so she sat up reading, praying, and asking God to baptize her in the Holy Spirit. Sometime in the middle of the night, she felt led to turn on the TV. Kenneth Copeland's program was on, so she began listening to him teach. In the middle of his message, he turned to the camera and said, "Go ahead. There's somebody out there—a lady who wants to be baptized in the

Holy Spirit. Go ahead and receive it right now. Receive ye the Holy Ghost!"

Anita's hands flew up, and she began praising God. She started in English, and then a heavenly language began to express itself. She was praising God and speaking in tongues at the top of her lungs in the middle of the night!

Although I had been sound asleep, I began to hear someone praying in the Holy Spirit. At first, I thought it was a dream, but when I sat up, I could hear that it was Anita singing and worshiping God in her heavenly language. I began praising God with her, and we had ourselves a camp meeting right there in our bedroom. Eventually, our daughters, Tara and Marissa, awakened by the joyful noise, ran in and jumped up on the bed. All four of us were worshiping and thanking God. It was wonderful.

Seeing my family all together in the middle of the night happily praising God and loving each other was such a tremendous sight. I realized that God truly had restored us and given us a new chance at life. Yet I sensed that this was just the beginning of what the Lord wanted to do for us.

Chapter Seventeen

MY NEW LIFE IN CHRIST

I was now starting a new life in Christ as a born-again believer, and for me to be fruitful and give glory to my heavenly Father, I had to base my life and my endeavors on the Word of God. In God's Word, salvation means preservation, deliverance, prosperity, and health. And I was determined to have all of them evident in my life. In Romans 12:1-2, God says, *"I beseech you therefore,e brethren, by the mercies of God, that ye present your bodies a living sacrifice, holy, acceptable unto God, which is your reasonable service. And be not conformed to this world: but be ye transformed by the renewing of your mind, that ye may prove what is that good, and acceptable. and perfect, will of God"* (KJV).God was to now have first place in every area of my life.

My new priorities and commitments were to meditate and study God's Word, pray in my heavenly language, and to praise and worship Him with a thankful heart. *"But seek first the kingdom of God and His righteousness, and all these things shall be added to you"* (Matt. 6:33 NKJV). Christ became my first love. Some days I would weep and cry as I soaked in His presence. I was on an *adventure in faith*, pursuing the Lord in His Holy Bible. I felt like a treasure hunter who was seeking nuggets of pure gold, yet I was seeking something more valuable—*eternal truth*. I was after the *heart of God*. In fact, I was more desperate to have *intimate fellowship* with Him than a drowning man seeking a breath of air to save his life. I would pray and sing in the Spirit, sometimes for hours, and then I would wait to hear God's voice speak to me. I thank God that I learned about the third person of the Trinity—God the Holy Spirit. The Holy Spirit would give me insight and wisdom regarding business matters and managing my family. In Proverbs 3:5-6, God says, "*Trust in the Lord with all your heart, and lean not on your own understanding; in all your ways acknowledge Him, and He shall direct your paths*" (NKJV).

Before my conversion, I manipulated relationships and forced situations to be successful. It was all about me, myself, and I. Now I realized that in God's Kingdom, it was "*not by might nor by power, but by My Spirit, says the Lord of hosts*" (Zech. 4:6b NKJV). As I walked with Him and obeyed His Word, He would build my life and house. Psalm 127:1a says, "*Unless the Lord builds the house, they labor in vain who build it*" (NKJV). Faith in Christ is the only sure foundation. In the parable of the wise and foolish builders, Jesus compared an obedient person's life to a house built upon a rock. When the storms came (sickness, disappointments, heartbreak, poverty, betrayal, etc.), the house survived because its foundation was solid. I was coming to the understanding that there is nothing more solid on which we can build our lives than Jesus' teachings.

> *Therefore everyone who hears these words of Mine and puts them into practice is like a wise man who built his house on the rock. The rain came down, the streams rose, the winds blew and beat against that house; yet it did not fall, because it had its foundation on the **rock**. But everyone who hears these words of Mine and does not put them into practice is like a foolish man who built his house on **sand**. The rain came down, the streams rose, and the winds blew and beat against that house, and it fell with a great crash* (Matthew 7:24-27 NIV, emphasis added).

When I read those verses, I finally understood why my life was in the condition it was in. I had based my foundation on the "shifting sands" of worldly possessions, accomplishments, and shallow relationships. No wonder everything collapsed.

While in prayer one night, God gave me a vision for my life. It was to have a dual purpose. I was to pursue business in the health and fitness arena and prepare for full-time Christian ministry. The Lord promised me that as I developed godly character and integrity and was a man of my word, He would *reverse every curse*; He would turn my *defeats into triumphs*; every *test into a testimony*; and my *debts into surplus*. My *mess* would become a *message*, and the message would become my *ministry*!

I knew that every day would be a F.A.I.T.H. (Fantastic Adventures In Trusting Him) walk. I also knew that I would face many battles from the devil's camp now that I had enlisted in God's army. My first battle was to make restitution to creditors. I had to clean up what I had messed up. The Lord showed me if you leave a mess, it follows you, and simply creates a new mess. I had to shed old habits and soul ties to be the man of integrity and responsibility that Jesus wanted me to be. God showed me that many people cannot fulfill their destiny until they eliminate the sinful relationships and issues in their lives—only then will they have joy and peace.

The moment I made the godly commitment to repay all my debts, the devil counter-attacked. My ex-partner's lawyers told me that they would not help pay any debt, and that I should declare Chapter 13 (Bankruptcy) because I was more than two million dollars in debt. The temptation was very appealing. They told me, "When you get off this religious high, call us. There is plenty of fast money to be made."

As I was driving home after my meeting with them, I began praying in the Holy Spirit. God spoke to me and brought these verses to my heart. First Corinthians 10:13 says, *"No temptation has seized you except what is* *common to man. And God is faithful; He will not let you be tempted beyond what you can bear. But **when you are tempted**, He will also provide a way out so that you **can stand up under it**"* (NIV, emphasis added). He said, *"Pay all your creditors. Be above reproach."* Romans 13:8a says, *"Owe no one anything except to love one another"* (NKJV).

Any doubts I may have had disappeared when I came home. Anita had been in prayer and she confirmed what the Lord told me. This was not an easy task. Paying these debts would take as much discipline and sacrifice as training for Mr. Olympia. The difference was, it was spiritual—not physical. As a baby Christian, I had faith and trust in a miracle-working God, and every day I stood on these Scriptures: *"...Have faith in God. For assuredly, I say to you, whosoever says to this mountain, 'Be removed and be cast into the sea,' and does not doubt in his heart, but believes that those things he says will be done, he will have whatever he says"* (Mark 11:22-23 NKJV).

I would speak to my million-dollar mountain of debt. This was part of the mess I had to clean up. Mark 11:24 says, *"Therefore I say to you, whatever things you ask when you pray, <u>believe</u> that you receive them, and you will have them"* (NKJV). Believe it and receive it; doubt it and do without it. God engraved this truth in my heart. I saw myself out of debt. In Hebrews 11:1, God says, *"Now faith is the substance* [the assurance, the confirmation, the title deed] *of things* [we] *hoped for, the evidence of things not seen"* (NKJV).

God also showed me that I must ask the people I had hurt to forgive me as well as make restitution to them. I immediately did the first and made arrangements for the latter. He also told me to forgive everyone who had hurt me and to "forget about it!" *"And whenever you stand praying, if you have anything against anyone, forgive him, that your Father in heaven may also forgive you your trespasses"* (Mark 11:25). My heart jumped inside me when I read Second Corinthians 6:14. In this verse God says, *"Do not be unequally yoked together with unbelievers* [In other words, do not make mismatched alliances with them or come under a different yoke with them, inconsistent with your faith]. *For what fellowship has righteousness with lawlessness? And what communion has light with darkness?"* (NKJV). Through this Scripture, the Holy Spirit was telling me to sever all past business dealings and relationships. That part was easy—as soon as word spread that I found the Lord, all my former so-called friends and associates deserted me. We had nothing in common anymore.

Through the eyes of faith, I saw myself at the debt-free finish line! I realized I had to remove the rearview mirrors from my life and focus on my tomorrows through the windshield of faith. Luke 9:62 says, *"No one, having put his hand to the plow, and looking back* [to the things behind], *is fit for the kingdom of God"* (NKJV). I was, however, able to look back and see what God had done. Now I could look ahead and see what He has begun. God gave me faith but I also had H.O.P.E.—which I describe as **H**eaven's **O**pportunities **P**ersonified **E**very day.

Anita and I spent almost every available moment reading and studying the Bible, Christian books on discipling, and listening to Brother Hagin's tapes, in addition to taking New Beginners' classes at our local church. Christian music filled our home 24/7. Ray McCauley continued to call to encourage us and pray with us. On several occasions, I phoned Ken Hagin, Jr. to seek advice and counsel. These fellows were great, discipling us, constantly assuring us that God knew where we were and would never leave us. "Keep standing on the Word," Ray counseled. "The answer is on the way."

After praying together one day, I said to my wife, "Anita, we've been trusting God, but we haven't seen any results yet."

"Well, Dennis, maybe this is the time to tell you..."

"Tell me what?"

"Well, I've got a little bit of money put away."

"How much money do you have, Anita?"

"Oh, probably about $17,000."

"Where in the world did you get it?"

"Well, some nights you'd come home completely stoned or drunk, and you'd be just about passed out on the bed. I would look at the pile of money you would put on the dresser and figured you probably didn't even know how much was there. So, I'd take a couple of hundred dollars—sometimes a little more—and stash it away. Over a period of time, I saved more than $17,000—and I've still got it!"

"Thank God, Anita. Now I wish you'd taken *all* the money from my pockets! But this will keep us going until our prayers for the future have been answered."

We took enough money to pay the household utility bills and buy groceries. Then we made a payment to my attorney, who was doing more legal work for me.

One of the lawsuits filed against me as president of the speaker manufacturing company went to court and was decided in favor of the plaintiff, John Vidal, the engineer and my former partner and stockholder. Even though the company's assets were frozen, his lawyer found some legal loophole, and John received a $50,000 judgment against me personally.

I met with John and his attorney after the final hearing. "The court says I owe you $50,000, John. Despite the fact that you were stealing from the company and doing other things that were wrong, I feel I should pay you what the court has ordered. I've become a Christian and I'm living for God now, and I want to make everything right from my past. I'm supposed to forgive, and *forget about it*! Please forgive me if I hurt or wronged you in any way. The only way I can pay you is if we set up a reasonable monthly payment schedule."

John and his lawyer talked it over for a few minutes, and then agreed to let me pay off the judgment at the rate of $1,000 per month, as I could. In addition, thanks to Anita's special savings, I was able to pay three months' payments at that time.

When we left court that day, I forgave John as I had asked him to forgive me. I walked away with peace and joy in my heart, because I knew I was being obedient to Jesus...and I made every payment promptly until the debt was paid.

Another Answer to Prayer

A few days later, I received a call from Doug Beaver, my bodybuilding friend who had helped me get the job selling Super Fitness products through the work-furlough program. "Dennis, you have some experience doing sales work—telephoning gyms and clubs—right?"

"Yeah, that's right."

"Well, I was wondering if you thought you could sell some used Nautilus equipment." At that time, Nautilus was selling about a million dollars a day in their new lines of exercise equipment. Naturally, I agreed. In fact, I got on the phone that very day, calling every health club operator and gym manager I could think of—in California and several other cities as well. In less than a week, I had sold enough used gym equipment over the phone to earn about $15,000 in sales commissions. The guy I was selling for was thrilled to death—and I was elated!

Not only had I earned a good chunk of money to apply against my debts, I also came up with the idea to start a gym equipment business. Ray

McCauley worked part-time in a health club and had a lot of friends and contacts, and frequently heard of people who were in the market for equipment. He started passing those leads to me.

I knew various individuals in California who manufactured gym equipment. They handled weights and plates, racks, benches, pulley systems—all kinds of gear. Moreover, they could make about anything a person might need. I worked out arrangements with a couple of manufacturers to buy at direct-dealer rates.

Then I got Pete Samra, my old friend and fellow believer, to help develop and call on leads. Pete, Ray, and I split the proceeds on all our sales. None of us got rich, but over a period of several months, we developed a consistent income.

Most importantly, God began to fulfill His promise to prosper me in the health and exercise business. I was on my way to achieving my goal of owning my own business!

Jumping Over Hurdles

The next big step was dealing with the Internal Revenue Service's claim that I owed them the preposterous amount of $800,000, a figure they had based on my ex-partner's outlandish boasts about how much money we were making, and his claims that we were going to take over the *Hollywood Free Press* and use it to control all the escort service and massage parlor operations on the West Coast. They had also conjured up inflated sales projections for our other companies and used those estimates to assess other taxes.

My attorney asked an accountant to assemble all the books and records for our various businesses, and then they met with the IRS agents who started wading through them, page by page. Of course, it soon became readily apparent that our legitimate businesses were long on potential and short on sales! Fortunately, Richard Caballero had always been insistent that we scrupulously pay taxes on all our escort service income. Because of the way our bookings were handled, we had very good records to support our case.

Over a period of several weeks, the IRS's claims were disproved and set aside. There were some discrepancies with payroll tax withholdings within two of the corporations, but Caballero and the accountant were able to demonstrate that the problems were computation errors, not fraud. The end result? The amount of $800,000 worth of tax claims was reduced to about $60,000. Caballero insisted that the IRS apply the value of the personal assets they had seized against the remaining taxes owed and accept payments on the balance.

Talk about a victory celebration! Words simply cannot describe the relief that came from having that burden removed from our shoulders.

Yet even though the IRS's claims and charges were largely based on rumor and hearsay, the agents still remained hostile and antagonistic to the end, never once apologizing or expressing regret for the persecution and hardship they had created for my family. Nevertheless, we forgave them—God insisted.

Anita and I were very much aware that God was at work in our finances. We simply applied the rules He had given us, and our needs were being met, with money coming in from completely unexpected sources. Anita conscientiously took ten percent—the tithe—from every dollar we received, and gave it to God—*first*—before we spent a penny on anything else. We could see that the promises of Malachi 3:10-11 were being fulfilled before our very eyes. God was "pouring out a blessing" in our lives and "rebuking the devourer" as we put His Word to the test.

Back in "The Biz"

Just as Ray McCauley had prophesied, the Lord did start prospering everything I put my hands to, and God began to shift circumstances in our lives.

For example, although I'd done several TV commercials back in New York, I hadn't been able to get a major assignment after I'd moved to California. God changed that! One day I auditioned for a Toyota spot, along with a hundred other bodybuilders. Later, the agency selected three guys for the shoot—Kalman Scalzak, a Mr. Olympia competitor, veteran champion Bill Grant, and me.

The commercial showed the three of us picking up a subcompact car, the Corolla, and bouncing it on its tires to show that it was a sturdy vehicle. Appearing in the commercial was very profitable—I received a lump sum, plus a small residual payment each time the commercial aired. Not only was it profitable, but the Toyota commercial also helped open the door for other work.

I signed with a new agent, and right away, I started booking assignments to pose in various bodybuilding shoots for various ad agencies as well as appearing in bodybuilding exhibitions and seminars. These events paid well, and God made sure I was in demand and working steadily.

In addition to the bodybuilding events, I began receiving invitations to share my testimony at Christian businessmen's groups, in prisons, high schools, church groups, and on radio and TV; and my photos and bodybuilding titles were used to attract unsaved people to the meetings. I was thrilled when individuals began making decisions for Christ after I gave my testimony. As the Holy Spirit prompted me to share some of the things I had been reading and studying at home, I found that I was incorporating even more spiritual truths in my testimony. I had never dreamed the Lord could work through me to minister to others. I prayed with many bodybuilders, athletes, actors, and entertainers; and many of them became strong Christians. This was another fulfillment of what the Lord had shown me about my new life in Christ.

An Invitation to Africa

Several months later, in the summer of 1979, Ray McCauley phoned from South Africa. Following his graduation from Rhema Bible Training Center, he had gone home to Johannesburg and started Rhema Bible Church and Training Center.

After beginning with about 20 people in his home, Ray then moved his congregation to a large auditorium, and the church continued to multiply. Within one year, more than a thousand people were crowding into the theater building for each service, hungry for the powerful gospel messages Ray preached and the bold faith he exhibited in ministering to people's needs for healing and deliverance. Miracles followed. He lifted a torch of love and reconciliation in the midst of a nation torn by the racial turmoil of apartheid. Ray ultimately built a successful Bible school as part of his 27,000-member church and helped establish multitudes of new churches in Africa and around the world.

Ray's letter invited Anita and me to come to South Africa to minister. He promised to set up a series of 20 bodybuilding exhibitions and seminars for me across the nation and also wanted me to share my testimony at evangelistic meetings he was planning, as well as assist him with the meetings.

Ray suggested that we plan to spend about a month with him and his wife, saying he would send us our plane tickets, and we could then pay

Miracle healing in Nigeria crusade

him back from the money we earned while we were there. We were very excited about the opportunity that the Lord had arranged for us.

First, I went to talk with my probation officer. To my surprise, he was very cooperative. "You've been doing swell, Dennis. You've never failed to check in with me, and everything you have told me has always checked out. Get me a letter confirming the plans, and I'll approve your leaving the country for a month."

Anita worked it out for one of my cousins and her husband to house-sit for us and care for Tara, and we took our youngest daughter, Marissa, to New York to stay with my grandparents. After a good visit with our relatives there, we caught a plane to South Africa.

What a great reunion we had with Ray and Lyndie! We stayed in their home in Randburg, along with an assistant pastor and his wife whom Ray had recently brought in to help with the church.

Raising the Dead!

A few days after we arrived, a workman was up on the roof repairing a leak. Suddenly, there was a terrible commotion, a frightened cry...then deathly silence. We rushed out to find the crumpled body of the workman on the ground. He had either slipped and fallen or had a heart attack and collapsed.

I ran over and examined him, and discovered that he wasn't breathing. There was no pulse or heartbeat. "Ray, I think this man is dead. You'd better call the police."

Instead, Ray and a few other people gathered around and began to pray. Anita and I looked on in astonishment for a few moments, and then joined in the intercession, asking God to restore life to this man.

I kept checking the man's pulse, watching for any signs of life. He was cold and clammy. Then, Ray laid hands on his forehead, commanded the spirit of death to release the man, and spoke healing to his body. As we watched in amazement, his body jerked, his chest heaved, and he began breathing again. His eyelids fluttered, and suddenly I felt his pulse come back!

"My God, Ray, he's coming back to life. He was dead! Now he's alive. Hallelujah, it's a miracle—he's alive!" I was so in awe, I was almost speechless!

"Yes, Dennis, the Lord has restored his life. God has raised him up from the dead!"

I'd never witnessed such a miracle before—and I knew Jesus had taken my faith and belief to a new level.

My first bodybuilding seminar was scheduled just a couple of days after we arrived. We barely had time to do a little sightseeing around Johannesburg, then we were off to Capetown, one of the most beautiful places I've ever visited. While there, Anita and I were also able to visit Cable Mountain and spend a little time at a private beach resort. At the seminar, I met Ash Kallos, a fascinating bodybuilder who had been Mr. South Africa several years before, and our host in Capetown.

I was amazed at how much interest there was in health and fitness in South Africa. Usually, more than a hundred people purchased tickets to my seminars, many of whom were very knowledgeable about bodybuilding and seriously interested in developing personal workout programs.

An absolute highlight of the trip was becoming personally acquainted with the legendary Reg Park, who had been one of my boyhood heroes. Ray had scheduled me to appear at a posing exhibition at the Mr. South Africa competition and to conduct a seminar at his health club. Afterward, I had dinner with Reg and his family. As we ate, I told him about how I had met him in New York when I was just a teenager. He had come to the Mid-City Health Club where I was working out, and the gym owner, Tom Minichiello, had arranged for me to visit his hotel room and meet his wife, son Jon-Jon, and a cousin. Reg had signed an autograph and posed for a photo with me—which I kept as a treasure for years. To this day, Anita and I continue to cherish our friendship with the Park family.

Anita and I were able to travel to most of South Africa's major cities—Soweto, Pretoria, Durban, in addition to Johannesburg and Capetown. During this time, I had the privilege of meeting several outstanding athletes who had been Mr. South Africa in various international competitions. The people of South Africa were warm and friendly—so genuine and down-to-earth, and I developed a real love and appreciation for all South Africans.

In addition to the seminars and exhibitions, Ray had booked me to be interviewed by reporters for several different newspapers and had arranged for me to be a guest on top radio and TV talk shows. After talking about my career and my bodybuilding achievements and titles, eventually the interviewer would ask what I was doing in South Africa. I was then able to use this as an opportunity to share my testimony and talk about the life-changing power of the gospel. We also found some time to indulge in the incredible delights of South African food!

Ministry With Miracle-Working Power!

In between my activities, I went with Ray on ministry trips to outlying areas. It was decided that our wives would remain behind because of the possible dangers. While traveling with him, I learned so much, watching him teach, preach, and witness. Even though I had seen him in action while he was in the United States, I was even more amazed at his boldness and fire. In addition, I was thrilled to see definite signs and wonders following his preaching.

One day we flew to Pretoria, near the border of Zimbabwe, and while there, Ray and I visited the military front and ministered to the soldiers who were patrolling the border, inviting them to come to a meeting that night.

When we arrived at the auditorium for the service, it was packed and jammed with people, including many soldiers. I posed and performed a few strongman feats, then shared my testimony. Ray preached a simple Gospel message and gave an invitation for those who wanted to give their lives to Christ. It seemed like the whole congregation responded! At least nine hundred soldiers accepted the Lord as their Savior in that one service.

On another occasion, we were ministering in a black township called Soweto. The building was not large, but it was jammed with three or four hundred people. I shared my testimony, and then Ray preached about God's divine healing power. Suddenly, he stopped and said, "There is a person here who has one leg that is much shorter than the other. In addition, he has a deformed back. I believe God wants to heal you tonight."

From the back of the building—from someone completely out of sight—came a sobbing cry, "Oh, yes, sir. That's my boy you're talking about. My son has been crippled and deformed all his life."

"Bring him up here," Ray said. Through the crowd came a heartbreaking sight—a young man, thin and weak, with a crude wooden shoe strapped to a withered leg. His shoulders were frail and rounded, and there was a definite hump on his back.

Ray had the youngster sit down in a chair, and then he knelt, unbuckled the built-up shoe, and tossed it on the ground.

"Father, in the name of Jesus, I ask that You make this foot normal." Before our eyes, the foot and leg began to grow, in both length and circumference. There was no pushing or pulling or manipulation. The leg simply grew some four inches longer!

Then Ray reached out, touched the boy's back, and prayed again. Instantly, there was a cracking and popping that could be heard all over the crowded building, and immediately the boy's shoulders uncurled like the petals on a flower and became wide and straight. The back straightened as if the boy had risen up from touching his toes!

The boy raised his hands above his head. Tears streamed down his face. He turned to his father, who was screaming, "My boy is healed! He is well! He is made whole!"

Pandemonium spread across that room—everyone was talking, pointing, laughing, and shouting! There was no doubt in anyone's mind that we had just witnessed a miracle of God's healing power. Waves of excitement swept back and forth across the room as people spoke to each other about what they had just witnessed.

Finally, Ray calmed down the crowd and said, "If you need to be healed in your body, raise your hands right now." A sea of hands went up. "Jesus, heal these people right now, I pray."

After Ray prayed for a few minutes, I opened my eyes. To my amazement, there appeared to be a cloud—like a light fog or mist—gently swirling about the room. I wasn't the only one who noticed it—people all over the place were caught up in wonder and amazement.

"Don't worry, people, that's the *Shekina*—the glory of God. It is a symbol of His presence with us. The Lord is in our midst!" As Ray said that, people started falling down on the floor...until almost no one remained standing!

Individuals were healed of all kinds of maladies. Tumors and growths disappeared. Deaf ears opened. Blind eyes regained their sight. Pain vanished. Walking canes were discarded. Arthritic joints loosened up. People were stretching, moving, touching their physical disabilities—and finding their problems gone.

After a while, Ray instructed the crowd to give God thanks and praise for what He had done, and in response, there was a tremendous outpouring of praise and joy. I found myself on my feet, arms upraised, tears streaming down my cheeks. I could sense the presence and power of God all around.

Nobody wanted to move—no one was in a hurry to leave. People just kept worshiping and praising the Lord. Moreover, there was a wonderful sense of peace and tranquility everywhere. After perhaps an hour, the cloud lifted...but the revival continued into the streets, where people were leaping, dancing, shouting, praising God—just like it happened in Acts 3:8—and testifying about the miracles God had performed.

Later, as Ray and I returned to his home, I was still awed and amazed at what I had witnessed. "Ray...?" I began.

"Dennis," he interrupted, "everywhere I go I *expect* God to move. I *expect* it!" He paused for a moment, and then gently added, "You're excited, huh?"

"Yes, very!"

"Keep that excitement."

And I did. Night after night, as we moved across that nation, I saw the supernatural manifestation and powerful moving of the Spirit of God. Thousands of people received the gift of salvation. One of the most amazing and moving events that I was a part of took place in the very conservative, restrained atmosphere of a prestigious Catholic boy's school.

In front of approximately 500 students, I started the meeting with some strongman feats, then posing, and followed up by doing push-ups with some of the largest students on my back. Then I spoke, sharing my testimony.

After Ray preached a very short, simple message, he gave a salvation invitation; and in response, the entire audience stood up and prayed the sinner's prayer with him. Then Ray said, "Raise your hands if you want to receive God's blessing of the baptism of the Holy Spirit." Every hand in the room went up! "All right," said Ray. "Get ready to receive the breath of God's Spirit." He then began to breathe on the crowd of students.

Everywhere I looked, I saw tearstained faces looking up to Heaven, hands reaching out expectantly.

In a moment or two, a sound began to hum and swell, like instruments tuning up in a concert hall. Then a flood of glorious music began—a thrilling anthem sung in many languages—as if God Himself were directing a spiritual orchestra. Then, starting as a gentle breeze that quickly grew in intensity, the mighty wind of God started at one edge of the room and moved all the way across. As the breath of God touched them, the students toppled over onto the floor as though they were a line of dominoes set on end.

Some of the boys began to rise, while others remained on the floor, but all were praising God and giving glory to His holy name in other tongues. As we left that evening, the students and the priests couldn't stop talking about what had happened to them; they knew their lives would never be the same. We left that school knowing that every student and priest were "on fire" for God.

Time to Go Home

A month flew by before we knew it, and during that time, Anita and I had the opportunity to visit a few tourist spots—diamond and gold mines, game preserves, and some of the most scenic and beautiful areas in the world. Even while we were sightseeing, there always seemed to be an opportunity to witness and minister, including three miles down in a gold mine where I ministered to African laborers, and on a safari to visit the Zulu tribes. We met wealthy, famous, and influential people—and some of the poorest, humblest people on the face of the earth. Our hearts were filled with joy to be part of the great evangelistic services reaching the masses, and to be able to witness to individual bodybuilders and lead them to Christ. It was the trip of a lifetime for both of us.

When we were getting ready to board our flight to London, Ray said to us, "Now, Anita...Dennis, expect God to bless you for what you've done. You've given a month of your lives to help minister to others. You've taken time to unselfishly serve the Lord when you could have been working and earning money to pay your debts. So, go home now and expect God to reward and bless you beyond your wildest imagination."

Anita and I were literally in a state of euphoria as we flew to London and traveled on to Wales, where we were booked for bodybuilding exhibitions and seminars. We were also humbled and grateful for what we had seen God do in Africa and for what He had done in our lives. I will always be indebted to Ray and Lyndie for allowing the Lord to use them to teach us so much and to impart His anointing and vision into our lives. We had been to the mountaintop—God showed us His glory! He had given us firsthand experience on how to rule and reign with the new impartation He had given us for His service.

And we couldn't wait to share it all with everyone we met. The trumpet had sounded in our hearts, and we were ready to proclaim His Word and believe in God for mighty signs and wonders, which would come by the power of the Spirit of the Lord (see Rom. 15:19).

When we arrived in Wales, we were met by my good friend, Mr. Universe-Mr. Wales Paul Grant and his wife, Christine. The weather was freezing cold, but it didn't bother Anita and me—we were "Sontanned"—on fire for God—and basking in His glory. As I posed and conducted a bodybuilding seminar at the Mr. Wales contest, the excitement and enthusiasm of the sold-out crowd gave us encouragement and confirmation that the Lord was guiding me and shaping me as I pressed toward fulfilling my vision.

My engagement in Wales was a financial success where we sold out our stock of t-shirts, pictures, and books. On a spiritual level, however, we suffered disappointment. When I shared about my newfound faith and spoke of the miracles I had seen in Africa, I was grieved in my spirit, for there was little or no interest in the things of God. People's hearts seemed as cold as the weather! Nevertheless, we had planted the seed, and as we prayed for the people there, Anita and I became even closer.

Anticipation was high as we headed back to New York at the end of our trip. We couldn't wait to see Tara, Anita's parents, and be reunited with our baby, Marissa. Soon, we were all together again in California. Both Tara and Marissa seemed to have grown so much in the short time we were away. We were full of joy, because Anita and I were expecting the divine intervention of God—we *expected* miracles and just couldn't wait for the prophetic words spoken by Ray McCauley to come to pass. We knew that God would take care of us.

Exceedingly and Abundantly

Late one night, after we'd read, studied, and prayed almost all day long, Anita said, "Dennis, I don't know how God is going to do it, but I feel like something miraculous is going to happen. Let's get some rest and just wait for God to work."

So, we went to bed and slept like babies. We knew we had done all we could do on our own. Now, we simply stood on the promises of God.

In the next day's mail, there was a royalty check from the Coronet paper towel commercial I had done years before in New York. The amount of the payment was more than I had received for doing the spot in the first place!

This money, in addition to the money from our trip to Africa was enough to make payments on the attorney bills and fund the payoff deals my attorney had worked out. Of course, first came the tithe. In addition, we were able to bless others and restock our shirt and book business. *And* there was enough left over to pay the mortgage and utility bills and stock up on groceries. What a wonderful feeling! More importantly, Anita and I were learning to walk by faith.

As we were praising and thanking God for coming through for us once again, Anita remembered what Ray McCauley had told us when we left South Africa. "We shouldn't be surprised, Dennis. Ray said we should be expecting God to bless us. But I never dreamed this could happen!"

When we added everything up, we had paid off well over a hundred thousand dollars of debt. Everything Ray had told us was coming true.

Chapter Eighteen

PARTNERS, PROBLEMS, PERSISTENCE, AND PRAYER

EVEN though I was on fire for the Lord, I still had dreams and the desire for competition within me, and I knew it was not yet time for me to give up this quest. I knew that in order to walk in my vision, I would have to return to competition for a short time and a season (see Eccl. 3:1) because God had blessed me with the talent for bodybuilding. The Lord also showed me that I would use the media to reach the masses.

I went to my lifelong friend Bill Pearl for counsel. He advised, "You're in great shape, Dennis, and you haven't reached your prime yet. With consistent training, you could win all the current competitions." Bill also pointed out that my popularity would help me sell many fitness products, which was a natural line of work for a bodybuilding champion to pursue.

Having already won every major bodybuilding contest in the world, including Mr. Universe, my sights were now set on the Mr. Olympia competition, the super bowl of professional bodybuilding events. Winning this one would be the crowning achievement of my career.

I must also admit that I simply loved competing—every aspect of it. Competing brought me joy and acceptance, and the energy and enthusiasm of the crowd took my total being to a place of indescribable splendor. Propelling my body to a point beyond known human potential, it released creative forces that enabled me to strive for physical perfection, setting a new standard for others who were to follow. Most importantly, competing and posing were now a way for me to display my God-given talent and give glory to the Lord for what He had done in my life.

Into the Snake Pit

Preparing for the 1980 Mr. Olympia contest would be my primary focus for the year, but there was another exciting development occupying my attention. Before I'd gone to spend a month with the McCauleys in South Africa, Bill Pearl had introduced me to someone he thought I should meet. Tom Moran was a wealthy and successful businessman who lived in Pacific Palisades. "Tom is a great businessman," Bill told me, "and he loves to work out with weights. Maybe you guys could be training partners at the gym. You could help him with his weight training, and he might give you some tips on developing your business."

During the next few months, I became well-acquainted with Tom. He told me that he had grown up in a Christian home and that his mom and dad were always praying for him and urging him to attend church. I sensed that Tom didn't have a strong personal relationship with the Lord, so I shared my testimony with him, and invited him and his girlfriend to go to church with Anita and me.

Tom was a very wealthy, successful businessman and entrepreneur, and as our friendship developed, I eventually shared my vision with him. God had given me the vision of manufacturing and marketing my own line of professional, state-of-the-art gym and cardio equipment, as well as related fitness products. With my professional reputation in the industry, I could do promotional appearances at grand openings and other events, in addition to conducting seminars for gyms and studios that bought our equipment. I had also written and published training booklets explaining my methods and philosophy of exercise. While in prayer, the Lord showed me that during the next ten years, thousands of gyms would be opening and need our equipment. This would put us at the crest of the fitness boom. It would also be a great way to increase finances *and* reach people with my Christian testimony.

Tom thought this kind of business could be tremendously successful. And we felt that with his sales and business experience and my professional expertise, we could create and market a superior product. After weeks of talking and planning, we were ready to put together a fifty-fifty partnership in a new fitness company.

"Unequally Yoked"

I called Ray McCauley in South Africa to seek his advice about our new venture. "Well, Dennis, the idea for the company sounds great. But the most important thing you have to be sure of is Tom Moran's spiritual condition. Is he sold out to Jesus one hundred percent? Don't get "yoked up" with an unbeliever—it will cause you grief. The Bible asks, "*Can two walk together, unless they are agreed?*" (Amos 3:3 NKJV).

Anita was also concerned and skeptical about getting involved in a partnership with Tom. "I don't know, Dennis. He's single and we're married. He's not really walking with the Lord, and we're totally dependent upon God. Is this relationship going to help him or hurt you? Will it destroy your testimony? Let's pray and be sure about this."

In the end, I decided to go ahead with the new project. I don't know if the promising potential of business success overcame my spiritual concerns or if I convinced myself that I would be able to influence Tom for the Lord. In either case, we launched the new company with high hopes.

The business started off great. We found a small company to take my design ideas and manufacture a full line of equipment. Using no advertising at first—just my contacts and leads—we started selling gym equipment "hand over fist"! In the first year, we had more than a million dollars in sales, including the outfitting of the first ten Gold's Gyms!

When I made appearances for the business, I also tried to schedule a speaking engagement or find the opportunity to share my testimony at an area church, school, prison, or civic organization. My schedule was full of meetings and appearances from early to late every day, but I found it exhilarating and fulfilling.

At the same time, my income had increased dramatically. Anita and I were able to live comfortably and still make substantial payments on our remaining indebtedness. Also, Tom loaned me a black Mercedes convertible to drive, and I frankly enjoyed tooling around town in that sleek, sporty automobile. Maybe that touch of the "good life" caused me to overlook some warning signs that all was not well.

Tom Moran was a hardworking, hard-charging, in-your-face, don't-take-no-for-an-answer type of guy. With Tom, what you saw was what you got. That's the way he handled business—and the way he lived his life.

But his bluntness and lack of tact caused him continual problems in personal relationships. He also lived a *Playboy* lifestyle—partying and womanizing all the time. And when he got in trouble, I got a call. I'd drop whatever I was doing and go counsel and pray with the guy. Sometimes he was vindictive, other times remorseful, or so depressed that he was almost suicidal.

One time, I got a call at three o'clock in the morning. "I need help, Dennis. I'm down here at the office—I just can't sleep. Can you come help me?"

"What are you doing?" Anita demanded. "Are you this guy's baby-sitter? He's got too many personal problems."

When I talked the situation over with Ray McCauley, he immediately went back to the basics. "Is Tom in the Word, Dennis? Is he praying?"

"Well," I said, "that's the one problem. He goes to church from time to time, but he's basically just a lukewarm Christian."

"Dennis, you know he's never going to find help until he surrenders his entire life to God. Be careful and don't get dragged down with him. If he's not willing to change, sooner or later you're going to have a decision to make!"

I knew Ray was right, but I didn't want to face up to it. Tom was such a great organizer and a skilled business manager. I was certain that together we could build the business into a real financial success.

And soon, we had a large complex in Westwood that housed our retail store, showroom, and offices. Business was good. I was busy on a whirlwind tour of promotional exhibitions for gyms buying our equipment, and speaking and ministering in two or three places in every city I visited. Before I knew it, the months had flown by, and it was time to prepare for the 1980 Mr. Olympia competition.

Despite all the demands on my time—family, church, office, and travel—I somehow managed to step up my training time, getting ready for the Mr. Olympia competition. My schedule was as full as one person could handle, and the erratic behavior of Tom Moran was becoming more and more of a problem. Like the Mother Goose character, when Tom was good, he was very, very good; but when he was bad, he was horrid.

By now, warning flags were flying everywhere I looked. The evidence of his ungodly practices and mentally unstable behavior could not be ignored. Yet our business was doing incredibly well, and I was still able to hold things together and protect Tom from himself most of the time.

At the same time, winning the Mr. Olympia title had become an obsession with me. Mr. Olympia was the only major bodybuilding contest I hadn't won; so, it became my one major goal, overriding all other interests or plans for my life.

Mr. Universe International!

Still rationalizing Tom's behavior, I put off making any decision or taking any action. By this time, I was well into the training process for the 1980 Mr. Universe International competition, which was to be in Caracas, Venezuela. I thought that if I could win this event, it might be the launching pad to prepare me for what promised to be the most significant Mr. Olympia competition ever, which would take place later in the year at the famous Sydney Opera House in Sydney, Australia. I was watching my diet and working out three hours a day. Tom worked out with me some days, and my good friend Doug Beaver directed my intense training.

During the building and conditioning process, Doug had me doing four reps of one-half squats with 675 pounds—the most I ever tried lifting. I was using 150-pound dumbbells to do incline bench presses—and my body was responding awesomely. I weighed 230 pounds and had less than five-percent body fat. I was in peak form.

The trip to South America was fantastic, and I thoroughly enjoyed every part of the competition. I felt good, looked good, and knew I was doing well at each stage of the contest against the top bodybuilders in the world. Being on stage, posing under the television lights for an enthusiastic and appreciative crowd was a great thrill. Easily winning my class in the pre-judging and finals boosted my confidence still more. Even so, when I was proclaimed the overall winner of the 1980 Mr. Universe International, I was elated beyond words! I met many international celebrities and important politicians...and made money as the winner!

I couldn't wait to get back home and back to training—this time, for the Mr. Olympia competition. Finally, everything was going my way, and I was on the brink of reaching my final goals in bodybuilding.

Every morning, I went to Joe Gold's World Gym in Santa Monica—*the* place to train. A veritable "Who's Who" in bodybuilding worked out there, and there was an electric tension in the air—an excitement that helped keep me pumped up mentally and motivated to do my best. And while I was there, Joe Weider helped me with my posing routine to bring it to a new level of perfection.

Because I was feeling and looking extremely good, I asked two leg-endary bodybuilding photographers, John Balik and Harry Langdon, to work on some photo shoots of my posing routines—the photographs were simply incredible. These shots were later used in *Muscle and Fitness* magazine and in my training manuals. Posing for the camera was some-thing I enjoyed. Not only was it a way to track my progress as a body-builder, but it was also a means to release my artistic expression.

The photos showed that I was obviously in tip-top shape, at the absolute pinnacle of my physical development. And I knew I was ready for the upcoming Mr. Olympia competition.

And then, my intention after winning the Mr. Olympia title was to retire. If I could just reach this last goal, I could step down and never look back!

Meanwhile, as I was training, I often saw Arnold Schwarzenegger working out—there were rumors that he was thinking of entering the competition and making a comeback. Most of us chose to ignore the

Dennis winning 1981-1982 Pro-Am Mr. Universe.

rumors because Arnold hadn't officially acknowledged them. And when he started training, he didn't look very good at all. He'd been out of competition for five years—since 1975 when he'd made the *Pumping Iron* movie. He just didn't have the definition and highly-conditioned massive bulk for which he was famous.

When someone mentioned that he might enter the Mr. Olympia contest, I said, "I don't care if he does compete. I'm good enough this year to beat anybody, no matter who it is. I can even chop down the 'Austrian Oak.'"

As usual, Anita was the first to know intuitively what was going on. "Dennis, you know I love you and that I'll do anything for you. But I have to tell you that I sense you're wasting your time with this competition."

"How can you say that? I'm Mr. Universe for the third time. I'm in the best shape of my life! My arms are more than 21-1/2 inches around. My posing routine is the best I've ever had. I'm ready to take on anybody!"

"Yeah, you look great! You've really got it—there's no doubt about that. But can't you see that the guys at the top don't want you to win? You don't fit in. By now you should know that the whole bodybuilding profession is a snake pit! We live a godly life now, with biblical values. Why do you want to put yourself back into the strife, confusion, jealousy, and anger that inevitably goes along with bodybuilding? We both know that the best man doesn't always win. Stick to your overall goal of being a businessman selling fitness equipment and a man of God using the media to share your witness. This competition is a distraction!"

The Snake Pit

I wanted to win the Mr. Olympia title so badly that I chose to ignore Anita's warning, and I kept on training. And when the entry deadline for the competition passed and Schwarzenegger did not submit his entry, I relaxed a little. All my friends, peers, and even the highly experienced Joe Weider agreed that this should be my year!

At the airport, I kissed Anita and my girls good-bye. We prayed for God's divine protection and favor, and I boarded the plane with many of the other contestants. Tom Moran would be at the contest with me but had flown to Australia on a different flight. On the plane, I sat beside Joe Gold. I was serene, confident, and at peace with God and man.

Upon arriving in Sydney, I checked into my room, took a shower, and had an early night. The next morning I went to the opening meeting of prejudging and saw that Arnold was there. When all the contestants arrived, he stood up and announced that he had decided to compete in the 1980 Mr. Olympia competition.

All the contestants were suddenly up in arms! We all knew that Arnold had not submitted his entry by the deadline. Mike Mentzer declared, "Well, according to the IFBB rules, you can't compete!"

Arnold loudly disagreed, and soon things developed into a full-scale argument.

I stepped between the two and pushed them apart. "Come on, guys— we don't need this! There has to be a better way to settle this. Maybe we should just let him compete. Let's all go out and let the best man win."

The others stared in disbelief that I was breaking up the argument, which was about to turn into a fight. The old Dennis would have let them rumble. The new Dennis became a peacemaker.

About that time, Ben Weider came into the room and informed everyone that the IFBB and the panel of judges had decided to accept Arnold's late entry. Therefore, he was an officially authorized contestant. The other entrants grumbled and complained, but there wasn't anything anybody could do about it. Weider said we could file an official protest later if we saw misconduct.

But even more telling was the presence of a Hollywood film crew—four or five cameras, a control booth, directors, floor managers—the place looked like a movie set. This was in addition to the regular news cameras and the ESPN video crew that was taping the competition for their cable network coverage. We soon learned that the crew was shooting a new Arnold Schwarzenegger movie titled *The Comeback*.

When Arnold made his first prejudging appearance onstage, posing to his familiar music theme from *Exodus*, he received a standing ovation. The Austrian Oak was back! And the audience was thrilled to see his first appearance in five years.

It appeared to me that in comparison with several of the other contenders, Arnold's physique did not stand out above the rest. And after the prejudging, I continued to hear grumbling among the competitors.

The evening performance went off smoothly, and I was impressed with the high caliber of the competitors. At the end of my posing routine, I received a standing ovation. It was obvious that I was one of the crowd favorites, and their response confirmed my belief that I was to be the next Mr. Olympia.

Nevertheless, the scoring for Arnold kept mounting higher and higher. And the crowd seemed bewildered to hear the judges continue to ask Arnold to step up and be considered in comparative poses with several obviously superior bodybuilders—including me.

"The Worst Competition Ever Seen"

Finally, the master of ceremonies announced the top ten winners. Although by then, I was well aware of what was happening, I was still bewildered and frustrated when I placed sixth. Former Mr. Olympia winner, Frank Zane, placed third, and in second place was a longtime friend of mine from New York, Chris Dickerson. Chris later went on to become Mr. Olympia.

Silence filled the auditorium—then came the announcement. "Ladies and Gentlemen, the winner of the 1980 Mr. Olympia competition is...ARNOLD SCHWARZENEGGER!"

After a split second of silence, the whole audience stood and booed! Broken beer bottles started flying everywhere! It was a mob scene on the verge of being out of control. Not only the audience was upset at the outcome, but the contestants were furious over the placing as well, particularly the choice of winner. I was grieved in my spirit and hurt beyond words that the sport I loved was discredited and shamed in front of the world.

The ESPN crew was beside themselves. "How are we going to show this competition on TV? Nobody is going to believe this!"

I shook my head and thought, *What am I doing here?* I went to my private locker room, undressed, and took a long, hot shower. *This is a joke,* I told myself, *except that it really isn't one bit funny.* I started praying, and I felt the presence of the Holy Spirit as He spoke, "The contest is over. You've done your best; now enter My rest."

Immediately, the passage in Galatians 5:16-21 became alive. Verse 16 says, *"This I say then, Walk in the Spirit, and ye shall not fulfill the lust of the flesh"* (KJV). Then I heard First Corinthians 13:1-13, which teaches that faith works by love.

"Pray for everyone involved in the contest," the Holy Spirit said. "Look back and see what I have done. Now look ahead and see what I've begun." Hallelujah!

When I slipped out the back door to return to my room, a guy tapped me on the shoulder and said, "Hey, Dennis, would you mind taking a picture with a couple of kids?" That's the last thing in the world I wanted to do, but as I looked down into the wistful faces of those little guys, I couldn't say no. So, I got down and posed with them for a couple of shots and talked with them one-on-one. Afterward, the father said, "Thanks, Dennis. I just want to tell you—for what it's worth—you should have won!"

I thanked the man, then caught a cab back to my hotel. I had to walk through a throng of newsmen and reporters just to get to my suite so I could call Anita. When I told her the results, she simply said, "Don't let the outcome discourage you, Dennis. You're God's champion."

My business partner, Tom Moran, was more upset than anybody. Following the contest, he'd gone for a long drive with Joe Weider and his wife, Betty. Even Joe was upset about the outcome, feeling that such an obvious "fix" was bad for the sport. Tom was so angry that he waited around the hotel lobby and picked an argument with Arnold and Franco Colombu when they finally returned after their celebration party.

Tom was still fuming the next day when he left to go back home. I stayed in Australia for another week to do some posing exhibitions and photo shoots with Bill Pearl. Then we flew home together.

About a week later, Tom and I went over to World Gym in Santa Monica to work out, where several of the Mr. Olympia contestants were looking at the photos Arty Zeller had taken in Sydney. These pictures and the articles in several bodybuilding magazines reinforced the fact that I was in the best physical shape of my life, and many spoke out, saying they believed I should have won. It was great to hear them say that, but nothing could change the outcome.

Deep in my heart I still felt that I had a shot at winning the Mr. Olympia contest—the only major competition I hadn't won. But Tom was insistent that I quit—that I didn't need bodybuilding any longer.

So he threw a "retirement" party for me in a fancy restaurant and invited several people who worked for our company and some of the big names at the equipment show. "From now on, Dennis is going to concentrate on business. Watch out for us now!" he declared.

I went along with the "retirement" because I had no arguments against most of the points Tom was making about the sport of bodybuilding. I realized that my time probably would be better spent focusing on the business. After all, I still had to finish paying off my old debts.

So, I let Tom talk me into "retiring"—at least for a while. Maybe the Holy Spirit was prompting me to try a new way of living.

Moving On

At first it was simple—it was time to rest my body from my grueling contest training. In fact, my whole body ached from head to toe. Besides, I realized I had been unfair to my wife and daughters. Everything our family did revolved around Dennis—my training, my business, my diet, my competitions. Bodybuilding had taken so much energy and discipline that, along with my work responsibilities, there was no time left for anyone else. Like every other "big-time" bodybuilder, at times I'd neglected my family because I had gotten caught up in the ego trip that is part of the sport.

During the hours that Anita and I spent praying and studying the Bible together, I began to realize that my priorities were not right. This was the time to spend *quality* time with my family—and to get refreshed and refueled in God's presence. The Lord emphasized that I needed to "shift gears." This was not an easy task, because the Mr. Olympia contest was hot news. Yet I focused in on my family, my business, and preparation for ministry.

The Mr. Olympia contest in Australia had opened my eyes to the harsh reality of the dark side of bodybuilding. I realized there was a great deal of evil in physique contests. Furthermore, I had *no* confidence in the fairness of the judges, or their decisions. Although it was difficult for me to accept, from this point on, contests had to become a tool for me to publicize my business endeavors. More importantly, contests were to be a platform for sharing my faith.

Instead of getting caught up in the strife that the Mr. Olympia contest produced, I had to rest in the Lord. Besides, I wasn't the only contestant who felt betrayed and frustrated; just about every major competitor in bodybuilding was now part of a newly formed "Bodybuilders Union." Their main objectives were fair judges, larger prize monies, and contractual agreements for product endorsements.

I was in total agreement with all the union objectives, but the Lord revealed that I was to remain apart from the union, because its efforts would be fruitless. In the Spirit, I saw that there was a devilish spider's web woven around the sport, while the bodybuilders were simply puppets on a string, being manipulated by promoters and the businesses that thrived on the sport. If the athletes wouldn't cooperate, their articles, ads, and posters would not appear in magazines, and they would be excluded from the contest and exhibition circuit, ultimately stopping them from making a living in the sport.

These were the dark clouds that hung over the sport of bodybuilding. So, in addition to keeping my business going, improving my relationship with my wife and family, and paying off old debts, I now felt I had to overcome corruption in the bodybuilding arena.

The Hat's Back in the Ring

In spite of my so-called "retirement," I really wasn't committed to giving up bodybuilding *completely*. I never stopped going to the gym and working out regularly, yet I just wasn't ready to turn loose. But only after a few months went by, I knew I wanted to compete again. So, I entered the 1981 Mr. Olympia competition—but this time I had no illusions about winning.

If the biggest muscle in the body is the heart, God had given me the "heart of a champion" and made me a warrior! I continued training and doubled my intensity with the purpose of empowering my life while improving upon my physique—which had been at a lifetime peak the year before. Because of my love for the sport, and the desire God had placed upon my heart, I was actually able to exceed last year's best—not for me, but for the glory of God.

When it was time to go to Columbus, Ohio, the site of the 1981 competition, I was ready. The Lord had shown me that this year's competition was to be a repeat of the 1980 Mr. Olympia competition, but He also told me that I was to later compete in the 1981 Mr. Universe contest. Where I had encountered defeat last year, I would walk in victory!

As Anita had told me the year before, I just wasn't part of the Mr. Olympia inner circle, and I would never be allowed to win. I knew that. But I also knew that the top competitors in the Mr. Olympia event automatically qualified for the 1981 IFBB pro-am Mr. Universe competition, which was to be held in Australia later that year. So, I participated.

The Mr. Olympia competition went just as I expected. All kinds of strife and bitterness went on behind the scenes. The new union had targeted the 1981 competition as a time to protest, and staged a general strike, urging all bodybuilders to boycott the event and not participate. I

stayed out of the battle and tried not to get caught up in the animosity. I just concentrated on doing a good job of posing and competing.

I was included in the top ten, which meant I was automatically qualified to compete for Mr. Universe. Just like the year before, my placing was not popular—as evidenced by the boos of the 5,000 spectators. Tom Platts was third, Frank Zane was second, and Schwarzenegger's perennial buddy, Franco Columbu, was the winner. He was named champion, despite being painfully out of shape, still not recovered from a serious injury he'd suffered some months before in a strongman competition.

The audience hated the decision and began chanting, "Fixed! Fixed!" Once again, bodybuilding took a blow. Instead of being upset with my low placing, however, I felt compassion for all the other bodybuilders—renowned champions—who had spent years of their lives sacrificing, training, and taking dangerous drugs and anabolic steroids in pursuit of a title that most of them would never win. I realized at that moment that my Christian walk now controlled my destiny and identity—not bodybuilding!

After the Mr. Olympia competition, I was eager to go back to Australia for the 1981 Mr. Universe contest. To me, training was not an ordeal but a labor of love. My body responded completely to every training technique, and all my muscle groups peaked out at exactly the right time for the show.

The competition in Sydney was intense. This group of Mr. Universe contestants were of the highest caliber, and for the first time in many years, I felt that this competition was different. The competitors were friendly and everybody seemed to be happy. There was camaraderie among the competitors that reminded me of my earlier competitions.

By the end of the prejudging, I was behind by about one point. One of the judges said, "If you want to win this, Dennis, you're going to have to give it everything you've got; you're going to have to go all out. It's down to you and Walker."

Between the prejudging and the evening finals, two of the other contestants, Steve Davis and Don Ross, came over to me and said, "You're going to win the Mr. Universe contest tonight, Dennis. We'd like to help you pump up and get ready!" Steve owned a World Gym in Van Nuys, California, and I had trained at his place a few times. He was really a tremendous encouragement and help to me that afternoon. He took me through my whole routine, offered a few suggestions, and helped me stay motivated to go out and do my best.

Every section of the competition was exciting and exhilarating. This was bodybuilding at its best!

My Final Title Victory

I felt that my performance in the final posing competition was the best of my life. The judges kept calling me out to pose beside various competitors, and I felt strong and confident each time. I just *knew* I was going to win—and I did! The master of ceremonies called off the names of the top ten contestants. Roger Walker, the local favorite, was second. And then the thrilling announcement: "Tonight's winner is...DENNIS TINERINO, MR. UNIVERSE FOR 1981!"

In a bit of irony, Arnold Schwarzenegger presented the winner's trophy to me. "Well, Dennis," he smiled, "I guess not *all* the results in Australia are bad decisions."

"All I know, Arnold, is that this is the *right* decision!" I replied, acknowledging the thunderous ovation of the crowd. Winning is always great, but this was an especially sweet victory.

After the awards ceremony, another of the judges came over to me and said, "Dennis, you were the best man this year. It was close between you and Roger Walker, but I chose you." I thanked the man for his support and started to walk away.

"Wait a minute, Dennis. You may not remember this, but I came to you right after the Mr. Olympia contest last year and asked if you'd have your picture taken with some kids—one of them was my son."

"Yes, of course, I remember. And you told me that you felt I should have won that competition."

"Yes, that's right. Well, once in a while justice is served, you see. I hope this victory helps make up a little for last year's disappointment."

As it often happens in life, an exhilarating victory is followed by a huge letdown. That letdown was the next phase of the Grand Prix bodybuilding competition circuit. These contests had not been promoted properly, and as a result, there was no prize money for the competitors. Instead, the assistant promoter suggested that we stage an exhibition and split the gate with him. That way, we could make *some* money as well as prevent a riot by the fans gathered to see a competition.

We reluctantly agreed, but I immediately demanded my purse for winning the Mr. Universe title. I learned that the promoter had my money, and he was "somewhere in Australia." My internalized anger propelled me through the exhibitions, and I fervently prayed that the Lord would somehow right this wrong. Therefore, it was not by coincidence that I should run into the promoter at the Sydney airport just a few days later. He apologized profusely, and promised I would have my money soon. I had no choice but to believe in God's promise and trust this man. My faith was rewarded one month later, when my Mr. Universe winnings arrived in the mail.

Before I left Australia, I had the privilege to be a part of another series of posing exhibitions with Bill Pearl, who was celebrating his 51st birthday. He was still in superb condition, and looked absolutely spectacular. It was obvious that the Australians respected and appreciated him, and I felt honored to be a part of one of his last series of exhibitions.

Decisions

I had many decisions to make regarding my career, family, and newfound faith. In prayer, the Holy Spirit gave me these verses from Jeremiah

29:11-13, "*'For I know the plans I have for you,' declares the Lord, 'plans to prosper you and not to harm you, plans to give you hope and a future. Then you will call upon Me, and come and pray to Me, and I will listen to you. You will seek Me and find Me when you seek Me with all your heart*" (NIV).

First Corinthians 6:19-20 also came to my mind: "*Do you not know that your body is a temple of the Holy Spirit, who is in you, whom you have received from God? You are not your own; you were bought at a price. Therefore honor God with your body*" (NIV).

Those words really struck a chord with me. Even though I had spent most of my life training and eating right, there was still the chemical issue—which definitely did not honor God. Although I was never a big steroid user, when I started to compete on the pro circuit, I began taking steroids three months before each upcoming show. I took them under medical supervision, while the rest of the time, I was drug-free.

I knew by the Spirit of God that it was time to leave the sport I loved so much. I had given my spirit, soul, and body to the sport, but God wanted me to be free from the bondages of bodybuilding—narcissism, pride, ego, vanity, self-gratification, and *steroids*. The Holy Spirit convicted me very strongly that I should no longer use them or encourage their use in any way—and that was that!

In terms of steroid use, the sport of bodybuilding is one hundred times worse than it was when I competed. Today's bodybuilders have become so dependent on chemicals that it is really out-and-out warfare! Both male and female competitors spend tens of thousands of dollars just to prepare for an *exhibition*! Unfortunately, steroids are readily available, and in addition to building muscle tissue, they unleash a variety of dangerous side effects on the body, mind, and spirit. In addition, these drugs are emotionally and physically addictive. I am sad to say that I have personally known about a dozen bodybuilders who became trapped in the world of steroids and other muscle enhancing drugs, and ultimately paid with their lives.

I thank God that over the years, I've been successful in helping many bodybuilders get off steroids and replacing them with valuable supplements. I am also grateful that unlike many bodybuilders, who become bitter and cynical when they leave the competitive circuit, the Lord gave me the grace to leave the sport without animosity. He set me free to move on.

Changing Seasons

Although my success in bodybuilding brought joy and fulfillment, there were hidden issues that began to surface. First, God was ending my season in bodybuilding competition and preparing me for full-time ministry; the next Mr. Olympia contest was to be my final curtain call. Secondly, the Lord showed me that my season of business partnership was to end. This was a major blow, because I considered this business to not only be my way out of debt, but my new career in the area of health and fitness.

Although Tom's family and I tried our best to keep him strong in his faith and encouraged him in his walk with Jesus, Tom constantly yielded to temptation. He brought ungodly unions into our business, and even bragged about his escapades and sins of the flesh.

As my ministry grew, I reached out to Tom, but he refused to repent and be delivered from his bondages. As Tom's spiritual indifference worsened, his personal problems began overshadowing his strong business abilities. I later learned that Tom had gotten involved with drugs, which drastically affected his moods and ability to reason.

In addition, we were encountering some serious business problems. The company that was manufacturing our gym equipment had started selling their own brand of equipment, which was a slightly altered copy of my design. When we had started working with them, the firm was working out of a shop the size of a one-car garage, but with our company's success, they had also grown and expanded into a major manufacturing operation. Now, by providing their own line of equipment similar to my design and cutting prices, they were unfairly competing with us.

The solution seemed obvious! We needed to find a new fabricator for our equipment and to cut all ties with the other company. I sought the Lord for direction in this decision as I did with all decisions. But Tom couldn't come to a decision. Because of his drug use, he was afraid to take any action at all.

One morning, as I was praying in the spirit on my way to the office, the Holy Spirit told me that I needed to go to Tom's other office, the headquarters for his other business in downtown Los Angeles. When I stepped off the elevator and walked into the front office, Tom's secretary said, "Oh, thank goodness, you're here! There's something wrong with Tommy. He's not acting right. I'm really worried!"

I was ready to break the door down, when I finally persuaded Tom to let me in. He was terribly distraught. He had managed to get an outside window open and was staring down at the street. "Everything's such a mess, Dennis. The best thing for everybody is for me to just jump and get it all over with!"

"No, Tom, you don't mean that. God loves you. He's bigger than any problems you might have. Nothing is worth taking your life over. Trust the Lord to help you. Turn your life over to Him." Gradually, by talking and praying, I was able to settle him down.

Obedience

Unfortunately, Tom never fully surrendered his life to Christ. As he continued to seesaw in his spiritual life, his personal crises continued to get worse...and more frequent. And I could see that the situation was going downhill—fast.

As I was praying about this situation one day, I became aware that the Lord was speaking to me. "Dennis, it's time for you to move on."

"But, Lord, I'm trying to help Tom. And I've worked hard in this business. What will I do for income if I just walk away? I'm still more than $100,000 in debt."

"You need to turn everything over to Me," came the reply. "Tom is entangled in a web, and he's just using you as a crutch. And as far as your personal needs are concerned, by now you should know not to seek provisions, but the Provider!"

I knew in my heart that the Lord was right. I had become "unequally yoked" with Tom—just as Ray McCauley had warned me. I could not compromise my Christian values—not even in an effort to reach Tom. The Lord assured me that I had done everything possible to help Tom, and his problems were not just affecting our business, but my family life as well. So a day or two later, I went over to end my partnership with Tom. The meeting didn't go well. Finally, I said, "Tommy, you're not listening to me. Can't you see that your life is messed up? You've got to change. I can't help you anymore."

"Well, I don't need you, Dennis. I don't need anybody! I'm just going to work it out by myself. I'm sorry I ever got involved with you in the first place."

"Well, Tom, I'll just turn my stock over to you and leave. Obviously, we're not in agreement anymore."

"Okay, what do you want?"

"Nothing, really. I'll just take the paintings I have on the wall in my office and the boxes of my bodybuilding books." In less than an hour, I had all of my personal belongings moved out of the office.

I walked away from a business that had the potential to become part of a multibillion-dollar company. I walked away from a guaranteed monthly salary. I didn't fully understand why I was doing what I was doing, but I was absolutely convinced that I was obeying the voice of God.

I drove home and related to Anita what had happened.

"What are we going to do, Dennis?"

"I really don't know. All we can do is just trust God. We don't have anyone else to turn to."

Chapter Nineteen

GOD WILL MAKE A WAY

DURING the year or so that I had been in the gym equipment business, my secretary had handled all my bookings and arrangements. Now, Anita resumed this responsibility. Without a regular income, staying busy with exhibitions and seminars was more important than ever. A weekend event, involving several appearances, usually was worth between $1,500 and $3,000 in fees, plus expenses.

There was an advantage to having Anita as my agent again. She often was able to schedule me to minister on Sundays in areas where I was conducting bodybuilding events. And as a committed Christian, she was able to communicate better with churches and organizations that wanted me to share my testimony and minister.

On the other hand, going from a comfortable salary to no guaranteed income at all was a jolt. Although Anita and I worked hard to keep me busy, it wasn't easy. Sometimes weeks would go by with nothing happening—no seminars, no exhibitions, no income. Meanwhile, our regular living expenses did not stop, nor did our monthly payments on an assortment of notes and payout agreements on my past debt.

Meanwhile, we kept praying, believing, and trusting God. We attended disciple classes and worship services and stayed involved in our church fellowship. We also read books by great faith ministers to build us up and maintain our optimism. Still, it was a real test of faith—a real trial. Eventually, our financial condition became so bad that we faced foreclosure on our house.

The pressure was becoming unbearable. One day, Anita told me that we had no food in the house, and no money to buy even a gallon of milk or loaf of bread for the children. Stressed out and in agony, seeing my family in need, I snapped at her. "What do you expect me to do about it?"

She snapped back. Before we knew what was happening, we were in a bitter, heated argument, and the kids ran into the kitchen to see what was happening. Thankfully, I realized that we couldn't let ourselves lose control in front of them. "I'm leaving for a little while—until we can both settle down a little," I said, heading out the back door toward the car. Marissa, our five year old, came running out after me. "I'll go with you, Daddy! Okay?"

"Yeah, sure. Come on."

I drove aimlessly for a while, not knowing where I was headed, and I prayed as I drove along, asking God to help me meet the needs of my family. I also prayed for direction and wisdom about what I should be doing to continue to pay off my debts and earn a stable income. Not even knowing what I should ask for, I let the Holy Spirit pray through me, and sensed a strong spirit of intercession at work on my behalf.

Eventually, I found myself pulling into a little shopping center where there was a fitness equipment store. I knew the owner and decided to go in and talk with him for a while.

When we got out of the car, Marissa ran over and picked up a scrap of paper lying on the parking lot. Then she began jumping and screaming in excitement. "Look, Daddy, look! I found some money! It's a hundred-dollar bill! Can we keep it?"

She brought me the greenback and it was, indeed, a hundred-dollar bill, crisp and new. I looked around the nearly deserted parking lot. There wasn't a soul in sight. There was absolutely no way to find the person who had lost the money.

I proceeded inside the store and talked with my friend for a few minutes. In response to his question, I told him that I was "currently in between projects," and that things were pretty slow at the moment. "Well," he said, "if you ever decide you want to build yourself another line of gym equipment, I know just the people to help you get it going. Contact this guy," he said, handing me a business card.

I barely glanced at the card. "Thanks a lot," I said, slipping it into my pocket.

As Marissa and I got back in the car, suddenly I was keenly aware of the presence of the Lord. *Dennis, you just prayed in the Spirit and asked for certain things. Here is your answer. Take the hundred dollars and give it to your wife. Call the person your friend referred you to, and you will begin receiving the answer to your prayers.*

Anita met me at the door. "I'm so sorry I fussed with you, honey. Forgive me. I know God is in control of our lives. We've just got to keep on believing and have faith to get us through these challenging times."

I apologized to her as well, and then told her the amazing thing that had happened. "I'll put back ten dollars for the tithe, Dennis. Then the girls and I are going shopping. God is so good to provide us with the money to get the food we need for this week!"

God Is at Work!

After Anita left with the girls, I took advantage of the solitude to pray, give thanks, and to continue seeking the Lord's guidance. As I waited in His presence, two Scriptures came to my mind. The apostle Paul's advice to the Philippians stood out to me—"*...in every thing by prayer and supplication with thanksgiving let your requests be made known unto God. And the peace of God, which passeth all understanding, shall keep your hearts and minds through Christ Jesus*" (Phil. 4:6-7 KJV). At that moment, Anita and I certainly needed the peace of God! We needed our hearts and minds to be kept through the Lord's power.

Then a great promise from Isaiah burst into my mind! "*When the enemy shall come in like a flood, the Spirit of the Lord shall lift up a standard against him*" (Isa. 59:19b KJV). Anita and I both felt overwhelmed by our needs and the oppression of the enemy. What an encouragement to remember that when this happens, God will lift up a standard—a flag of victory—to overcome the enemy!

As I meditated on these Scriptures, I walked over to the bookshelf and pulled out a book. It was entitled, *Living in Divine Prosperity* by Jerry Savelle. I flipped it open and started reading. To my utter amazement, the page I opened to contained the same two Bible verses that had just come to my mind—and the author's comments confirmed my exact thoughts!

I realized that God was already at work. *Wait a minute—this means we're coming through this thing! The devil has thrown his last shot. If you stand, you'll see victory! The house may be in foreclosure, but we're not going to lose our home. The devil is not going to take anything away from me, rip off my family, or cause us to be defeated. For everything the devil has stolen, God will pay us back sevenfold! He will make a way where there doesn't seem to be a way. Something **good** is about to happen!* (see Prov. 6:30-31).

About an hour later, while I was still prayerfully meditating, the phone rang. "Dennis, this is Wayne Lassiter from Oklahoma City. I called you several months back about having you appear on my TV show on TBN and give your testimony. Do you remember?"

"Yes, I remember. It's good to hear from you again."

"Well, Dennis, I hope you understand what I'm about to say. As I was praying today, God told me you were having a need, a money problem right now. He told me to call and tell you that I'm sending some money in the mail."

"Praise God, Wayne. I do have some big needs right now. Thank you for responding to the leading of the Spirit."

"Listen, I still want you to come to Oklahoma City. You and your wife can both come. You'll be on the program with me, and I'll get you lined up to speak in a church I know. The people will enjoy your ministry, and I believe they'll be a blessing to you." We picked a date, and he said he was sending two plane tickets!

When Anita arrived home, she was thrilled to learn about what was happening. We both sensed that we were seeing a real spiritual breakthrough. The Provider we had sought so faithfully was making provision for all our needs!

The next day, I phoned George Arsenault, whose business card was in my pocket. I spoke with him about manufacturing a new line of gym equipment, and he invited me to come see his factory. He was very interested in what I wanted to do. I showed him pictures of my earlier equipment and pointed out changes and improvements I wanted to make. He began drawing sketches on the spot and made other suggestions to better the product line. George was amazing! He also offered to put together a proposal on what it would cost to tool up and get ready to fabricate the new line.

A few days later, Anita and I flew to Oklahoma City. We had a great time of fellowship, and I appeared on Wayne Lassiter's telecast. I shared my testimony of salvation and deliverance, and the response from viewers was tremendous!

The next day during lunch, Wayne asked how we were getting along. We shared some of our current needs, especially the pending foreclosure on our house. We had less than two weeks left to make a substantial payment or we would lose the house and all the money we had paid over the years.

"I wish I had the money to lend you personally," he said. "But I have a feeling that God is at work on your behalf. I want to agree with you in faith, right now, that God will meet your every need." And we prayed together right there at the table.

After we prayed, Wayne asked, "Is there anything you'd like to see or do around town?"

"Yes, as a matter of fact," I replied, "I'd like to go to a gym."

Within an hour, I was at a neighborhood health club. As I started working out, several people at the club recognized me and came by to talk. After a while, the manager of the gym came over to get acquainted. He was very interested in my workout routine and asked about some of the competitions I'd won over the years.

Making a Sale!

Somehow the conversation turned to gym equipment and I mentioned that several of his weight machines were in really bad condition. In fact, all of his equipment was substandard considering the gym was a fairly new facility and was in a prime location.

"Yes, I know it's bad," he said apologetically. "But we're starting to look for new equipment, and we're planning to replace all our weights and machines."

Something clicked in my mind. "Really? Well, I'd sure appreciate it if you would consider my company to supply your equipment. I've installed gym equipment in several Gold's Gyms and other top health clubs across the country."

The manager went to make a call to the head of the company, and by the next day, I was sitting across the desk from the chairman of the board of a large chain of gyms I'd never heard of before! He was impressed with the brochures and catalog sheets from my previous equipment companies, and I threw in publicity appearances and fitness seminars as part of the deal.

He asked a few questions about prices, terms, and delivery schedules, and said, "It sounds good to me. I'll make some financing arrangements, and you'll be getting my order."

Anita and I flew home the next day feeling cautiously optimistic—wondering if the company would really come through with the kind of order we had been discussing. We didn't have long to wait for an answer.

Within a week we received the call. "Dennis, let's get going on that equipment. We need it bad! And we need it fast. I'm mailing you a check today for the 50 percent deposit you requested on the first order. As soon as this installation is finished, we'll talk about ordering equipment for some of the other gyms."

Talk about celebrating! Anita and I had a marathon praise service right in our front room, thanking the Great Provider for meeting our needs. And as we prayed and thanked God, both Anita and I felt a strong sense that a supernatural supply of finances was on the way, greater than we could ever imagine.

Everything fell into place. The check arrived from Oklahoma City, which was used to pay George Arsenault for the tooling costs and to make a deposit on the first order of equipment.

And there was enough left over to get my house out of foreclosure and pay some other bills as well.

By the time that first order was filled and delivered, we had already sold our second installation, and had leads on two or three other good sales. The new equipment company was already assured of success.

With a thankful heart, I bought my plane ticket to London to participate in what would be my very last bodybuilding competition—the 1982 Mr. Olympia contest.

My Bodybuilding "Swan Song"

Winning the title of Mr. Universe in 1981 in Australia had truly been a gratifying experience, and had actually rejuvenated my career in bodybuilding. A current or even recent champion is always in more demand for seminars and exhibitions.

Following my victory in 1981, I continued to stay in good shape, while a Christian friend from my church, Nick Taylor, became my training partner. He helped me polish my routines and reach really awesome physical form. So when the entry forms for the 1982 Mr. Olympia competition arrived in the gym where I worked out, I decided to give it one more try. Maybe the sixth time would be a charm—I would finally capture the elusive Mr. Olympia title.

Anita just shook her head when I told her of my plans. "Honey, you know how I feel about bodybuilding. But if that's what you want and need to do, go ahead!

Nick went with me to London. I was relaxed and confident—totally prepared. I did great in every phase of the competition, and every time I went on stage, the audience gave me a standing ovation.

However, everything else about the contest was absolutely awful! There was an atmosphere of discord and bickering backstage that had simmered to the boiling point. Most everyone involved in the event—the promoters, judges, and contestants—seemed to be edgy and irritable all the time.

During the finals, the judges engaged in a loud, angry argument that was obvious to all present. In the end, Chris Dickerson became Mr. Olympia, and Frank Zane was second. Both were veteran bodybuilders, who competed in lighter weight divisions than me. Apparently, the judges liked the smaller contestants that year.

At a time when I was still at my physical peak, in excellent shape, with a superior posing routine, I placed ninth! Although disappointed, I was not angry or despondent over the situation. By now I understood that this was simply another example of the controversy and confusion that had surrounded the Mr. Olympia contest from its beginning. I had come to terms with the fact that my exposure and publicity in the sport would help me in business and keep me motivated for training. I realized that my life didn't revolve around contests—there was far more to life than body-building!

As Nick and I headed out for dinner that night, we heard a loud commotion down in the lobby of our hotel and found a crowd watching two bodybuilders fight—literally punching each other in the face!I was totally disgusted. At that moment, I realized that never again did I want to have anything to do with this sordid, rancorous lifestyle.

After dinner, I called Anita and told her what had happened both during the competition and afterward. She listened for a few moments, than quietly asked, "Have you had enough of this?"

I sighed in resignation. "Yeah, I have finally had it, Anita. I'm throwing in the towel. I promise you I'll never compete again." And I never did.

The Real Purpose

Before I left London to return home, I had the opportunity to travel around the city and meet various people I had met over the years who were associated with bodybuilding. I witnessed to many of them, and prayed with several. One woman, who recognized me when I walked into a hotel lobby to meet some friends for lunch, came over and said, "You're Dennis Tinerino. I met you years ago when you won your first Mr. Universe title—you were dating a girl who I knew."

We chatted briefly, and then she asked, "Is it true that you are a believer—that you've accepted Jesus?"

"Yes, it is," I assured her.

"Then why would you still have an interest in bodybuilding—this God-forsaken sport? The only reason I stay involved is because my husband is a judge. There is so much unhappiness and misery involved in it. I have never seen so many wives who have been neglected and abused. And there have been so many broken marriages and heartbreaks due to this sport. If you're out of it, why don't you stay away from it?"

I paused for only a moment—the answer was very clear. "Perhaps I am here today to tell you that God can change your life the same way He has changed mine," I told her. Right there in the hotel lobby, I witnessed to her and asked if she would like to accept Christ. The tears streaming down her face were her answer. What a thrill to lead her in the sinner's prayer, and ask God to help her and change her whole world!

At that moment, I realized that I was finally doing what I was supposed to be doing with my life. Everything that had happened to me was only in preparation for the ministry God had planned for me. The joy of doing God's work was greater than any fame or notoriety I had ever known.

A New Beginning

I was happy to get back home to California and be with my family. I also was ready to finally devote all my time and energy to my business and ministry. Anita and I had recently invested in a new business—a tanning salon and fitness center called Get Tan.

To my surprise, both my gym equipment company and the new Get Tan store opened doors for me to meet many local celebrities, including TV and movie people. I would begin talking with them about fitness and tanning equipment, and when they recognized me or discovered my bodybuilding background, I had the perfect opportunity to share my testimony. Time after time, I was able to witness for the Lord, often leading people to salvation or ministering to great personal needs in their lives.

In fact, I found myself drawn more deeply into ministry. Doors were opening and opportunities were available for me to share the love of God—not just in my daily routine, but also in my old neighborhoods and in other countries as well!

After a few weeks of almost full-time ministry, I found that talking, teaching, praying, and preaching were even more satisfying and fulfilling to me than bodybuilding had ever been! Consequently, I set out to prepare myself for a whole new calling and lifestyle—studying and praying for hours every day—just as I had once sweated and strained in the gym. I was determined to be just as dedicated and devoted to preparing my heart and mind for ministry as I had been committed to training my body for competitions.

And I had a feeling that it was going to be a lot more exciting!

Sold Out—A New Career

I've always been an all-or-nothing kind of guy.

When I was a competitive bodybuilder, I prided myself on being totally committed, totally dedicated to my sport. I trained faithfully, often for two or three hours a day; I disciplined myself to eat properly and to fortify my body with extra vitamins and mineral supplements that could make me even stronger and healthier; and I constantly sought for ways to improve my training techniques and posing programs. My goal was to achieve my full potential and be the best I could possibly be.

When I was living a life of sin, involved in crime and a worldly lifestyle, I deliberately sought to push my personal behavior to the most outrageous extremes possible. As a partner in crime, I would attempt the most daring robberies and strive to be the toughest, meanest guy on the street. I could talk louder, dress flashier, and party heavier than anyone. I managed to get inside the most exclusive clubs and traveled in style with big-name celebrities all over the world. And whether the topic was drugs, sex, violence, criminal activities, or even flirting with organized crime, I could say without exaggeration—"Been there...done that!"

So, perhaps it was to be expected that when I became a Christian, I was determined to be as totally dedicated and sold-out to Jesus as I had been to the devil. And just as Jesus described in the parable to Simon the Pharisee, perhaps I loved God the most because I had been forgiven the most (see Luke 7:41-43).

So, I did not become a "nominal" Christian. I didn't go halfway or part-time. With all the power within me, I literally tried to give my entire self, my whole being, my all, to the Lord. To some people I probably seemed like a radical or fanatic—but I didn't know any other way to be.

Many did not understand my new commitment to Christ. When I talked with my old friends and told them what had happened to me, they shook their heads in amazement. "Dennis, it sounds like you've been totally brainwashed."

"You may be right," I told them. "And you know what? My brain really needed to be washed. Maybe you should give it a try!"

I threw myself into an intensive Christian disciple training program as enthusiastically as I had ever trained for any bodybuilding competition. I was hungry and thirsty for truth, and I wanted a life of integrity and godly character. When I didn't have to be working on an equipment sales project or a fitness seminar to earn a living for my family, I spent every spare minute studying the Bible and praying.

I read my Bible at least an hour a day—sometimes more—and was amazed at how the Word of God was opening up to me. There had been times when reading the Bible was a real chore for me—empty words and boring, confusing passages. But no more! I found that the more I read, the more I understood.

In addition to all this preparation, I soon discovered that I seemed to learn the most when I spent time in prayer, seeking the wisdom of the Spirit of God. At first, praying five minutes seemed impossible. I didn't know what to say or how to say it. Soon though, I found myself communing with God through a spiritual force deep inside me. And once I began to flow with the Spirit, I could pray for two hours and feel as though it had been only a few minutes!

I sensed that I was growing in understanding and faith. At that time, Anita and I were active in a tremendous church in southern California, Cornerstone Agape Faith Center. For some reason, a large number of athletes and bodybuilders began coming to that church, and I found myself drawn to them. I understood them, and was able to minister to them and help them.

My pastor, Ed Longshore, mentored me and gave me opportunities to learn how to minister—to teach, speak, and counsel with people. I loved it all. I never got tired of sharing what I had learned or of leading individuals to make their own personal decision for Christ.

Soon my weekends were full—speaking to youth groups, sharing my testimony, teaching and preaching at various meetings. In the meantime, Pastor Longshore continued to counsel and help prepare me for each new opportunity.

Eventually, Anita and I decided to sell the Get Tan business. Although it was doing well, we felt it took too much time for the amount of income it produced. In addition, the equipment sales business and my personal appearances generated more income related to the time spent, and allowed more time for ministry activities.

Chosen for Ministry

When Ray McCauley occasionally came to the United States, I spent as much time as I possibly could with him. And while he was here, he took me with him to his services and trained me how to minister, encouraging me to share my testimony, witness, counsel, and pray with people.

He also introduced me to Jerry Savelle, who also had a tremendous influence on my developing ministry. I had read several of his books and knew he was a strong man of faith, but I learned even more by observing him in action. We would talk for hours at a time, and he would answer my questions, often referring me to various Scriptures for further study. I spent time in his home with his family and discovered that the man lived what he preached. Not only does Jerry have a heart for helping Christian athletes and entertainers, he is a great missionary, evangelist, and humanitarian. Most of all, Jerry is a real friend to me.

In 1984, Ray McCauley and Jerry came to Los Angeles to attend the Olympics and to witness to the people they met at the various events. During the time they were in L.A., these two ministers conducted a crusade together at Cornerstone Church. Jerry would preach one service, and Ray the next. Hundreds of people attended the meetings, including many well-known people in the television and film industries. Many of them were touched by the power of God, and made decisions for Christ.

For me, the highlight of the crusade was a special ordination service that these two wonderful men of God conducted for me as I was licensed and accepted into the Inter Conference of Faith Ministers. They laid hands on me and commissioned me to go forth as a minister of the Gospel and do the work of an evangelist. From that moment on, they told me, I was to expect God to direct me and use me in His service.

This service was a truly momentous event for me. I felt a whole new chapter of my life was opening up before me, and I was finally prepared and ready to go out in full-time Christian service. I believed with all my heart that God was going to do great things in my life and through my ministry.

Ministry Trip to Korea

Actually, my first real missions trip had already taken place several months before when I had gone on a trip to Korea. This happened when I was still deep in debt and my house was about to go into foreclosure.

My pastor, Ed Longshore, called me one day and said, "Dennis, I know a fellow named Brother Gus who has been supporting a bunch of orphans in Korea. He says God gave him a vision of going to Seoul to visit the kids in the orphanage and to minister to the Korean people. In his vision, he saw three other men going with him. He has asked me to go, and Frank Smith from the church also wants to go."

"That's wonderful," I said. "I hope it works out for all of you. I'm sure it will be a wonderful trip."

"Well, here's why I'm calling," he said hesitantly. "We feel like you're supposed to go with us."

"Pastor, that's just not possible. You know the financial trouble I'm in. There's no way I could afford to go to Korea."

"I know all that," he said. "I was reluctant to even mention it to you. But I feel so strong in my spirit that you're supposed to go with us. Why don't you just pray about it and then let me know what you decide."

Knowing it wouldn't take long to pray about this deal, I told Pastor Ed I would give him an answer by the next day. That afternoon, I went out into my backyard to pray. "Lord, I've been asked to go to Korea to minister, but there's just no way I can do it in the midst of this financial crisis. I'm sure Your will is for me to decline and just pray for those who do make the trip."

Dennis' first mission trip to Korea

I knew I had prayed very sensibly—but somehow it just didn't feel right. I was definitely not at peace inside. Suddenly, I sensed that God was impressing something on my mind, speaking to my spirit.

Dennis, you saw Me do the miracle of the hundred-dollar bill when you had no money for food. I gave you direction into the fitness business. You saw me do a miracle through Wayne Lassiter in Oklahoma City when he called you and sent money to you. Now, I am about to work another miracle in your life. Yes, I want you to go to Korea and speak to the whole nation on radio and TV. You will speak prophetically by My Spirit. I am sending you there, but you will have to walk by faith.

Initially, I resisted what I was hearing in my spirit. I was terrified that I might be letting my own desires and wishes influence me. How could it be right to do something that appeared so irresponsible—to leave my family alone in a time of critical need? Surely, I was mistaken about what the Lord was saying!

As I continued to pray and ask God to guide me, the message I kept receiving was to go to Korea! I was stunned! Then I remembered a Scripture I had read a few days before: "*And every one that hath forsaken houses, or brethren, or sisters, or father, or mother, or wife, or children, or lands, for My name's sake, shall receive an hundredfold, and shall inherit everlasting life*" (Matt. 19:29 KJV). And that seemed to be the last word on the subject. Speaking to the whole nation of Korea on TV and radio was all I could think about. Millions would hear what the Lord would give me to speak!

Needless to say, when I told Anita what had happened, she was not overjoyed. Her objections and concerns sounded exactly like my protests to the Lord as I was praying. I listened, and then said, "Anita, all I know to do is to ask you to pray about it and see if the Lord speaks anything to your heart."

She agreed, and after an hour or so of prayer, came back to me—laughing! "What's so funny?" I demanded.

"I remember once hearing Oral Roberts talk about how he sowed seed and trusted God for a thousandfold return. Well, after praying, I feel like God wants you to go to Korea. So, I'm going to sow *you* into this mission. I'm going to trust God and see what I can get for 230 pounds of Mr. Universe! We'll just have to believe and see the miracle God will do!"

A few minutes later, I was on the phone with Ed Longshore. I told him that after a considerable amount of prayer—as impractical and irrational as it seemed—I would go to Korea. And I was full of questions for Ed. "What are we going to do when we get to Seoul? Who are we going to see or work with there? Where are we going to minister?"

"Dennis, I don't know any of that! The only thing Brother Gus knows for sure is that he wants to visit the orphanage where he's been supporting several orphans. He says the Lord has promised him that when we get to our hotel, God will reveal the next step we're supposed to take."

Chapter Twenty

MINISTRY OF MIRACLES

IT was a giant step of faith for me to be planning a two week long trip to the Orient with no itinerary or schedule. Before all my bodybuilding trips overseas, I always knew what hotels I would be staying in, what time various events would take place, and what my schedule of exhibition appearances would be. Furthermore, I always had two or three typed pages of instructions to carry with me. This trip was certainly different!

A day or two after I made the decision to go, Pastor Ed called to tell me the date we would be leaving. Less than a week later, I turned on the TV and saw a news flash that a Korean 747 airliner, Flight 007, had been shot down by the Russians. Everyone on board, some 300 people, had been killed. Later, the news showed the chaos in the streets of Seoul, caused by the anger and anguish of the people. Anita and I were shocked and grief stricken by this tragic event.

As I watched the news, suddenly the Lord spoke to my heart. "Now you know why you are going to Korea. You are going to speak light to those people. I will open up a supernatural door for you and give the Christ in you an opportunity to preach to the entire nation. Christ overcomes every crisis, so do not be discouraged by obstacles. I will help you overcome them all; I will turn obstacles into opportunities." I immediately thought of the apostle Paul's comment in First Corinthians 16:9, "*A great door and effectual is opened unto me, and there are many adversaries*" (KJV).

When it was time to leave, I didn't have any extra money, and I was concerned about how Anita and the children were going to make it while I was gone. "Don't you worry, Dennis," she said. "God will take care of us. I feel completely at peace about this." I left her with what little money we did have, and showed up at the airport to spend a week in Korea with only ten dollars in my pocket!

The first leg of our flight was to Alaska, where we changed planes to fly on to Seoul. Waiting for our flight in the airport at Anchorage, I struck up a conversation with a young man who had just graduated from Oral Roberts University. "I remember seeing you on the Richard Roberts TV program," he said. "You were on with another bodybuilder from South Africa, a guy named Ray McCauley who became a pastor."

"Yeah, that's right," I said. What are you doing here? What are your plans now that you're out of school?"

"Well, I'm going to an island called Ek Chong, which is off the coast of Korea. I'm going to be involved in missionary work there. I don't have an appointment or have any organized support yet. I'm going *totally* by faith."

"Well brother, I believe in that. In God's plan, money follows ministry. Here, let me give you this," and I handed him my ten-dollar bill, the only money I had. Now, I was going totally by faith! Before we parted, we all prayed for each other and took communion together.

Because of our excitement, sleeping on the long flight to Korea was virtually impossible, and when we finally got off the plane and stepped onto Korean soil, we could hardly wait to find out what God's plans were for us!

Led by the Spirit

Someone had recommended that we stay in a hotel that was located very near Rev. Paul Yonggi Cho's great church. We had no trouble getting rooms there, even though we had no reservations. As soon as we checked in and went upstairs, I started feeling that we were in the wrong place. So I called the four of us together and said, "Let's pray. Something's not right here, and we need to know that we're in God's perfect will. Let's get in agreement. The Bible says, "*For where two or three are gathered together in My name, there am I in the midst of them*" (Matt. 18:20).

As we prayed together, there was a word of prophecy about dwelling high on a hill. I said, "Brother Gus, I believe the Lord wants us to go to a hotel up on a hill."

So we carried our luggage downstairs, told the desk clerk we were in the wrong hotel, and checked out. Then we walked out onto the sidewalk, not knowing where to go!

I looked over at a line of cabs and saw a tall black driver dressed in Western clothes. It was very obvious that he was an American. I called out, "Hey, yo! We need help over here. We need to go to a big hotel on the hill."

"Where you from, Gumba?" he asked as he started loading our luggage in the trunk of the cab.

"I'm from L.A., man."

"Yeah, sure. You sound like you're from New York, just like me!"

"I grew up in New York. What are you doing here in Korea?"

"I was in the army here. I like it in this part of the world, so I retired here. Now I drive a cab just to make some extra money. Get in the car, man. I'm going to take you to your hotel on the hill!"

In a few minutes, the cab was going up a very steep grade, winding around a tall hill to the beautiful Hyatt House hotel. When we started unloading our bags, we noticed that there was a long line of people waiting to check in. The line went from the desk, all the way across the lobby and out onto the sidewalk.

"I hope you got reservations, man," said the cabby. "This place has a big convention going and the word is that they overbooked!"

"Yeah, we're covered. I'll go check us in."

I looked at the long line and thought to myself, *in Deuteronomy 28:13, the Word says that I am the head, not the tail. I'm above and not beneath. I don't think I'm going to wait out here.*

I walked past all the people in line, went right up to the desk, and just stood there. The Korean clerk said, "Sir, what is it that you want? If you are checking in, the line is over there."

"No, that's okay," I said. "I have a reservation." I slid a bodybuilding photo of myself across the desk. "My name is Dennis Tinerino. I'm Mr. America—Mr. Universe."

He hit a few keys on the computer keyboard and said, "We don't have a reservation for Tinerino."

"Then they are probably listed under the name of Jesus," I said.

"The name of Jesus?"

"That's right. God sent us here from America. We're on a mission for God. We need two double rooms."

The clerk moved over to look me straight in the eye. "I thought you would never come," he said. "You are an answer to prayer! I've been asking God to send some of His servants from America to our country on a divine assignment. I will take care of you."

Within a few moments, I had the keys to two double rooms and vouchers for free meals in the dining room. As I autographed the picture I had given the clerk, I said, "We're trusting God to open up some doors for us to minister. We don't know exactly what we're supposed to do, but the Lord has promised to direct our path" (see Ps. 119:105).

"I will pray about it with you," he said. It turned out that the clerk was a member of Pastor Cho's church and believed completely in the leading of the Holy Spirit. Hallelujah!

Following God's Schedule

Our little group went upstairs, weary from the long trip on the plane and the harried activities involved in getting a room and settling in. However, we decided to pray together for a while before we rested. As we prayed, the Lord released the spirit of prophesy to speak to me: *Tomorrow night, you will be on national television, and this is what you are to tell the people of Korea....* I scribbled down some notes from that prophetic word, then exhausted, we all fell into our beds.

A few hours later, the phone rang. Nobody in the world knew where we were—not even my wife. I couldn't imagine who would be calling. To my surprise, it was the desk clerk from downstairs.

"Mr. Universe!" he said breathlessly. "You'll never believe what just happened! The president of the International Federation of Body Building in Korea just came into the hotel to eat lunch. I told him you were here, and he is very excited. He says he always works with the visiting bodybuilders to set up meetings and exhibitions for them. Is it okay if I send him up to your room?"

Soon, the Korean IFBB president was in my room, offering to set up appearances for me around Seoul and in other nearby areas. He knew who I was, and knew of all my records and achievements. "It is a great honor to have a champion like you in our country," he said. "I will make all the arrangements for you right away."

Then he asked what I was doing in Korea, and why I hadn't contacted him before I arrived. I told him we were there on a mission for God. The other fellows with me began to share their testimonies and talk about the Lord. Within an hour, the guy was on his knees in my room, asking Jesus into his life. He had an amazing encounter with God, and was filled with the Holy Spirit, weeping and speaking in tongues on the same day he accepted the Lord!

He told us that he was separated from his wife, a Pentecostal Christian from New Jersey, and she had been praying for him to accept the Lord. She had told him that some day God would send someone he could relate to who would minister to him. Now it had happened!

After a time of fellowship and prayer together, he said, "Dennis, not only will I set up bodybuilding appearances for you, I'm going to see if I can get you on a television talk show—it's the Korean equivalent of the "Tonight Show" in America. It's our top-rated program, and reaches 20 million viewers. I will get back to you in the morning.

True to his word, he called the next day with good news. "You're going to be on TV tonight!" He said. "They had the opera singer Pavarotti scheduled, but he has a sore throat, so you're going on in his slot! And that's not all! I went by the Far East Broadcasting radio station, and they want to interview you on the air. I can't believe how easy it has been to make the arrangements. It's like they were just waiting for me to call!"

"They were, my brother," I told him. "God had already told us that we would be on TV tonight!"

During the radio interview, which reached into communist North Korea and China, I had the opportunity to share my Christian testimony and say whatever I wanted. The host was very gracious and cooperative, and I sensed the anointing of the Holy Spirit upon me as I spoke. The words just seemed to flow, and I instinctively knew what to say.

In the afternoon, I approved several bodybuilding appearances my new friend had arranged for later in the week. I then spent some time praying and preparing myself for the TV program. Later, I met with a Buddhist woman who was to be my interpreter on the show. She laid out an interview that would be structured around my worldly background and my professional accomplishments. Instead, I handed her a list of questions to ask me that would give me the opportunity to share my testimony and deliver the message God had laid on my heart. Looking her in the eyes, I said, "If you cannot do this, I will have to request that I work with another interpreter."

I could feel the intense spiritual confrontation going on in and around her. Finally, she looked up and said, "All right. I agree. I cannot fight the most high God."

During the program that night, I did answer lots of questions about my bodybuilding accomplishments as well as my New York and Los Angeles experiences, including my involvement with celebrities on the party scene and my criminal activities. After some posing and strongman demonstrations, I talked about the movies I had been in—*Hercules* with Arnold Schwarzenegger and a bit part in *Shamus* with Burt Reynolds.

The interpreter then asked one of my questions. "What has been the greatest event or moment in your life?" I shared my testimony of how God had sent Jesus, His Son, to forgive me of all my sins and give me eternal life. I spoke of how the Lord had saved and delivered me, and was commissioning me to go out and do His work in the world.

Preaching to the Nation

I turned to the host and asked, "Is it okay if I talk directly to the people of Korea for a few minutes?" He nodded his head.

As I began to speak, I sensed the Holy Spirit's gift of prophecy upon me, giving me words to say that I had not planned. I referred to the tragedy of Flight 007, and said there was even more serious spiritual warfare going on in the heavens. I told them not to despair, that God's power would triumph, and Korea would be one of the first nations in the world to be predominantly Christian. "You, the people of Korea, will help evangelize the rest of the nations!" I ended by asking viewers to give their hearts to God and to pray right where they were. Then I led in a simple prayer of salvation. Even the TV host prayed with me.

It was an amazing moment. All of our team said they could sense a tremendous moving of the Spirit of God. The people in the TV studio were very reverent and respectful, as they sensed the presence of God and the power and reality of the ministry that was happening. Many had tears flowing from their eyes as they prayed.

Afterward, a man came over, paid me the show's regular $175 appearance fee and said, "We enjoyed having you on the program so much. I would like to present you with gifts. He was holding out very nice gifts for all four of us.

By the time we returned to our hotel, calls were coming in from all over the country. Doors of ministry opened everywhere, and our team received more opportunities to go preach than we could accept. We then went to Pastor Cho's church, and he took us into his office, which looks out over the city. In that beautiful and anointed place, we prayed together. Afterward, we visited Prayer Mountain, where 10,000 people gather to fast and pray—often for weeks at a time—clustered in little huts on steep slopes.

Later, we took a tour of the notorious "DMZ"—the demilitarized zone between North and South Korea—escorted by a U.S. military convoy. I wore a tank top, which revealed my bodybuilder's physique, and we quickly attracted a crowd of soldiers stationed near the DMZ. I witnessed and prayed with them as hundreds accepted Christ.

As we were praying, another crowd of Korean people also gathered around us. Some were carrying sick people on their backs to our service to receive prayer. We were told later that some of them had been carried for miles. We prayed for as many as we possibly could, and heard testimonies of dramatic, miraculous healings and deliverance. It was awesome!

I made several bodybuilding appearances during our stay and held posing exhibitions and seminars, which always included part of my personal testimony and a time for preaching. I also had the chance to speak to various civic clubs filled with politicians, world leaders, and businessmen, and to youth groups and several churches. We became national celebrities, and our activities were reported in the newspaper, on radio, and several times on the TV news.

After the first day, we were booked solid for the rest of the time we were in Korea. We even went to one special revival that began at midnight and didn't break up until eight o'clock in the morning! Thousands accepted Christ as Savior. The people were so hungry for Bible teaching and to see the power of God in action. We had a real Holy Ghost camp meeting!

After all these exhilarating experiences, we finally headed to the orphanage that Brother Gus had come to visit—the only part of our trip that had been planned before we left! Cramped in a small cab, we drove for hours through rough mountainous terrain to reach the orphanage, and we all wept as we saw the abject poverty the children were living in. Brother Gus had brought a generous gift for them, and their appreciation was overwhelming. Touched as they shared a meager meal of rice with us, we ended up giving them all we had—my watch and jewelry, and the money from the talk show—and yet, we knew in our hearts it would make only a dent in the massive needs of the orphanage. It was so difficult to comprehend that a government could let its children live in such conditions. We were told that babies, mostly female, were abandoned on their doorstep on a weekly, sometimes daily, basis.

As we drove away, crying children, begging us not to leave, followed us. Our hearts were breaking, and we wished we could bring them all back with us. Yet the knowledge that we were able to preach the Gospel on national radio and TV to Korea's 20 million people filled our hearts with joy! The simple message that Jesus loved them was eagerly received throughout the nation.

We all were exhausted as we headed to the airport to catch our flight home. None of us were looking forward to being cramped up in the plane for hours. But imagine our surprise and joy when we checked in at the counter and found that because the flight was so full, the four of us had been upgraded to first class! We could almost hear the Lord whispering in our ears, "*Well done, thou good and faithful servants.*"

The Man With Nine Lives

After takeoff, I began talking with the man seated next to me. He told me that he was from New Jersey. I said, "You're the man with nine lives, aren't you?" I had no idea why those words came out of my mouth!

The man did. "How did you know that?" he exclaimed. "I was just saying that to myself. You see, I was originally booked to come to Korea on Flight 007, the plane that was shot down by the Russians. I got to the gate late, and the plane was just pushing back. I had missed the flight by a few seconds, and I cussed and yelled at the airline people because they wouldn't call the plane back to let me on."

He was quiet for a moment, obviously struggling with his emotions. Fighting back tears, he whispered, "Of course, in a few hours, I realized that fate—or something—had intervened and spared my life. I don't understand exactly what happened, or why."

"I think I know," I said. "May I explain it to you?"

"Please do," he said. "I know it had to be more than just an accident."

"God spared your life, my friend. He loves you. He has His hands on you, and He wants you to come into the Kingdom of God. He must have something very special for you to do. I believe He wants you to accept the Lord Jesus right now."

Five minutes later, the man was openly weeping, eagerly looking at my Bible as I pointed out some key verses from the Book of Romans. When I took his hand and asked if he was ready to pray, he nodded silently, tears splashing down on our hands. He repeated the sinner's prayer after me and accepted Jesus Christ into his life. His conversion was a miraculous conclusion to a miracle-packed trip.

Amazingly, Anita's expectation of a thousandfold return from sowing her 230-pound husband into God's field was quickly realized. Only a few days after I returned home from Korea, we learned that we were getting a $65,000 settlement from one of the speaker company lawsuits—a totally unexpected financial breakthrough!

A few months later, Anita's mother passed away in New York. All of our family felt a great sense of loss. Although we lived on the other side of the country, and had not been able to spend much time with her, we loved and respected her as a woman of strong principles and deep faith in God.

To our surprise, Mom had left us a substantial inheritance, including the house in Astoria. We were overwhelmed by her love and generosity. The gift was totally unexpected.

The check from the speaker company lawsuit arrived just as Mom's house sold and the estate was settled. The total amount received was astounding!

I told Anita the good news. We both just sat in awe for a moment. We suddenly realized that the long financial nightmare was finally over. Truly, we were receiving a supernatural financial supply—more than enough to pay off the complete balance of the $100,000 debt. We were free and clear—totally out of debt and in the black!

Making War in the Heavenlies

Shortly after I began working in full-time ministry, I became involved with an organization called the Inner City Youth Training Ministry. This organization targeted street people in the slums and ghettos of America's major cities, gang members, drug dealers, and users—basically the outcasts of modern society. Because of my own background during my childhood and teenage years, I had a soft spot in my heart for this ministry. JoJo Sanchez, a fearless minister, helped direct the work, and Rosy Grier, Meadowlark Lemon, Little Richard, and Wendell Tyler of the San Francisco 49ers were all involved from time to time. Several major evangelistic ministries helped underwrite the work of the Inner City Youth Training Ministry, including men of God like Ken Copeland, Jerry Saville, and others.

In 1986, I was speaking at one of their rallys in Lancaster, California. And by this time, Anita and I were blessed to have a third child, a son who was about two months old. I had been spending a great deal of my time on the road in meetings, traveling alone much of the time; so, I asked Anita if she and the children would like to attend the service with me and spend some time with our friends. Anita thought it was a terrific idea. "That sounds great, Dennis. We've really missed you lately."

We loaded up the family van with our luggage, including a travel crib for Dennis, Jr., who we called D.J. We prayed for safety on our trip, and that the Lord would give us journey mercies. Anita drove so I could pray and prepare for the service that night—and maybe catch a little nap. While in prayer, the Lord gave me a word from Matthew chapter 11: "*And from the days of John the Baptist until now the kingdom of heaven suffereth violence, and the violent take it by force*" (Matt. 11:12 KJV). "Force? Violence?" Although at that moment it was a puzzling word, I believe that the Holy Spirit gave me that word as a warning of what was to soon come.

As Anita drove towards Lancaster, it began to rain, and eventually, I dropped off to sleep. Sometime later, I awoke to hear Anita screaming at the top of her lungs, and I could feel the van swerving and lurching down the rain-slicked highway.

Anita had been driving along at 60 miles an hour, and had just past Magic Mountain when the van suddenly began hydroplaning, hurtling out of control on a treacherous sheet of water.

Oh God, what are we going to do? How can I stop this runaway vehicle? Instantly, I realized that we were under a spiritual attack of the enemy—I was living Matthew 11:12!

The Spirit of God spoke to me, *When you don't know what to do, open your mouth and I will give you the words you need.* Immediately, I heard my voice declaring authoritatively, "I bind you, satan, in the name of Jesus. I take authority over you. Spirit of death and destruction, you shall not touch my family. I break your power in Jesus' name!" (See John 10:10.) The Holy Spirit poured into me as I continued to pray in tongues, and Scriptures poured from my lips. "No weapon formed against me shall prosper! I release the angels!" (See Isaiah 54:17 and Hebrews 1:7.)

As I reached over and tried to help Anita rein in the vehicle, it seemed the harder I prayed, the more the van surged out of control! The next thing I knew, the vehicle hit the center divider of the freeway, did a 180-degree turn, hit the center divider again, then careened over an off-ramp, and flipped upside down and all the way over on its left side.

When the van first hit the center median, I was thrown out of my seat, across the van, and on top of my wife. When the vehicle spun and hit the median again, we both were thrown back across the van into the passenger seat. My body broke the armrest and Anita landed on top of me, semiconscious.

I knew the van was still moving and that no human being was driving. As the Dodge Caravan hurtled across the ramp and flipped over, I sensed that my children were being tossed around like rag dolls. I continued to pray in tongues to bind the work of the devil, and to speak forth the promises of Psalm 91:15, calling upon God for deliverance, and Isaiah 54:17.

Then I heard the windshield smash, and all the windows on the left side just disintegrated. Finally, with a dizzying whirl and a sickening thud, the van finally came to rest on its side, jammed into the side of the mountain. Although the vehicle was totally destroyed, its engine was still running.

Surely, the angels of God protected us in that van (see Ps. 91:11). In spite of the shock my body had sustained, I had the peace of God in my heart—and no fear, for I knew that God was with us! (see Ps. 23:4). And there was an aroma of roses permeating the van.

To this day, I have no idea how I got out of the van. I saw that Anita was barely conscious but breathing. Tara, my 12-year-old daughter, was terrified, but she didn't seem to be seriously hurt.

I ran to the back and picked up little D.J., who was lying face down in the water and mud oozing into the backseat. I saw blood on his head, and tried to wipe it away with my hands. A man came running up to me out of nowhere, and I put my son in his arms to be taken to safety. The man was saying, "I never saw anyone drive like that! You missed every other car on the road!" He simply stared in disbelief when I told him that no one had been driving the van.

By this time, cars were stopping on the freeway, and a lady and another man came running over to the van through the pouring rain. I was just opening the back door to check on my 8-year-old daughter Marissa, when I saw her twisted neck and body. Her head had slipped under the back seat, and she wasn't moving at all.

I could hear a woman screaming, "My God, that child is dead! Oh, God, it's awful! She's dead!"

With superhuman strength, I pushed on the back of the seat until the bottom tilted up enough that I could drag Marissa's head out from under it. There was blood oozing out of her ear—it was smeared all over the side of her head. I pressed my fingers to her neck, then to her wrists, but there was no pulse. I put both hands on her clammy, cold face and began shouting, "I break the power of death over my child. She shall live and not die, and shall declare the works of God! I speak life to her in the name of Jesus! I release the gifts of miracle, healing, and faith!" I had no fear—only faith.

Nothing happened—nothing at all! As I stood holding her in the pouring rain, praying and quoting Scripture, Marisa was lifeless and still. Yet I kept praying and rebuking the power of death. Suddenly, I heard the woman next to me shout, "Oh, look! She's moving! Her eyes are opening. She's alive!"

Marissa suddenly came to and began screaming and crying. Then she said, "Daddy! I saw ten thousand of God's angels fight the dark angels. They came from everywhere and told me everything's going to be okay because God is with us." Someone wrapped her up to keep her dry and warm until the ambulance arrived to take her to the hospital.

Miraculously, after we all were examined at the hospital and cleaned up, none of us were found to be seriously injured. My ribs were really sore and banged up from slamming into the armrest of the passenger's seat, but that was the worst of it.

I called our pastor back home to pick us up, and I phoned the church to let them know we had been involved in an accident on the freeway and wouldn't be there that night.

The next day, I gathered my family together and told them we were going back to the crusade. I was especially concerned about my daughters. I didn't want fear to enter their hearts. "Tomorrow, the whole family will go to church and testify about how God spared our lives," I told them. "I don't want you to be afraid. The enemy tried to stop us—even kill us—but God kept us in His divine protection. Now it's time to give Him praise and let people know how great His power really is." (See Revelation 12:10.)

The crusade director called and said we didn't need to come to the meeting if we didn't feel like it. "Oh yes, we do!" I said. "We'll be there. I believe God wants to do something miraculous in that service."

And so, we went to Lancaster that night. My family testified and I preached that life and death are in the power of the tongue, and about God's divine protection and intervention in our lives. There was an altar call, and many people came forward to accept Christ and do business with God—including the man who believed that God was steering our van!

Victory Over Demons

After the altar call, JoJo Sanchez, the crusade director, spoke a word of knowledge from the Lord that there were five people in attendance who were in need of special deliverance. "I'm not talking about ordinary problems," he said. "This is not for those who are just discouraged or have a headache or would like things to go better at work. This call is for those who have reached the end of the line. You have tried every other source of help. You have exhausted every resource. You are up against the wall. You feel like you just can't go on another day. If God doesn't step in tonight, it's all over for you."

As he spoke, five people came forward. JoJo asked me to pray for them. I went to each individual and prayed. There were some critical needs there, and I felt the power of God moving as I prayed for each of the first four. I don't remember the details of their needs or even exactly what happened to them.

But when I stepped in front of the fifth person, a young girl, I suddenly sensed an ugly, evil power. In the spirit realm, I saw an ugly, diabolical creature—similar to the one in the movie *Alien*—wrapped around the girl's body. The gift of discernment (a spiritual gift of discerning of spirits) showed me that this creature was a spirit of witchcraft and divination. I put my hand on her forehead and said, "Come out in the name of Jesus!" At that instant, a flashing, burning, surging sensation—God's anointing—shot through me and slammed into the girl, and she dropped like a rock to the floor. As she fell, there was a shrill, piercing screech, then a guttural, choking, and unearthly sound, like the sound of the baying hounds of Baskerville. The girl's body convulsed, then she screamed. A short time later, she began to quiet and get still.

By then, I guarantee that the attention of every person in the building was focused on what was happening to that young woman. They saw that after my hand touched her forehead for an instant, nobody had touched her again. Yet, her body had twisted and shook, and the noises that burst from her lips were strange and inhuman. She was being delivered!

A man in the crowd stood up and began shouting, "That's my daughter; that's my daughter!" He made his way to the front and began to tell his story to some of the prayer counselors.

His daughter was demon-possessed, and had been growing steadily worse for months. When the evil spirits would torment her, foul language would pour out of her and she would do gross, unspeakable things to her body, including cutting and mutilation, like in the movie, *The Exorcist*. He had been trying to get help for her for many months. An American Indian, he had gone to a tribal medicine man, to Catholic priests for exorcism, and to various new age religions and cult groups. But nobody had been able to help his daughter. He said that he stopped at a gas station that morning where he was a regular customer, and a man he had never seen before pointed to a poster advertising the meeting and said, "Go there.

Take your daughter. She will be set free." Then the man disappeared. Hallelujah! The Lord had sent an angel.

True to God's word, the evil forces were broken from this girl, and the demon spirits left her during this meeting. After a few minutes, the girl got up from the floor, tears of joy streaming down her face—she was normal, rational, and overcome with emotion. "I'm free! I'm free! The devil has left me!" she yelled. As we prayed with her for the Lord to come into her heart and fill her with His Holy Spirit—to cleanse her and keep her from that night forward—her face glowed like that of an angel!

Seeing this dramatic, miraculous transformation, I had no doubt at all that the wreck the night before was a last-ditch effort by satan to prevent me from accomplishing God's ministry and to stop the crusade service where this girl would find deliverance and many more would find healing and salvation.

Making the Break—For Good

Next, I headed for London to assist Ray McCauley with a ministers conference he was conducting in various churches. "You'll really learn a lot at these meetings, Dennis. And I believe God will use you on this trip."

Ironically, I ran into several bodybuilders at the airport. They were on their way to Belgium to compete for the title of Mr. Olympia, 1986. Because I was favored to win, they were incredulous when I told them I wasn't competing! They tried their best to get me to join them, but my heart was set—I would go to the meetings with Ray. "Sorry, boys," I told them. "I'd love to, but I'm doing God's work now."

The conference was a tremendous experience. In addition to Michael Bassett and Ray, the other speakers included many great teachers and evangelists.

Ray had arranged for me to speak at some meetings on the outskirts of London, and when I arrived, I noticed posters advertising me as a speaker at the meetings. And next to those posters were posters promoting Arnold's new movie, *Commando*. Even more ironic was the location of the church—next door to a theatre showing the film, with Arnold's name emblazoned on the marquee. On the church door was a large picture of me and the statement that I would be sharing my life-changing story for Christ that day. Arnold and I were once again side-by-side. There was a lot of confusion at first—people thought I was there to promote the movie. So, when people asked for my autograph, I invited them to my meeting!

Approximately one thousand English, Irish, and other European ministers gathered around the stage at the first service. I started by simply sharing part of my personal testimony. Soon, however, I felt the anointing of the Holy Spirit come upon me, and I began to preach. Words I had never practiced came flowing out of my mouth; truths I had never thought of before flooded my mind. Then, in a few minutes, I sensed it was time to invite people in the audience to come forward and pray. There was an immediate response, with scores—maybe hundreds—moving in close to pray and seek the Lord.

I then saw a young bodybuilder in the crowd and made my way through the throng to speak to him. He told me that he had seen my picture on some conference posters and wondered what a former Mr. Universe would be doing at a religious meeting. "Why have you disappeared from the sport of bodybuilding?" he asked. "Arnold Schwarzenegger's movie, *Commando*, is showing at the theatre next door. Why aren't *you* making movies? What are you doing here talking about Jesus?"

"Because God has called me to help people like you," I told him. As we talked, he admitted he was on steroids and other drugs, and that his life was a mess. "I'd do anything to be like you," he said. "Listen to me," I said. "Now you can see that the important thing is not winning body-building titles or becoming a movie star. The important thing is to learn about Jesus Christ and to invite Him into your life." And then, the young man did just that! I saw him as he was led away for more information with the other new converts, tears streaming from his eyes. Seeing this young bodybuilder won to Christ was worth the whole trip!

It really is true that life will pass, and only what one does for Jesus will last! When Ray and I left the meeting that afternoon, we both looked at the crusade sign, then the movie marquee. One stood for eternal life; the other—violence, disguised as entertainment.

"What Are You Guys Doing Here?"

I was thrilled to have been invited to participate in a major outdoor crusade in Florida. There were meetings scheduled in the Little Havana section of Miami (predominately Cuban), Miami Beach, and then, Liberty City—right in the middle of one of the worst ghettos in the world—certainly in the United States.

There were no "good sections" in Liberty City—it was all bad. Crack and other drugs were for sale on every corner. Ten and twelve-year-old kids were out selling dope. The streets were lined with pool halls, bars, and ragged-looking hangouts—all filled with drunks and addicts. Even the people on the sidewalks were high on pot and cocaine or were stagger-ing drunk. It was like the land of the living zombies. Pimps and hookers plied their wares, unashamed and unafraid. Some of the prostitutes were barely teenagers. Every block seemed worse than the last—filled with stench and trash, cluttered with broken, hopeless human debris.

To illustrate how bad conditions were, on the day our crusade started, Wendell Tyler and I were walking down a street in the area, handing out fliers and inviting the people we met in the streets to come to the meeting. And as we were walking along, two squad cars pulled up and several police officers got out and stopped us. One of them said, "I know you— you're Dennis Tinerino, Mr. Universe!" Of course, they all recognized Wendell Tyler. His team, the 49ers, had beaten the Miami Dolphins the year before in one of the playoff games before the Super Bowl.

They began talking all at once. "What are you guys doing here?" "Can't you see that this is a violent, crime-ridden area?" "This is not like New York, or L.A., or San Francisco! This is the worst place in America!" "You're putting your life on the line just being here!"

"Well, I don't know about all that," I replied. "All I know is that God loves these people. We're here to tell them about Jesus and how He wants to set them free."

The cops shook their heads in dismay. "You're wasting your time down here. These people are a lost cause. Nothing and nobody is going to help them!"

Wendell looked the most vehement one in the eye and said, "Officer, you need to come to the meeting. You need Jesus in your life."

"Yeah, yeah, I know. Well, don't say we didn't warn you. I hope we don't have to come back and pick up your bodies after these punks stomp you in the mud!" They jumped back into their squad cars and drove away.

Back in my hotel room, I began to pray and prepare my heart for the service that night. I felt such sorrow and compassion for the people, and

I was agonizing before God, interceding for the Lord to pour out His Spirit and be merciful to the poor people of this terrible place.

The Lord began speaking to me as I prayed. *Dennis, you know about faith, and tonight the gift of faith will be shown to the people through your ministry. Do not look at what is seen! Look into the realm of the Spirit and see faith moving the things of the natural to bring about My glory!*

I had no idea what that meant, and I kept seeking God for direction and wisdom. However, I *did* sense that something unusual and dramatic was going to take place that night.

When I arrived at Liberty Park, there were already about 4,000 people who had gathered out of curiosity to see what was going on. The streets were lined with convertibles filled with young punks, boom boxes blasting away in the background. Even before the service began, the crack of gang-related gunfire rang out on side streets not far from the park.

As I looked out over the crowd, I saw something that puzzled me. "What are all these people doing with umbrellas?" I asked.

JoJo replied with a grin, "Well, Dennis, we're in the path of a hurricane, and everybody's expecting a violent rainstorm to flood us out and shut us down."

Rebuking the Rain

The service began, and in a couple of minutes, Wayne Cochran began to sing. He started with one of his most popular secular hits, substituting Christian lyrics. He hadn't even finished his first song when it started pouring rain!

The rain was coming down so hard, I wondered if the water would short-out the microphones and speaker system. *Maybe we **are** going to get shut down by the rain*, I thought, looking across the park and seeing people beginning to scatter in all directions. At that moment, I remembered what the Lord had spoken to me about not focusing on what was seen, but to expect the power of faith to move on the things of the natural and change them for the glory of God. I began to pray softly, under my breath, in the Spirit.

JoJo leaned over to me and said, "Dennis, the Lord shows me that you have something to say."

"Yes, I do!" Grabbing a microphone, I hurried to the front of the platform and began screaming at the top of my voice, "Look up! Look up now! Look up! Everybody look up! Don't leave—you're going to miss the miraculous power of God. Look up! Look up!

The people obediently looked up into the torrent of rain flooding down. Even some who had started to leave stopped and peered up into the sky. But I knew I wouldn't have their attention for very long.

Remembering what the Holy Spirit had spoken in my room about the gift of faith and miracles, I simply opened my mouth in faith. "I come against you, prince of the power of the air!"

WHOOSH! Immediately I felt a surge of power rise up within me so strong that I could hardly keep my feet on the platform. My fingers were tingling, and I was trembling all over in anticipation of what was about to happen. "I come against the spirit of the environment, and I COMMAND THIS RAIN TO CEASE IN THE NAME OF JESUS!"

You see, I didn't know much about hurricanes. I didn't know that the rain was part of an immense storm system that could wipe out entire neighborhoods and destroy complete cities. I was just doing what I felt the Lord was directing me to do. And because the rain was threatening to stop a service that could bring salvation and deliverance to thousands of sin-sick souls, I commanded the rain to stop in the name of Jesus.

The miraculous part of the story is—IT STOPPED! It did not lighten up or taper off. The instant I said "in the name of Jesus," the rain was suddenly on the other side of the park, moving away from us. Like God parted the Red Sea for the children of Israel in Moses' day, God parted the storm clouds in Miami and left us high and dry! Not only did the rain stop, but the sky itself got light—so bright, it felt like a spotlight was shining down on the platform and the open field where the crowd had gathered.

Everyone was staring in amazement, pointing up into the sky, shaking their heads in wonder, and chattering in excitement.

"What you have just seen is the power of God!" I declared. "You know that no earthly power could stop that rain. God did it to prove to you that He loves you and is concerned about you! Now, if you know you saw a miracle right here in this place tonight, come give your life to Jesus! Step out now! Come on down and pray with us. The power of God is here to save and deliver you from all your sins—to set you free from drugs, devils, and demons. Come on, people. Come to Jesus!"

Out in the crowd, people began throwing down their umbrellas and moving toward the platform; some knelt right where they were. The believers in the audience raised their hands and started crying, "Hallelujah!" and "Praise the Lord!"

Behind me on the platform, Wayne Cochran and other team members started singing a song of invitation as I kept urging people to come give their lives to Christ Jesus. By this time, a steady stream of people were making their way forward, and it looked as if the entire crowd was responding to the invitation!

Out of the corner of my eye, I saw a huge black man running from the back of the crowd all the way down to the front. I began watching him as he came. As he got closer, he raised his arms over his head. To my shock, I saw he had a gun in one hand, and he was lowering down to point straight at me!

Strangely enough, I felt no fear. I prayed, "Lord, deliver that man now!" As I looked into the man's face, I could see that he was visibly shaken from God's powerful presence and the Spirit of God was dealing with him mightily.

The man's arm moved suddenly, and seconds later I heard something bounce and then felt a glancing blow off my shoe. I looked down and realized what had happened. The man had thrown his gun up on the platform. I kicked the gun over to JoJo and said, "Take the clip out of this .22 and put it in your pocket. You may want to frame it to hang in your office later!"

Then I turned back to the man, who was sobbing at my feet. "I want to get right with God," he cried. "I need to be delivered." I prayed with him, and then directed a personal worker to come to his side.

I went back and forth across the platform, praying with people, praising God for the great harvest of souls. We later determined that some 380 people gave their lives to God in that service.

On the opposite side of the platform from the man who had thrown the gun, I saw an attractive black woman with her two young daughters. Suddenly, I felt drawn to her. Kneeling down, I said, "I have a word from the Lord for you." She simply looked at me in surprise. "You haven't seen your husband for a long time now, for more than a year."

"That's right. My daughters and I came forward to renew our commitment to the Lord and to pray for my husband and their father."

"Your husband was called to preach, but he got caught up in alcoholism, right?"

"Well, yes, that's right—but how did you know?"

"The Lord showed me. Now I want you to look way over there at that man who is crying and praying. He just threw a gun up on the platform a little while ago. Isn't that your husband?"

She looked across the sea of faces until she recognized her husband. "Oh, my God, it is him! It's a miracle! God has answered our prayer—that is my husband!"

Personal workers in the crowd helped the lady and her daughters work their way through the mass of people. What a tremendous scene it was to see that family reunited, crying with joy and celebration at the altar!

So many wonderful things happened that there is no way to relate all of them. Drug addicts and drunkards were set free. Prostitutes were washed clean by the blood of Jesus and were given new lives! People who were sick, broken, and hurting in their minds, bodies, and emotions were healed and made whole. Others who had been oppressed and possessed by evil forces were dramatically delivered and set free.

Once the move of God's Spirit began, it swept across the entire park and divine dramas took place virtually everywhere you looked. We heard reports of one miracle after another. It was the most powerful meeting I'd ever seen or been a part of!

And this was just the beginning! We continued our crusades in New York, Arizona, Oakland, San Francisco, Nevada, and throughout the world—Hallelujah!

Chapter Twenty-one

THE ADVENTURE CONTINUES

I live the most exciting life of anybody I know. My family has been led by the Holy Spirit for more than 20 years, trusting God to provide for our needs and our living. I've been privileged to meet and work with some of the most interesting and exciting Christian leaders in the world, and my life has been deeply enriched by their testimonies and ministry.

A major highlight of my life was traveling with Tom Sirotnak and his Champions for Christ to Japan. We literally covered the nation, witnessing to sumo wrestlers, esteemed educators, wealthy industrialists and businessmen, and top social leaders, as well as the ordinary people we met on the streets, on buses, trains, and in hotels.

Tom also arranged for us to minister to the Dodgers, the Detroit Pistons, the L.A. Lakers, various other professional football, basketball, and hockey teams, as well as the top college teams. We have ministered together on many college campuses and have been involved in tag-team preaching in open-air services. We have also spoken in literally dozens of chapel services at the University of Southern California.

Going Home!

One of the most satisfying ministry trips of my life was going back to my old neighborhoods—Brooklyn, Queens, Manhattan, Coney Island, and Harlem—for an extended time of ministry with JoJo Sanchez and several of his team members. We started off in Union Square on 14th Street in an open-air meeting. I'll never forget witnessing the healing of an old Puerto Rican man, a deaf, homeless derelict who lived in a cardboard box. Two team members—young girls from Riverside, California—laid their hands on his ears and prayed for him. Instantaneously, God opened this poor man's ears and he could hear again. He testified at the crusade, and many more people sought prayer for healing. There were a great many testimonies of healing and deliverance from drugs.

From Union Square, we moved to Greenwich Village, a place made famous in the '50s by "beatniks," smoking dope and reading strange poetry in dark dingy crowded coffee houses. Later came the hippies, and the '60s—Timothy Leary and LSD, flower power, the Beatles, and eventually, the Woodstock crowd.

I had spent lots of time in the village listening to great jazz musicians like Dave Brubeck and Herbie Mann playing in the nightclubs. This, of course, was during some of my wilder days, when I fought in the streets and woke up in strange women's beds.

My purpose for this visit was quite different as I joined the team in walking the streets to hand out literature and witness to everyone who would listen. I also had the opportunity to talk with several bodybuilders and share my testimony. We even were able to help some runaway teenagers find safe shelter and persuaded some of them to make contact with their parents to go back home.

Because there were professional athletes and celebrities in our midst, we were interviewed and articles were written about preachers and stars working together to help clean up various areas of New York.

I especially enjoyed our work in Times Square, site of the nationally televised annual New Year's Eve celebration—where the giant lighted ball drops at the stroke of midnight to mark the arrival of the New Year. I'd been to Times Square so many times as a teenager and young man, attracted by the lights, excitement, and glamour. Of course, going to the gyms and bodybuilding shows, the discos and dark, smoky clubs, and gambling on the streets were major attractions for me as well! I had often gone to the movies in magnificent cinemas and watched parades of luxurious limousines delivering celebrities and movie stars to the premiers. I had even attended an occasional Broadway show in the nearby theatre district. Now, I worked Times Square's stained and tawdry streets for Jesus, handing out tracts and preaching to whoever would listen. I had never realized that there were so many hurting people—hungry for love and hope and help.

Times Square had undergone many changes since I lived and played in New York. It had gone from an eclectic, yet dingy kaleidoscope of porno shops and gay bars to specialty stores, boutiques, and trendy restaurants. The sidewalks continued to be a teeming slice of raw humanity where our ministry team encountered a total cross section of people— young and old, rich and poor, from the down and outcast to the up and outlandish! We spoke with pimps and hookers, hustlers and transvestites, pushers and addicts, strippers and Chippendale dancers, actors and musicians, businessmen, tourists, beggars, and thieves—every shape and color of people imaginable. We prayed with street people who hadn't had a bath in weeks. We prayed with socialites covered in mink and dripping with diamonds. But no matter who they were, they all had the same basic spiritual needs, and God was able to touch them all with His life-changing power.

Then it was on to Harlem, rotting and festering with vacant buildings and crack houses, stripped-out cars, gangs, junkies, vandals, and just plain thugs. The spiritual darkness and need there was almost overwhelming. We met a group of kids who told us about dragging a bum over onto the railroad tracks. He never woke up because a train came by and decapitated him! The kids were laughing and making jokes about it. We introduced the local pastor to them who said he would give them help

We also encountered many members of the Black Muslim organization and other cult groups. I saw the notorious Rev. Ike driving by in a Rolls Royce. We soon realized we were down in the trenches, doing all-out spiritual warfare.

Then a guy came up to me and said, "Hey, I remember you from the old days. I lived in the same projects you did. Where's your brother Salvatore—where's Larry?

A kid who was saved during the meeting came over to talk to me. "I remember when you were Mr. America and Mr. Universe," he said. "I thought you were a real hero then. Now I have new respect for you because you didn't forget the people you came from—you came back to the neighborhood. You're really doing a good thing, man. I'm glad you got Jesus!"

"Thanks, buddy. I'm glad you got Him now too. Remember, you're a real champion when you accept Jesus in your life!"

The Harlem meeting brought a tremendous breakthrough, with multitudes of desperate people reaching out for help. It was a perfect illustration of Romans 5:20b—"*But where sin abounded, grace did much more abound*" (KJV). People were saved, set free, healed, and delivered. In a racially charged environment, we saw undeniable evidence that the bloodline overcomes the color line.

The next day we moved the crusade to Coney Island and set up right by the Ferris wheel, the merry-go-round, and the music park. Anyone who came to the amusement park area saw our meeting, and lots of curiosity seekers came over to check us out. We tried to attract people with as many celebrities as possible. I was onstage with other famous athletes and popular musicians—anybody we thought could help draw a crowd. Once people came to see us, we could start pointing them to Jesus.

Coney Island has always been a very special place to me. It's where I would come as a kid to get away from the dreariness of the projects and hang out with my bodybuilding friends. We would flex, pump iron, and pose to impress the young ladies. We danced under the boardwalk, chased bikini-clad girls, and surreptitiously watched gangsters and their "gumadas" from Little Italy. Our neighborhood gang had gotten involved in a bloody fight here one day that easily could have ended up in tragedy. It was also here that I came with my best girl to celebrate winning the Mr. America title. I had even come out in January to watch members of the Polar Bear Club shed their coats and strip down to bathing trunks, then dive into the frigid winter surf.

We attracted some big crowds at Coney Island, and just as in the days of my youth, throngs of people came out from the housing projects to see what was going on at the beach.

During the day, all of us would hit the streets and hand out fliers and tracts. We nailed posters to every pole along the boardwalk and up and down the side streets, and we tried to talk to everybody who went by. I also found a boxing gym at Coney Island, and one afternoon I ran into a bunch of boxers out jogging. One of them said, "Hey, that's Tinerino! Dennis, my man, what are you doing?" And I stood there and witnessed to those guys, inviting them out to the service that night.

During the time I was in New York, I tried to go back to all the old neighborhoods and all the old hangouts where I had spent time as a kid growing up, and as a young punk. I met lots of old friends, bodybuilders I used to work out with, and guys I used to fight in the streets. Many of the storeowners remembered me from the days when I came in to buy Italian sausages, hero sandwiches, calzone, pizza, and cokes. When I went by Nathan's for a hot dog, a grizzled old guy shouted out, "Hey, there's the muscle man! How you doin', Dino? Where's Reno and Tarzan?" As you may recall reading, Dino, Reno, and Tarzan had been the nicknames for me, my brother Sal, and a friend of ours named Mario Schosek. This guy still remembered our wild and crazy antics from the past. We all had a lot of laughs as he told story after story.

Everywhere I went, I tried to share my testimony and witness for Christ. Some people rejected what I had to say, and made fun...sure. But some didn't. There were lots of people who were hungry to hear about God, desperate for some good news. I was so thankful that God made it possible for me to return to my roots and minister the Gospel. For a long time, I had felt like it was something I really needed to do.

During the time I was there, I also had the opportunity to spend a little time with my family, especially my brother Larry and my father. We had a great time of fellowship together, reminiscing and remembering some of the good times—and bad.

Dad even went with me to some of the services and shared his testimony with one crowd of how he was healed from paralysis of the face. "My son prayed for me and I was healed! We prayed on the phone, and he said, 'Dad, when I come to New York, you will be totally healed.'" Dad delighted the crowd by showing how he could once again move his face into any position. He also seemed fascinated at the boldness of our team, who were always willing to talk about God and introduce people to Jesus.

One afternoon I asked, "What do you think about this, Dad?"

"Well, son, I just don't understand why you're not a movie star. You always had the looks, the talent, everything. You worked so hard to do it. Why is it that you're not in the movies or doing lots of commercials or whatever?"

"Yeah, I know, Dad. I really thought I'd make it in the movies or TV. But it hasn't happened. Maybe it still will come about someday, but this is what the Lord has me doing right now. I'm just trying to reach out and help some people."

"I know, Denny. And I want you to know, I'm very proud of you. Just keep on doing what God wants you to do."

Witnessing on Land, Sea, and Air

Exotic places are not just great locations for movie shoots. Just like the rest of the world, the people in these areas also need to hear about Jesus. Europe, Japan, Singapore, Thailand, The Philippines, South Africa, South America, Africa, Australia, Greece, Cyprus—these are just a few of the places we have visited over the years.

Recently, my family also had the opportunity to go to Hawaii and conduct several evangelistic meetings on the islands of Hawaii, Maui, and Lanai. In addition to the scheduled services in various churches, we all went out on the beaches and personally witnessed to groups of young people. One of my proudest and most fulfilling moments was to look up the beach and see my wife and both of my daughters praying with people and sharing about the Lord.

My son, D.J., and I also spent a week on a navy ship, the U.S.S. Arkansas, traveling from Pearl Harbor to Alameda, California. While it was a grand and unforgettable adventure for him, he caught on in a hurry that we were actually there on a mission. As we witnessed to the sailors on the ship, we saw backsliders repent and come back to the Lord, and unbelievers humbly kneel and confess their sins to Jesus, asking Him to come into their hearts. After one prayer meeting out on a windswept deck, D.J. looked up and said, "Wow, helping people accept Jesus is really neat, Dad!"

Before leaving Hawaii, my family and I were invited to visit the set of the Kevin Costner hundred million-dollar movie, *Water World*. Watching the production and seeing the famous movie stars was interesting, but to me, the best part of all was getting to meet the movie's stuntmen and having the opportunity to pray with them.

The Power of Prayer

Since I gave my heart to Jesus, my life has been a classic example of the scriptural truth that *"the steps of a good man are ordered by the Lord"* (Ps. 37:23 NKJV). Time after time, the Lord has directed my path, sending me where I should go at just the right time, and other times protecting me when my life was in peril.

One time, I was returning to Los Angeles after finishing meetings on the East Coast. I was rejoicing over the transformed lives of those whom I had ministered to and was looking forward to sharing with my family all the great things I had experienced. What I didn't realize was that in a few hours I would be staring death in the face. Shortly after the pilot announced that the plane was starting its descent into the Los Angeles area, just moments away from landing, chaos broke out. The plane began vibrating and shaking violently, then plummeted toward the earth, and passengers began to scream in terror.

The pilot made an announcement to prepare for a crash landing, and flight attendants were helping people get buckled into their seats, giving them pillows and showing them how to put their heads between their knees to prepare for the shock of a crash. Passengers were crying and cursing as fear and panic swept through the cabin. It was pandemonium!

Following the orders of the flight attendant, my head and hands were between my knees. (There are people familiar with flight safety regulations who will humorously remark that when you are in this position, it means you can "kiss your butt good-bye.") Well, I started to reflect about my life as if it were my last moments on earth. The spirit of fear, death, and destruction had consumed the passengers who believed they were going to die without the knowledge of Christ. Feeling God's Holy Ghost fire burning through my bones and a supernatural anointing upon me, I boldly got out of my seat and raised my hands. I then shouted, "Devil, you're a liar." I began praying loudly and quoting Scripture. As one of the flight attendants hurried by, I grabbed her arm and said, "Sister, you don't have anything to worry about. I'm a Spirit-filled believer, and the Lord has shown me that we're going to have a safe landing. I'm praying and binding the prince of the powers of the air in the name of Jesus."

She smiled and said, "Praise God, brother. I'm in agreement with you. I'm a believer too. Let's just pray and agree together." And we did, taking authority over the spirits of destruction, the principalities and powers of the air. I knew that Heaven would back up the words I was praying. Looking back, I believe that the car crash and other life threatening situations had prepared me for such a time as this.

After we prayed, the stewardess went to her seat praying in tongues and praising God with a smile on her face. As the runway rushed up to meet the plane, the aircraft was wobbling and pitching around like mad. Below us I could see the flashing lights of ambulances, fire trucks, police cars, and other emergency vehicles. In addition, the runway had been covered with foam—they were prepared for the worst.

About ten seconds before impact, the plane shuddered violently, and the wings rolled from side to side. There were renewed screams and curses from terrified passengers and cries of "We're crashing!" "Oh dear God, save us!" and "I don't want to die!" I shouted, "Jesus has provided us divine protection! This was a United Airlines flight, but I realize this plane has become a TWA (Traveling With Angels) flight. Thank You, Jesus!" Then we touched down without the use of the wheels due to malfunctioning of the landing gear. In only a few seconds, the plane slowed to a stop—no crash, no damage, no injuries. I realized I was still standing up with arms lifted up praising God, as we landed. After exiting the plane, many people asked me to pray for them to accept Christ. Others said when I prayed, peace came upon them and fear left them. Still others said that my loud and bold prayers comforted them and blocked out the cussing and screaming of passengers. I cannot express in words how thankful I am that the Lord has redeemed my life from destruction.

As I entered the airport, my friend Eddie Dalcour who had come to pick me up, came running up to me. "Man, Dennis, if you could have seen that plane coming in the way I did—the way it was bumping, twisting, and turning in the air—you'd have known it just had to crash and be totally destroyed! But somehow, at the last minute, it thumped down and straightened out. Praise God! What a miracle!

'That's right, Eddie," I said. "A manifested miracle of God's divine protection."

There have been so many other examples of how God has divinely protected me and my family. I guess I'll never forget what happened on January 17, 1994. At 4:30 in the morning, a massive Los Angeles earthquake hit and literally knocked me out of my bed and onto the floor! While preaching in Fontana the day before, the Lord had given me a prophetic word about an earthquake coming to California—that there would be devastation, but He would protect those who praise Him, honor and dwell with Him in the secret place. Little did I know He meant it would happen the next day!

In spite of our panic, Anita and I instinctively knew what had happened, and I realized that this was the word I had been given the day before. As we prayed, a sound like a freight train rumbled through our house. It was actually very short, but it seemed like forever before it stopped. We could hear glass breaking, walls falling down nearby, and watched as the walls of our home and everything in it danced and swayed violently. "Oh, my God!" she cried. "This must have been the big one!"

"Are you okay?" I asked.

"Yeah, I'm fine," she said, running to check on the children. We could hear them screaming in fear, but we found them all unhurt.

Outside there was widespread devastation. There were gas leaks and fires, and no electricity for miles. Just four blocks from our house, an entire shopping mall was completely destroyed, reduced to trash and rubble in a matter of seconds. Our daughter Tara was supposed to work at the mall later that day. To the south, east, and north of us, there was a billion dollars in damage in the Northridge area alone. People were trapped in buildings, some with serious injuries, waiting for help that didn't come for hours. We learned later that some 40 people were killed just a few blocks away from us.

Although Anita and I didn't have any earthquake insurance on our house, we soon discovered we didn't need any. Except for some fairly minor items, our home was virtually untouched. We gathered our family together and read the promise from God's Word, that we had prayed when the earthquake started. "*Because thou hast made the Lord, which is my refuge, even the most High, thy habitation; there shall no evil befall thee, neither shall any plague come nigh thy dwelling. For He shall give His angels charge over thee, to keep thee in all thy ways"* (Ps. 91:9-11 KJV).

Chapter Twenty-two

LIFE IS A JOURNEY— NOT A DESTINATION

I faced many challenges during the writing of this book. As I was reading through the first draft, I began to experience stomach cramps as well as abnormal fatigue. Anyone who knows me also knows that the word "tired" simply is not in my vocabulary.

Then, my left elbow became severely swollen and filled with fluid, which had to be drained. The doctor ran tests and discovered that I was anemic; however, I was told that my blood would have to be monitored because they were unable to find a cause for the anemia. I kept telling the doctor that I was having stomach cramps, but they never ran a CAT scan on my stomach. Not only was there a spiritual battle with the sickness but also with the doctors who were unable to detect the cancer. My wife and I both felt that the doctors weren't administering the correct tests. I spoke His Word every day. "Jesus bore my sickness and carried my pain. Sickness and disease have no power over me, for God sent His Word and healed me." (See Psalm 107:19-20.)

In spite of my symptoms, I continued with my ministry for several months, blaming the stomach pain on abdominal exercises and fighting fatigue. While ministering at a church in New Jersey on a Sunday morning, I felt faint and experienced some vision impairment near the end of the service. Nevertheless, the Holy Spirit urged me to pray for the sick in the congregation. In spite of the crushing weakness in my body, I prayed for all those who came forward that day. In fact, as I prayed for the sick, I began to feel better. And after the service, I took the afternoon to rest, eat, and pray.

When it was time for the evening service, my fatigue was still overwhelming. In the audience that night was a good friend who had driven from Pennsylvania—Pastor Fritz Matthews. He came to me after the service to let me know that the Lord had sent him to pray for me, and that he felt in his spirit that I was suffering from a life threatening illness.

It's a Mystery

Upon my return home, Anita listened as I told her how I felt, and was shocked to see how pale and exhausted I looked. She pleaded with me to check into a local hospital for tests. For once, I listened to my wife! The doctors then told me that I had been losing blood internally from a GI bleed. In fact, the doctors said I had lost so much blood it was a miracle that I was alive, let alone traveling and ministering at such a frenetic pace!

Blood transfusions and more diagnostic tests followed, but the doctors still were not able to determine what was causing the bleeding. It seems they ran every test in the book—except the right one! Their first thought was a bleeding ulcer. When that turned out to be incorrect, they went back to anemia. My friend John and I pleaded with the doctors to do different tests. We both felt that satan was having a hand in all these "unclear" test results and "misdiagnoses." Unfortunately, our protests fell on deaf ears, and the doctors again said they would continue to monitor my blood.

After a ten-day hospital stay and a blood transfusion, I felt great! So, I decided to keep my commitment for a two-week ministry trip to Canada. I spoke at Bible schools, churches, and was overjoyed to have an old friend—a World Gym owner who had driven for miles in freezing weather to get there—respond to the altar call at my first meeting. We wept together as he received Christ. A short while later, he went home to be with the Lord.

The meetings in Canada were tremendously powerful and filled with signs and wonders. I also appeared on 100 Huntley Street, a Christian TV show on that trip. Multitudes were saved in Toronto, Niagara Falls, and Stratford-on-Avon.

Battling for My Life

For the next five months, I was in what seemed to be perfect health. Then, while on a ministry trip to the East Coast, I noticed a lump on the left side of my stomach as I finished my workout. To be honest, I figured I ate too much Italian food that day, and didn't give it another thought. After all, I was feeling great and working out—I just had been keeping a very hectic schedule.

The night that I returned home from the New York trip, severe abdominal pains awakened me. Almost immediately I was cold and shaking, as though I was coming down with the flu. My solution was to take a hot bath and go back to sleep. I stayed in bed until mid-afternoon, then jumped up to start my day—except I wasn't standing—I was lying on the floor, looking up at my wife and daughter, who were praying over me.

Then suddenly my spirit left my body and I was looking down on them. I felt the awesome eternal presence of God's Kingdom with indescribable peace and light all around me. I knew that I had died and I believe that I was on my way to glory. The light that I was sensing was God's angels. I could not speak and I could not pray audibly. But my inner man was praying, praising the Lord.

Because of this experience, I've learned that believers in Christ can have great confidence in the Scripture that says *"to be absent from the body is to be present in the Lord."* (2 Cor. 5:8) Any split second, I could've been in the Kingdom of Heaven seeing my Lord and Savior face to face. I then heard Anita pray, "You will not die but live and declare the works of God. I bind you spirit of death. Go from him now in Jesus' name. I loose divine health, healing, faith, and miracles" (Ps. 118:17). As they prayed these words, my spirit went back into my body. I knew their prayers brought me back from death.

Looking at the faces of the paramedics, friends, and family, I knew I was fighting for my life. Actually, my body was in severe shock due to internal bleeding. All I knew was that I felt as though I was in a freezer and that my life was slowly slipping away. Although I tried to speak and pray in the ambulance, I was too weak. My inner man was able to pray, however. "You are my Healer, Jesus! I trust You, Lord!" my spirit cried out.

At the hospital, the diagnosis was not good. A CAT scan of my stomach revealed a Lyomyosarcoma—a cancerous inter-muscular tumor the size of a grapefruit—on the outside of my intestines. The doctors said the internal bleeding had been caused by two ruptured blood vessels attached to the tumor, and that time was of the essence.

After emergency surgery to remove the tumor and more than a foot of my intestine, and to repair the ruptured blood vessels, I awakened later that evening looking into the face of my doctor. "Well, I guess we found out what was wrong!" he joked. But looking in his eyes, I knew he did not have a good report for me. He told Anita and me that they believed the cancer had spread, and that I had only two weeks to live.

Upon hearing their dire report, I began to sing, "*The joy of the Lord is my strength; a merry heart does good, like medicine*" (see Prov. 17:22). Much to their amazement, I had NO FEAR! I told my family and all the doctors that I was going to live and not die. Shaking their heads, the doctors said they had heard patients say this before, but unfortunately, they all died. "There is no cure for this type of cancer," they informed me. "Not even radiation and chemotherapy will have any effect. Actually, we have never seen this type of cancer in anyone before. This is quite bizarre. When we saw the tumor, we were amazed. This is a very rare type of cancer."

I heard their words, but in my heart I knew the truth. This cancer was an attempt by the devil to kill me before my appointed time so that I couldn't complete the divine destiny God had for me. I quoted Psalm 91:16, "*With long life will I satisfy him....*" I realized that up until this point, I had always relied on my gifts of physical strength and mental toughness. But now, in my weakened condition, out of my spirit, I quoted Zechariah 4:6—"*Not by might nor by power, but by my spirit....*" I had to depend on God's promises for my life—for the healing touch from Heaven's power plant—and get ready to receive a miracle!

Making War in the Heavenlies

My family and I understood what the doctors didn't understand—there was a spiritual battle taking place. Yes, there was my body against the cancer, but that was a subtext. The real war was the Master Physician against the master destroyer! Satan was determined to kill me, but I was on God's operating table now, and by overcoming this disease, I would be able to inspire those who would face similar battles—and show them how to win! God would use this circumstance for the good and to save many people (see Gen. 50:20.)

The words of Psalm 118:17 poured out of my spirit. *"I shall not die, but live, and declare the works of the Lord!"* (KJV). I confessed. From that point on, the Holy Spirit told me to pray only with people who had great faith to believe for a miracle healing, and to even be on guard about who was allowed to visit.

My wife and children stood at my bedside, and we sang, "Whose report do you believe? We shall believe the report of the Lord! His report says I am filled. His report says I am healed. His report says I am free. His report says VICTORY!"

When my nurses heard this, they were stunned. They began asking us to pray for *their* illnesses and situations, and soon we had a hospital revival! Many who worked there accepted Christ during my stay.

Numerous Christian friends and ministers were praying for me, and I continued to claim my healing by faith—on the phone, in person, and, of course, with Anita and the children. I believed in the power of prayer; and through prayer networks, my situation was lifted up around the world. The 700 Club, T.B.N., and my church were all praying for me. I also received many prophecies during this time. One I remember particularly was from Kim Clement. He said that satan had thrown a "fiery dart" to bring me down and to try and stop my ministry—but he would not succeed!

While I was in the hospital, I developed a blood clot in my left ankle, which was *also* life threatening! Consequently, I had to take blood thinners to dissolve the blood clot before it could travel to my heart. Obviously, the enemy felt he had to have a backup plan in case the first one failed!

When the doctors felt they had done all they could do for me, they sent me home—so they thought—to die. Anita and D.J. helped me into a wheelchair. And because of the blood clot, I had to ride with my leg straight out. I was 30 pounds lighter than when I had gone into the hospital—the lightest I had been in 30 years!

When I arrived home, Anita and I set up the "war room." It was a place for God and me to do battle with the enemy. I would listen to healing verses on cassette 24/7, and every day, according to First Peter 2:24, I declared that my body was healed. Videos on the subject of healing played around the clock; and Psalm 103:2-3, *"Bless the Lord, O my soul, and forget not all His benefits: who forgiveth all thine iniquities; who healeth all thy diseases"* (KJV), were continuously on my lips.

Then the bills began to arrive! Not intimidated, I continued calling my body healed. Because I did not have medical insurance, I also confessed every day that the $120,000 in medical bills were paid in full.

Meanwhile, Anita had searched the Internet every night while I was in the hospital, looking for alternative cancer treatments and other useful information. Many of the so-called "cures" we found online were based on new age beliefs. Not only were they not of God, they were very costly and had no proven record of success. Also, many of them seemed to be taking advantage of all the people in the world with incurable cancers, who did not know about or had no faith in Christ's healing power.

Anita and I made a decision that I would receive my healing by faith, and forget about all the alternative treatments we found.

After my release, we went to see a Christian nutritionist, who gave me advice on supplements, antioxidants, juices, and healing foods. Of course, he also said that supplements and food could not cure or prevent this type of cancer—or keep it from coming back. Nevertheless, I drew upon my knowledge of nutrition and fitness as well, and designed a nutritional program to strengthen my immune system and cleanse my body. Using a diet of organic foods, lots of water, fruits and vegetables, herbs and antioxidants, and absolutely *no* processed food, I began to rebuild my body. The first sign of success? The blood clot dissolved! And every day, I called my body healed.

Twice, I traveled to Mexico to OASIS, a Christian clinic for cancer patients...and twice the doctor had an emergency and could not see me! Instead, I spent my time praying for the other terminally ill patients at the clinic. From the moment my family and I arrived at the clinic, I felt a burden to pray for people with cancer. My heart was filled with compassion and my eyes filled with tears, looking upon the faces of dozens of people, young and old, in the last stages of cancer. I would go from room to room, praying with patients, comforting children as they cried out for their parents to not die, meeting ambulances as they brought in the sick. Occasionally, I would take notes as a cancer survivor would give their testimony and speak about nutrition for healing. I knew we were on the right track.

Next, a friend made an appointment for me with a top oncologist at Scripps Clinic in San Diego. Other than being amazed that I was still alive, the doctors again said there was nothing they could do for me. In their opinion, I had a time bomb inside of me. Yet, after evaluating my records and examining me, they were confused. "You should have been dead in a matter of weeks," they told me. "But here you are, and you're looking well. You should be wasting away, but you've gained back the 30 pounds you lost! This is the most bizarre thing we have ever come across. We can't find any sign of cancer anywhere! Of course, this type of cancer always comes back. At some point, your cancer will return."

We knew better. Sickness will not return a second time (see Nahum 1:9); and he who the Son makes free is free indeed! (see John 8:36). We had our miracle!

The Lord not only provided a healing miracle, he also did wonders in our financial situation. When the hospital's collections department demanded payment of $140,000, Anita went in to speak with the woman in charge. As it turned out, the woman had the same maiden name as Anita and grew up in the same town as Anita's father in the Philippines. They were relatives! Boy was Anita excited now. Anita's new found relative was able to adjust our debt, reducing it to less than $10,000— Hallelujah!

The Other Side of the Battle

In retrospect, the toughest battle I faced was not just cancer. The second part of the battle was in the realm of my mind!

Throughout my fight with cancer, there were many who prayed for me. Their voices, lifted in prayer, were the sweetest sounds a man could hear. There were, however, other voices—demonic voices that filled the lonely nights in my hospital room—voices saying, *You're going to die! Where's your God now? Look how you wasted your life! Where's your health now, Mr. Universe? Why don't you take a few more supplements? You did this yourself, you know...taking steroids to be stronger!*

When those tormenting voices would strike, I would jump from my bed, saying, "Satan, you are a liar! You accuser of the brethren, you have no right to condemn me! I bind you, you harassing and tormenting spirits from hell! Be gone in Jesus' name! The Word of God says that by His stripes I am healed! (See First Peter 2:24 and Isaiah 53:5). God said it, I believe it, I receive it, and that settles it!"

However, the enemy was not finished yet. Realizing that I was standing in faith for my healing, he then attacked three of my closest friends. Not only were these wonderful people stricken with cancer, they all were people of faith, believing for their healing. Each of them lost their battle, and each of their deaths caused me to doubt and question God's divine healing power—but only for a moment. I was standing on His promises. *"For God hath not given us the spirit of fear; but of power, and of love, and of a sound mind"* (2 Tim. 1:7 KJV). And the Lord spoke to me while I was in prayer, "Son, do not allow what you see or what others tell you to hinder your faith walk with Me."

Satan couldn't have my mind, so he went for the finances. Having cancer creates a bit of a problem with jobs and ministry—it's called lack of income from months of no work! Our family had to place our trust in the Lord, not men (see Jer. 17:5). We focused on Philippians 4:19, *"My God shall supply all your need according to His riches in glory by Christ Jesus"* (KJV).

All my life, I had enjoyed optimum health and supernatural strength...until now. I was believing God to restore it all back. People were spreading all kinds of rumors—that I had a brain tumor or that my cancer was a punishment for how I had lived in the past. Others said that bitterness, disappointment, and lack of forgiveness could have caused the cancer. I spent a great deal of time soul-searching and crying out to the Lord, to search my heart for any area where I might have bitterness or animosity toward any man—or any area that was not pleasing to God. I could relate to David in Psalm 51:10.

Some well-meaning, but biblically illiterate person said that this was God's way of dealing with me. Whereas another man asked me to thank God for the cancer! Needless to say, I didn't allow the opinion of man to cause my faith to waver. Instead, I trusted the truth that was in my heart—the truth of God's Word regarding healing.

You see, nothing aggravates the enemy more than watching each of his plans go down at the touch of the Master's hand.

You may ask, "Why would God allow His servant to suffer through so many trials? In His Word, it says, *"Many are the afflictions of the righteous: but the Lord delivereth him out of them all"* (Ps. 34:19). His Word also says, *"When Jesus heard that, He said, This sickness is not unto death, but for the glory of God, that the Son of God might be glorified thereby"* (John 11:4).

Fast-forward

The medical "experts" were wrong. The cancer did not come back.

My family had a second chance to enjoy the beautiful land and people of Greece. Once again, Bill Damovoletes made all the arrangements, but just before we were to leave, he began to get severe headaches. A CAT scan revealed a tumor in his brain. Guess who was trying to stop this ministry trip? Ha! We prayed, a miracle occurred, and the tumor disappeared.

It had been five years since our last trip to Athens. Our final destination this time was the island of Crete, and during our travels we met many pastors who told us that the prophecies and words of knowledge I had given by the leading of the Holy Spirit had come to pass. Many testified of miracles in the areas of finances, family, health, and ministry.

Our four meetings in Crete were awesome! The church was filled with people who had gathered from the war-torn nations of Bosnia, Iran, Hungary, Slovakia, Czechoslovakia, and Albania. People accepted Christ in large numbers, and many also received healing and prophetic words. Hallelujah!

Upon our return to Athens, Pastor George Patsaouras told me that the prophetic word I had given him five years before regarding a new building had manifested, and I had the honor of ministering in it that night!

We were blessed to witness a mighty move of God in Kavala, Phillipi, and Thessalonia. During one meeting, the Lord gave me a word that soon Christians from around the world would gather in Athens to pray for revival in Greece, and that the Lord had instructed them to break strongholds. I told them that I had learned that powerful, intercessory prayer is the only thing that will change the spiritual climate of a nation.

Following that meeting, an Australian pastor tearfully told us that God had sent him there to organize just such a worldwide gathering! What a wonderful ending to an extraordinary assignment from the Lord!

Over the years, I have ministered with many ministry organizations, and at one time, Jackie Yockey, COO of the High Adventure team, invited me to minister throughout England with them. Our first meeting was to be at Heathrow Hilton Hotel. After a long flight, I immediately went to my room to prepare for the meeting, and in my time of prayer, I heard the Holy Spirit say to me that this meeting would affect the royalty of this nation.

During the meeting, after ministering the Word of God, I prayed for people individually, not knowing what the Lord had next. I then noticed a small shy petite woman who looked out of place. By the unction of the Holy Spirit, I said, "You've never been to this type of Christian meeting before." She responded, "You're right." I then said, "God sent me here to tell you that He loves you and that your work as a hairdresser and make-up artist for the Queen Mother at Kensington Palace is a divinely orchestrated plan from Him, so that you can share the Gospel and pray with her.

Before she reaches one hundred years old, you will pray with her to accept Christ."

She was immediately engulfed with God's presence and wept, as God spoke to her in detail about her life and the assignment that God had for her. Afterward, the pastor and her friends confirmed that everything I said to her was indeed true.

The following year, I once again was in England to minister at Pastor Martin Phelps' church. After the meetings, we decided to go to one of our favorite places to spend the afternoon. As we were touring central London, we all felt it was the most spectacular, beautiful day we could remember.

On August 4, 2000, we witnessed seven thousand troops from various military regiments, a military airplane salute, marching bands, farm animals, choirs, racehorses, camels, dancers, and floats—the reason for this pageantry was the one hundredth birthday of the Queen of England.

While riding in a cab with Martin, John, and my son, Dennis, I started to share the story about my ministry the previous year with the English woman who was the personal assistant to the Queen. I then prayed, "Lord, allow me to say, 'Happy birthday' to the Queen Mum face-to-face. I know the woman has prayed with You to accept Christ."

Immediately, our unbelieving cab driver said, "Can't you see—that would be impossible with all the security and all the multitudes of people."

"My God is a personal miracle-working God who answers prayer," I responded.

The cab driver, continuing to speak doubt and unbelief, then turned his cab into a restricted lane, which miraculously ended up alongside the Queen Mum's limo, no more than two and one-half feet away from her. And with my window opened, I said, "Happy Birthday, Mum. I know

Jesus is in your heart." The cab driver was in shock, to say the least, as were my two friends and son.

My son said, "Dad, with all the multitudes of security and people around, God supernaturally answered your prayer. He's a miracle God." And then, the taxi driver asked, "How do I accept this miracle God?"

⸺⸺⸺⸺⸺

Over the years, I have maintained friendships with many former bodybuilding competitors—one of those individuals has been Arnold Schwarzenegger. Anita and I were excited when we received an invitation to the inauguration of Arnold being sworn in as Governor of California. Reflecting back on the years that I have known Arnold, I think politics was the last thing on his mind. Indeed, ministry was the last thing on my heart. We pray for him and Maria continuously and correspond with him as the Lord leads. We thank God that we are able to touch many influential people in many different arenas of life.

Faithful to the Call

Just a few short months ago, my ministry celebrated 25 years. Twenty-five years—where has the time gone? Life is like a vapor—here today, gone tomorrow. I know that among these years, there were seasons where God was pleased with my faithful service to Him and my calling. When I surrendered my life to Him 25 years ago, I found the pearl of great prize. He took me out of darkness and put me in His light. He became my Lord and Savior and gave me a purpose and direction. I thank God He called me to minister His Word. I put my hand to the plow and have never looked back. I thank the Lord for His grace in anointing me these years to fulfill my destiny.

He has opened doors (see 1 Cor. 16:9) to minister His Word throughout America and the nations of this world. I've been faithful to run my race (see Phil. 3:14; 1 Cor. 9:24; 2 Tim. 4:7). I have witnessed God's power firsthand, just as the apostle Paul did. In Africa, I have seen the deaf hear, the blind see, and the crippled walk out of wheel chairs. I have heard testimonies of people healed of diseases from AIDS to cancer, and from many who were raised from the dead. When I preached to 80,000 starving destitute people, tears rolled down my face as multitudes gave their lives to Christ. The Lord has given me favor through every form of the media in several continents, nations, and states where I have traveled—Korea, Japan, Canada, Alaska, Australia, Europe, and South America. Hundreds of millions have heard my testimony and of the great things God has done for me. I receive praise reports every week from those whose lives have been transformed.

All these years, I have received His divine favor and guidance, and I've seen His hand divinely protect me in plane crashes and car accidents. He's the God who has met all my needs; He's more than enough.

The nine gifts of the Spirit that I've seen flow through me have broken every demonic yoke imaginable. Standing on His principles by faith has always released His promises. I can't count all the churches, TV appearances, prison ministries, or how many people I have prayed for, or how many times I have mentioned the name of Jesus, but the Lord knows. It's in His name and His name only that the sinners will be set free. His name releases miracle power. His peace and rest are available to us.

I'm pressing forward to finish my race. I'm not looking to the right or to the left. I've taken the road less traveled, the narrow road, with His Holy Ghost fire upon me. I'm blazing a trail that will give God the glory.

Looking back on what He's done, I can now look ahead and see what He has begun.

It's a battle to stand for the cross of Christ and be a godly warrior enlisted in His army, but when the battle gets tough and I get weary, I can go into His secret place to worship and praise Him. It is there, in His presence, where my weakness is exchanged for His strength. What a mighty God I serve and will serve. I'm pressing forward to finish my race.

My friend, be diligent to fulfill your destiny. Run your race. The rewards are not the applause of man (and I have received much of that over the years), but the applause of the King of kings Himself saying, "Well done, My good and faithful servant." The gun has sounded. The race has begun. So be faithful to your call.

Joy in the Journey

Teddy Roosevelt once said, "Far better it is to win glorious triumphs even though checked by failure, than to live in the gray twilight of those who know not victory or defeat!"

On my mantle and surrounding shelves are trophies—the rewards of countless hours of sweat and toiling, day in and day out, year after year, in every imaginable and sometimes unimaginable place, in different cities and different nations. These same trophies can also be seen in my photographs and on dozens of magazine covers—waved high, with my hands over my head in victory. What you don't see in those captured moments is the constant dieting, the aching muscles, the mental and physical strain, the sacrifices, and the anguish I experienced when someone else was announced the winner.

However, as I look at those photos of various competitions, I can see these same trophies as symbols of fulfilled dreams and accomplishments that released incredible elation—an emotion that surpasses all of the negatives put together. Disappointment, sacrifice, and pain fade away in that moment of glory in the winner's circle.

Those trophies contain a world of memories for me—the sights and sounds of different cultures; pleasant aromas from restaurants and kitchens, and the not-so-pleasant aroma of hundreds of locker rooms; jubilant celebration with friends and family, crying because my efforts were finally being rewarded; the mishaps, the challenges, the words of acceptance, and the mocking, which all sound the same in different languages; being a hero to some, and a villain to others.

Now the trophies and medals are tarnished. Yesterday's victories and defeats that were cheered by some and booed by others are mostly forgotten, like yesterday's news. The rewards of men are lost in the memories of yesterday's fans. But I am blessed that I have discovered how to earn an eternal medal of gold. *"You've all been to the stadium and seen the athletes race. Everyone runs: one wins. Run to win. All good athletes train hard. They do it for a gold medal that tarnishes and fades. You're after the one that's gold eternally"* (1 Cor. 9:25, The Message).

What many people don't know is that without having God in their life, all the accomplishments in the world won't bring true happiness and peace (see Luke 12:15). Without the Lord, they most likely will simply repeat some or all of the mistakes I made along the way. But if they will put Him first, He will show them that although the medals and trophies tarnish, there is a crown that will never tarnish or fade (see 2 Timothy 4:7-8).

To anyone who chases glory and seeks a reward in any profession, know this: The Lord is your exceedingly great reward (see Gen. 15:1). Without knowing Him, what you achieve is only temporary and will be forgotten.

I have been so many places in my life, and I have done so many things; yet to know that I am a vessel for Him to use is the most amazing thing of all. I am a father, a husband, a speaker, a bodybuilder, a minister...I have become a man who uses the talents and gifts he has been given to serve the One who gave me eternal life. I am the clay, and He is the potter who molded me into a champion for Him.

You see, bodybuilding was the vehicle that would drive me down the freeway of success in life—but in my zeal to succeed, I left life's greatest Navigator at the starting line (see Matt. 6:33). Still, He never left me. He stuck with me through everything, and when I finally ran out of gas, He filled my tank with "Holy Ghost Hi-Octane"!

God is so good. He is "Heaven's Paramedic," who rescued me when I crashed, breaking the speed limit with my fast living and sinful lifestyle. I crashed, but I didn't burn, because He carried me in His arms and brought me to "Heaven's pit crew"—other believers who led me to a personal relationship with Him. He set me out in front of the pack—as the head, and not the tail (see Deut. 28:13). He restored my soul and sent me back into the race of life to fulfill my destiny.

How could I ask for anything more than to have the most interesting and exciting work any man could have? Why should I worry when the Lord supplies all my needs and protects me from every danger? What better life could there be than living the adventures of faith?

I could fill another entire book with accounts of the amazing things I've seen and the great moves of God I've been part of across America and around the world during the past two decades. I've seen the power of God moving in people's lives from prisons to palaces. My life is certainly an ongoing adventure for the Lord. I never know for sure what God will have me to do when I get up in the morning. The only thing I do know is that if I follow His leading, the adventure will be exciting and productive for the Kingdom of God.

The finish line awaits—the journey continues. Whatever happens in between is up to the Lord. And when I reach the finish line, I want to be able to say: "I have fought the good fight. I have finished the race. I have kept the faith." And as I receive my crown of righteousness, I will hear Him say, "Well done, my good and faithful servant."

I am so thankful for the opportunities I have been given. There are only a handful of people in the world who have had the privilege to live this kind of life. I am also extremely grateful for the knowledge and wisdom I have acquired in my years as a competitive bodybuilder. Working out, nutrition, and supplements have enabled me to keep my body strong and healthy through the years, and that's something you cannot put a price on. Nor can you put a price on knowing the love of God. Without Him, there *is* no joy in the journey.

EPILOGUE

September 11, 2001

The World Trade Center is in ruins. The Pentagon has been pierced. Sound bites and tearful faces fill the airwaves. America has been attacked. Shock turns to anger, and fear turns to faith.

January 1, 2002

Now, more than ever, the world is searching for answers. Our nation is at war. Flags are flying over businesses, homes, and on cars. Bookstores are selling out of Bibles. People are praying, and crying, and praying. And everywhere, you see the phrase, "GOD BLESS AMERICA!"

The answer is clear—we must turn back to God, our source, our healer, our deliverer. Only then will we find the perfect peace that passes all understanding.

He Has Called You—Will You Answer?

Do you have a personal relationship with the Lord? Obtaining it is simple. God's plan of salvation has not changed over thousands of years, and will never change. The choice, however, is yours—which path will you take? There are many forks in the road, and each one requires a choice or decision for you to make. One leads to mistakes, failure, and pain; the other to joy and peace.

My friend, God has a plan for your life, and has given you a destiny to be fulfilled. He is not a respecter of persons. The God who healed me of cancer is the same God who wants to heal you. The God who delivered me from the pit of hell and saved my soul from destruction is the same God who sits at the right hand of the Majesty on High praying for you to be saved.

The God who protected us from death and devastation in the Northridge earthquake, the plane crash, and the car accident is there to release His angels from Heaven's aircraft carriers for your preservation. The God who guided me through His principles of finance so I could be debt-free is there for you. The God who picked me up when I was down, turned my life around, and gave me a new life with a new beginning wants to do the same for you. The God who spoke His words through me to reveal His miracle healing power is there for you.

This same God, named Jesus, who died on the cross at Calvary, is waiting to write your name in Heaven's Book of Life. Let Him be #1 in your life. Simply pray this prayer with all your heart.

Prayer of Salvation

God in Heaven, I come to You today because it says in Your Word, John 6:37, that You will never, no never, reject anyone who comes to You. So, I know that You will not reject me, but take me in.

Your Word says in Romans 10:13 that everyone who calls upon the name of the Lord will be saved. I am calling on Your name, Lord, and I know that You will save me now.

You also have said in Romans 10:9-10 that if I acknowledge and confess with my lips that Jesus is Lord, and in my heart believe that God has raised Him from the dead, I will be saved, for it is with the heart that a person believes, and so is justified, and with the mouth he confesses and confirms his salvation.

I believe in my heart that Jesus Christ is the Son of God, and that He became my substitute on the Cross, died for my sins, and that He was raised from the dead and lives forevermore. I repent of my sin and receive the gift of God's salvation in Jesus Christ. I thank You, Father, that I receive forgiveness and the gift of eternal life and am now a new creation in Christ. Amen. (See John 3:16, John 3:3, and Second Corinthians 5:17.)

TITLES & AWARDS

1964 Mr. Brooklyn

1964 Junior Mr. Metropolitan

1964 Mr. New York City

1964 AAU Outstanding Bodybuilder

1964 Mr. Eastern America

1965 Mr. Metropolitan

1965 Mr. Teenage America

1965 Mr. North America

1965 Junior Mr. U.S.A

1965 Mr. East Coast

1966 Mr. U.S.A

1967 Junior Mr. America

1967 Mr. America

1967 Most Muscular Man in America

1968 Amateur Mr. Universe (NABBA)

1975 Mr. Universe (Pro-IFBB)

1978 Natural Mr. America

1980 Pro-Am Mr. Universe International (Caracas, Venezuela)

1981 Pro-Am Mr. Universe (IFBB)

1981 Italian American Sports Hall of Fame

1988 Natural Bodybuilding Man of the Year (ABCC)

1989 ABA Hall of Fame

1989 Natural Bodybuilding Man of the Year (ABA)

1990 Legend of Bodybuilding (ABA)

1995 Pete Maravich Award (AIM)

1998 Amateur Athletic Union (AAU) Hall of Fame

2006 IFBB-Bodybuilding Hall of Fame

2006 Oldetime Barbell & Strongmen Hall of Fame

MINISTRY CONTACTS PAGE

Dennis Tinerino Ministries
PO Box 280326
Northridge, CA 91328-0326

Phone 818-885-5711
Fax 818-885-5712
Website: www.tinerino.com

Additional copies of this book and other book titles from DESTINY IMAGE are available at your local bookstore.

Call toll-free: 1-800-722-6774.

Send a request for a catalog to:

Destiny Image® Publishers, Inc.

P.O. Box 310
Shippensburg, PA 17257-0310

*"Speaking to the Purposes of God for This
Generation and for the Generations to Come"*

For a complete list of our titles,
visit us at www.destinyimage.com